The State as C[illegible]
Practice

Mark Bevir
and
R. A. W. Rhodes

OXFORD
UNIVERSITY PRESS

OXFORD
UNIVERSITY PRESS

Great Clarendon Street, Oxford, OX2 6DP,
United Kingdom

Oxford University Press is a department of the University of Oxford.
It furthers the University's objective of excellence in research, scholarship,
and education by publishing worldwide. Oxford is a registered trade mark of
Oxford University Press in the UK and in certain other countries

First published 2010
First published in paperback 2015

Published in the United States of America by Oxford University Press
198 Madison Avenue, New York, NY 10016, United States of America

British Library Cataloguing in Publication Data
Data available

Library of Congress Cataloging in Publication Data
Data available

ISBN 978–0–19–958075–0 (Hbk.)
ISBN 978–0–19–960448–7 (Pbk.)

The State as Cultural Practice

Contents

Preface and Acknowledgements

In our earlier book, *Interpreting British Governance* (2003), we outlined an interpretive approach to political science and used it to explore changes in British governance. We emphasized the importance of interpreting governance by examining practices from the bottom up, and noted the lack of such studies. *Governance Stories* (2006) sought to fill that gap with ethnographic fieldwork. We emphasized that practices of governance arise out of actions based on beliefs informed by traditions. *Governance Stories* located its ethnographic work in a broader account of traditions in the study and practice of politics.

The aim of this book is to develop a novel theory of the state as 'meaning in action'. This theory directly challenges the new institutionalism, probably the most significant present-day strand in both American and British political science. We seek to move away from such notions as modernist-empiricism, 'path dependency', and 'bringing the state back in'. We argue for anti-foundational analysis, ethnographic and historical methods, and a decentred approach that rejects any essentialist definition of the state and espouses the idea of politics as cultural practice. To decentre is to focus on the social construction of a practice through the ability of individuals to create, and act on, meanings. It is to unpack a practice as the disparate and contingent beliefs and actions of individuals. Therefore, we argue the state is a diverse set of practices rooted in varied beliefs about the public sphere, about authority and power, which are constructed differently in contending traditions. A decentred approach appeals to the notions of tradition and dilemma to explain changing conceptions of state and governance. It seeks to develop a more diverse view of state authority and its exercise. It develops the idea of politics as historical practices arising out of the conjunction of state and civil society. Our stories show how ministers, civil servants, and citizens construct and reconstruct the stateless state.

In brief, we have three aims:

- to develop an anti-foundational theory of the state (Part I); and
- to develop a new research agenda around the topics of rule, rationalities, and resistance (Part II); by
- exploring empirical shifts and debates about the changing nature of the state and showing how anti-foundational theory leads us to see them differently.

We draw on several essays previously published jointly and singly since 2002. We list them below in date order.

'Putting the People Back into Networks', *Australian Journal of Political Science* 37 (3) 2002: 399–415.

'Historicizing the New Institutionalism(s)' (with Robert Adcock and Shannon Stimson), in R. Adcock, M. Bevir, and S. Stimson (Eds.), *Modern Political Science: Anglo-American Exchanges since 1880*. Princeton, NJ: Princeton University Press, 2007, pp. 259–89.

'The Everyday Life of a Minister: A Confessional and Impressionist Tale', in R. A. W. Rhodes, P. 't Hart, and M. Noordegraaf (Eds.), *The Ethnography of Government Elites: Up Close and Personal*. Houndmills, Basingstoke, UK: Palgrave-Macmillan, 2007, pp. 21–50.

'So What? The Prospects and Pitfalls of Being There' (with Paul 't Hart and Mirko Noordegraaf), in R. A. W. Rhodes, P. 't Hart, and M. Noordegraaf (Eds.), *The Ethnography of Government Elites: Up Close and Personal*. Houndmills, Basingstoke, UK: Palgrave-Macmillan, 2007, pp. 206–33.

'The Life, Death, and Resurrection of British Governance', *Australian Journal of Public Administration* 65 (2) 2006: 59–69.

'Central Government' (with Paul Fawcett), in A. Seldon (Ed.), *Blair's Britain 1994–2007*. Cambridge: Cambridge University Press, 2007, pp. 79–103.

'Historical Understanding and the Human Sciences', *Journal of the Philosophy of History* 1 (3) 2007: 293–317.

'Reinventing Westminster: How Public Executives Reframe Their World' (with John Wanna and Patrick Weller), *Policy and Politics* 36 (4) 2008: 461–79.

'Anti-foundationalism', in M. Flinders, A. Gamble, C. Hay, and M. Kenny (Eds.), *The Oxford Handbook of British Politics* (Oxford: Oxford University Press, 2009, pp. 115–37).

'Scenes from the Departmental Court', *Public Policy and Administration* 24 (4) 2009: 437–56.

'Interpreting Territory and Power', *Government and Opposition*, vol. 45, no. 3, pp. 436–56

We have incurred many debts. Pride of place goes to our various co-authors: Robert Adcock, Paul Fawcett, Paul 't Hart, Mirko Noordegraff, Shannon Stimson, John Wanna, and Patrick Weller. They also commented on several other chapters. We thank them for their help, criticism, and above all their graciousness in allowing us to use their work in this book.

Several colleagues commented on individual chapters: Asaf Kedar (Chapter 1), Alan Finlayson, Mike Kenny, and Anna Marie Smith (Chapter 3), and Kevin Orr and Mirko Noordegraff (Chapter 6). Eilidh St John checked the references. Laura Bevir compiled the index. We thank them for their help if not their agreement.

Our greatest debt is to the ministers, permanent secretaries, and twenty members of the Private Offices in three Departments who agreed to taped interviews and allowed us to watch them at work. They needed extra work like they needed a hole in the head, yet they tolerated us with great good cheer and were unfailingly helpful. We are all too well aware of the demands of 'the diary'. We are most grateful and, should they read this book, we hope they think their efforts were not in vain. Chapters 6 and 9 were read and commented on by the major participants in the study and are anonymous at their request.

Berkeley and Hobart
September 2009

Tables

Abbreviations

APS	Australian Public Service
APSA	American Political Science Association
CM	Correspondence Managers
CSV	Community Service Volunteers
DG	Director-General
DS	Diary Secretary
FWNB	Fieldwork Notebook
GCSE	General Certificate of Secondary Education
GP	General Practitioner
HM	Her Majesty
NPM	New Public Management
NHS	National Health Service
OPSR	Office of Public Services Reform
OTA	Occupational Therapy Assistant
PASC	Public Administration Select Committee
PCO	Privy Council Office
PCT	Primary Care Trust
PIU	Performance and Innovation Unit
PMDU	Prime Minister's Delivery Unit
PMFSU	Prime Minister's Forward Strategy Unit
PMSU	Prime Minister's Strategy Unit
PPS	Principal Private Secretary
PS	Private Secretary
PSA	Public Service Agreement
PSG	Public Services and Growth
PSX	Public Services and Expenditure

List of Abbreviations

RCAGA	Royal Commission on Australian Government Administration
RIPA	Royal Institute of Public Administration
SAFF	Service and Financial Framework
SpAds	Special Advisers
SSRC	Social Science Research Council
WRVS	Women's Royal Voluntary Service

Chapter 1

Introduction

In this book, we propose new responses to old questions about the nature of the state and how to study it. We argue that political scientists should think of the state as a series of contingent and unstable cultural practices, which in turn consist of the political activity of specific human agents. We also argue that political scientists should explain these cultural practices by reference to the meanings embedded in them, where these meanings arise against the background of contingent historical traditions and dilemmas. This chapter sketches the roots of theories about the state. We trace the shift from idealism to modernist-empiricism, and to a radical historicism and anti-foundationalism.

The study of politics has long concentrated on the state as a sovereign authority. This concept of the state arose gradually and contingently during the Renaissance and Reformation, culminating in the great texts of Bodin and Hobbes. However, once the concept of the state as sovereign authority had arisen, it proved to be remarkably powerful and remarkably resilient. It inspired political actors to remake the world in its image, most famously in the Treaty of Westphalia, which enshrined it as a principle of international relations. Moreover, as this concept of the state became more and more entrenched in political life, so many students of politics began to take it for granted, treating it as a natural development.[1]

The theory of the state dominated political science in the nineteenth century. In America and much of Europe, the central place given to the state was in part a response to, and a catalyst of, various forms of state-building. The important place given to the state also reflected its role as one of the key principles in the developmental historicism that then dominated the social sciences. The state made sense of historical developments: statehood was the consummation of the history of nations that were held together by ties of race, language, character, and culture. The state played this guiding role in traditions of scholarship as diverse as Hegelian idealism, Comtean positivism, evolutionary theory, and Whig historiography.

Proponents of all these different forms of developmental historicism typically agreed on several key points. First, they believed the state expressed, or at least could express, the common good of a people bound by cultural and ethnic ties. Second, they thought the social sciences could explain the character of any particular state through a historical narrative about the emerging political organization of a cultural and ethnic nation. Third, they believed that representative institutions, perhaps alongside a constitutional monarchy, could enable citizens to hold accountable political actors who embodied, acted on, and safeguarded the common good of the nation.

Developmental historicism often led to a view of the state as akin to an organism. A state embodied a spirit or culture that itself had a progressive teleological history. Thus, for example, Bosanquet (1965, 172) famously argued that the state was not just an institutional reality but also an ethical one. Following Hegel, he saw the state as a nest of interconnected social relations and institutions of which it was the ethical core and guiding spirit. The state was greater than a particular set of political institutions. It embodied the general will of its people. For Bosanquet to ask whether the state was just a set of institutions was like asking whether a person was just a set of physical organs. Just as an individual's will and intentions guided and governed his or her body, so the public interest and general will of the people informed the public policies and historical development of a state.

Bluntschli is a neglected figure, yet his classic *The Theory of the State* was probably the single most influential work of political science in the nineteenth century, acting as a founding text for the discipline in Germany and America. Bluntschli, like Bosanquet, believed in a developmental historicism in which the state was a 'moral and spiritual organism' (Bluntschli 1885, 54). He began by rejecting those existing theories of the state that gave it only a partial role. He attacked the legal conception of the state, arguing that it limits the role of the state to the protection of the rights of citizens; it ignores the state's ethical role in promoting social justice and public welfare. He also attacked those concepts of the state, notably the 'socialist' one, that he thought gave it too much power. Then he turned to detailed discussions of representative democracy and constitutional monarchy. In both cases, he traced the historical development of a set of political institutions that arose as the expression of the moral organism. He paid particular attention to the link between these institutions and the historical cultures of specific nations.

Today the idea of the state as an ethical organism is alien to most of us. It was decisively undermined by the First World War, which eroded faith in progress and therefore developmental historicism. The war led American and British scholars to distance themselves from the German philosophy and political science that was the basis for much of this theory of the state.

If the state is not an ethical organism, how should we think about it? If political scientists can no longer believe in developmental historicism, how can they make sense of the state and governance? Throughout the twentieth century, most political scientists responded to these questions in ways indebted to modernist-empiricism and positivism. Modernist-empiricists see the state as a set of formal and informal institutions and behaviour, and they try to explain these institutions by appealing to ahistorical structures, classifications, correlations, and mechanisms.[2] Behaviouralists are far more critical of the concept of the state, often rejecting it for sociological terms such as 'system'.

Modernist-empiricism and positivism

Since the collapse of developmental historicism, the study of the state in political science has been dominated by a modernist-empiricism mainstream that shades into positivism. We will briefly review these approaches to the state, looking at the forms of explanation and empirical topics they favour.

Modernist-empiricism

Bluntschli's decline from a pre-eminent voice to a neglected one reflects two overlapping but separate trends in political science. Although these two trends tended to reinforce one another, each had its own roots, and belief in one did not require belief in the other. The first trend saw modernist-empiricism replace developmental historicism as the dominant approach in the social sciences. Developmental historicism had located actions, cultures, and institutions in broad temporal narratives governed by largely fixed principles such as those of liberty, reason, and statehood. This developmental historicism was undermined by the crisis of faith in reason and progress associated with the First World War. This crisis encouraged the rise of modernist-empiricism. Modernist-empiricism treats institutions such as legislatures, constitutions, and policy networks as discrete, atomized objects to be compared, measured, and classified. It adopts comparisons across time and space as a means of uncovering regularities and probabilistic explanations to be tested against neutral evidence (see Bevir 2001). Political scientists such as Herman Finer (1932) and Friedrich (1937) broke the state into its constituent formal-legal institutions to provide comparative analyses of institutions and politics across modern states.

The early twentieth century witnessed a second, overlapping trend in political science: the rise of new empirical topics. Political scientists began to look beyond the topics associated with institutional history, constitutional law, and the general theory of the state. They believed that these older agendas reflected a pre-democratic Europe, and were no longer relevant to the mass-based politics that developed with an expanding mass suffrage. In their view, modern societies could be understood only if the dynamics of policy making, mass-based political parties, and public opinion were studied alongside formal government institutions. Political scientists wanted to study how policy making, political parties, and public opinion worked. The most important such study was Bryce's *The American Commonwealth* (1888), which moved relatively quickly through historical and legal issues to devote hundreds of pages to parties and public opinion. Bryce's work inspired other political scientists, including most notably Harvard's Lowell, who later repaid the transatlantic debt with *The Government of England* (1908).

It was when political scientists turned to modernist-empiricism to examine the new empirical topics that they crafted what would now be called the 'old institutionalism'. Many of them continued to understand the state as both a set of formal and legal institutions and the ideas embedded in these institutions. Today many people treat this institutional approach to the state (*staatswissenschaft*) as the historic core of political science. They tout the study of formal and legal institutions as the defining feature of political science. Eckstein (1979, 2) is a critic of the old institutionalism, objecting that its practitioners were 'almost entirely silent about all of their suppositions'. Nonetheless, he recognizes the importance of this 'science of the state' with its focus on 'the study of public laws that concern formal governmental organizations' (Eckstein 1979, 1, 2). Indeed, in an earlier article, he pointed out:

> If there is any subject matter at all which political scientists can claim exclusively for their own, a subject matter that does not require acquisition of the analytical tools of sister-fields and that sustains their claim to autonomous existence, it is, of course, formal-legal political structure. (Eckstein 1963, 10–11)

Similarly, Greenleaf (1983, 7–9) argued that constitutional law, constitutional history and the study of institutions constitute the 'traditional' approach to political science.

As the old institutionalism broke with developmental historicism, it turned towards both modernist-empiricism and new empirical topics. First, the main forms of explanation typically became increasingly ahistorical. They were often cast in the form of cross-temporal and cross-cultural regularities or patterns. Legal rules and procedures often served as the independent variable with the functioning of democracies acting as the dependent variable. For example, Duverger (1959) criticized electoral laws on proportional representation because they fragment party systems and undermine representative democracy. Second, old institutionalists expanded the range of terms such as 'state' and 'constitution' far beyond the older focus on textual documentation and attendant legal judgements. For example, Herman Finer (1932, 181) defined a constitution as 'the system of fundamental political institutions'. The old institutionalism came to cover not only the study of written constitutional documents but also the associated 'customs' (Lowell 1908, 1–15). The distinction between constitution and custom has since recurred in many related guises, most notably in the distinction between formal and informal organization.

The old institutionalism promoted comparative and inductive studies of states and their histories (Rhodes 1995, 43–6; and for the usual caricature see Thelen and Steinmo 1992, 3). Finer (1932) is a fine exponent of the comparative approach (and see Eckstein 1963, 18–23; Bogdanor 1999 for more examples). While Finer broke away from the older state-by-state approach to compare institution-by-institution across states, he still located his institutional analysis within a clear theory of the state. For Finer (1932, 20–2), the defining characteristic of the state is its legitimate monopoly of coercive power (see also Sait 1938, chapter 5). He surveys the main political institutions 'not only in their legal form, but in their operation' (Finer 1932, viii), as they evolved. Political institutions are 'instrumentalities' which embody the 'power-relationship between [the state's] individual and associated constituents' (1932, 181). Then, and only then, Finer compares the political institutions of America, Britain, France, and Germany. His analysis covers the parts of state organization, including democracy, separation of powers, constitutions, central–local territorial relations, and federalism. Finally, he turns to 'the principal parts of modern political machinery, namely, the Electorate, the Parties, Parliament, the Cabinet, the Chief of State, the Civil Service and the Judiciary' (1932, 949). His approach is grounded in a theory of the state and explores key institutions and their operation.

The old institutionalism was also inductive. Its proponents claimed the great virtue of institutions was that we could 'turn to the *concreteness* of institutions, the *facts* of their existence, the character of their *actions* and the *exercise* of their power' (Landau 1979, 181, emphasis in the original). We can draw inferences from repeated observations of these objects by 'letting the facts speak for themselves' (Landau 1979, 133).

Finally, while the old institutionalism turned away from historicist forms of explanation, it often continued to take a historical perspective, looking at the historical development of states and forms of government. History is extolled as 'the great teacher of wisdom' because it 'enlarges the horizon, improves the perspective' and we 'appreciate... that the roots of the present lie buried deep in the past, and... that history is past politics and politics is present history' (Sait 1938, 49). Because political institutions are 'like coral reefs' which have been 'erected without conscious design', and grow by 'slow accretions', the historical approach is essential (Sait 1938, 16).

In America and Britain, the formal-legal analysis of the old institutionalism remains alive and well. It dominates many textbooks, handbooks, and encyclopaedias. Major works are still written in the idiom. Sammy Finer's three-volume history of government (1997) combines sensitivity to history with a modernist-empiricist belief in comparisons across space and time, regularities, and neutral evidence. He attempts to explain how states came to be what they are with a specific emphasis on the modern European nation state. He searches for regularities across time and countries in an exercise in diachronic comparison. He sets out to establish the distribution of the selected forms of government throughout history, and to compare their general character, strengths, and weaknesses using a standardized typology. He provides a history of government, from ancient monarchies (about 1700 BC) to AD 1875.

Formal-legal analysis also remains prominent across continental Europe. It was the dominant tradition in Germany, although challenged after 1945. The challenge is yet to succeed in, for example, Italy, France, and Spain. Here we can only give a flavour of the variety that is French political science, and establish it as a distinctive endeavour that runs at times in a different direction to, and at times parallel with, Anglo-American political science.

There is a strong French tradition of constitutionalism. It is descriptive, normative, and legalistic, focusing on the formal-legal aspects of institutions, but not on case law. Chevalier (1996, 67) argues that 'the growth of the French liberal state in the nineteenth century led to the predominance of the law and lawyers stressing the guarantee of citizen's rights and limits on state power'. These jurists monopolized the field for nearly a century and remain a major influence (see, e.g. Chevalier 2002). So, despite various challenges, the 1980s witnessed 'the resurgence' of 'legal dogma' with its focus on the state's structures and functions (Chevalier 1996, 73).

Outside the tradition of constitutionalism, the French approach to the study of institutions remains distinctive, and does not engage with the Anglo-American literature. An early example is Duverger (1954; 1980). Although his work on electoral systems and semi-presidentialism is probably better known outside France than inside, nonetheless it was a major challenge to the academic lawyers and it influenced a younger generation of scholars. Latterly, 'the strategic analysis of institutions' focuses on electoral systems and core political institutions (such as the presidency) and tries to identify how institutions, singly and in combination, affect behaviour (for citations see Elgie 1996). Its main proponents include Duhamel and Parodi (1985). Parodi explains the changing nature of the Fifth Republic's political system by identifying, for example, how the direct election of the president with a majoritarian electoral system for the National Assembly bipolarized the party system.

Behaviouralism

Bryce and Lowell introduced new empirical topics associated with mass-suffrage societies, but they typically continued to conceive of the state as the sovereignty of a collective will. This concept of the state began to lose ground to pluralist alternatives only after the First World War. The new trend arose through transatlantic exchanges, for while American pluralism later developed a distinctive hue, it initially owed much to British scholars, especially Laski who spent several years lecturing at Harvard and Yale. Laski brought the term 'pluralism' and British debates about sovereignty into the American academy. Equally, his time in America made it central to his democratic theory (Gunnell 2007, chapter 7). In the first decades of the twentieth century, pluralism combined with the new empirical topics to transform the theory of the state. The older idea of the state as a sovereign authority became less popular. In its place, there arose studies of pressure groups within which sovereignty and authority were dispersed among various organizations. A string of future presidents of the American Political

Science Association (APSA) built their careers on studies of pressure groups – Herring (1929), Odegard (1928), and Schattschneider (1935). By the 1950s, the concept of a pressure group was also applied to British politics by the recent Harvard PhDs Beer (1956; 1963) and Eckstein (1960) alongside Finer (1958) and Mackenzie (1955). During the interwar period empirical research on public opinion, parties, and pressure groups was known collectively as the study of 'political behaviour'. The APSA's review of the state of the discipline in the 1940s stressed the pervasiveness of this phrase. It even claimed 'political behaviour has largely replaced legal structures as the cardinal point of emphasis among political scientists' (Griffith 1948, 224). Even if this claim was an overstatement, it rightly suggests that the study of political behaviour was prominent in American political science before the onset of the 'behavioural revolution'.

The behavioural revolution thus represented less a change in empirical topics than the rise of a new theory that stood in sharp contrast to modernist-empiricism as well as the earlier developmental historicism. In other words, to specify what was new about behaviouralism, we must remember the new empirical topics had arisen long before. Many behaviouralists had substantive interests in public opinion, pressure groups, and topics other than formal government institutions, but these interests simply extended an intellectual trend dating from the turn of the century. Behaviouralism got much support from the Committee on Political Behaviour, which was established in 1949 by the Social Science Research Council (SSRC). The Committee's main goals were not, despite its name, to promote the study of behavioural topics; rather, the common theme of the articles arising from the Committee on Political Behaviour was the call for a political science that was 'systematic' (Garceau 1951, 69–85; Leiserson 1951, 29–32; Truman 1951, 37–9; Eldersveld *et al.* 1952). The focus was on *how* to study politics, not *what* topics to study.

The Committee on Political Behaviour (1950, 20) had two declared goals: 'development of theory' and 'improvement in methods'. Although behaviouralism is often remembered for the second goal, the first was as important. The failure of the specific theories advanced by behaviouralists in the 1950s and 1960s to win lasting support should not obscure the revolutionary impact of behaviouralism on conceptions of the character and role of theory, especially in American political science. Behavioural theory was broadly positivist, ethically neutral, and orientated to empirical science more than political practice.

Up into the 1940s there was little dispute about what theory was or should be. Political scientists on both sides of the Atlantic understood 'theory' principally to mean the study of the history of the political thought that had shaped modern institutions. Most political theorists spent more time studying, teaching, and writing about historic texts than attempting to produce novel theories. Political theory combined moral philosophy and constitutional history with the theory of the state. From moral philosophy, it inherited the idea of training young elites to take their place in the world by teaching them a canon of great texts. From constitutional history, it inherited a concern to study law, authority, and institutions through the study of legal and historical documents. From the theory of the state, it inherited a concern with classifications of types of government and institutions.

The rise of modernist-empiricism and the new empirical topics in the first half of the twentieth century did not challenge this approach to political theory. A view of science as fact gathering and objective reporting gave political scientists no reason to question the epistemic standing of historical research. While fewer and fewer political scientists outside the subfield of political theory did historical research, they did not see their theory colleagues as obstacles to a scientific discipline. To the contrary, political theory complemented the rest of political science. Political theory gave students both a historical survey of ideas set against the backcloth of evolving institutions, and a guide to the concepts used by contemporary political scientists. Thus, the generalist scholar still flourished. Barker (1915; 1944; 1956) in Britain and Friedrich (1941; 1952) in America wrote about both political ideas and institutions. They produced comparative institutional studies, histories of ideas, translations of canonical texts (Aristotle 1946; Kant 1949), and many other works. Modernist-empiricism offered little warning of the theoretical departures that positivism later inspired in American political science.

Positivist theory took varied forms in the different subfields of political science. In the study of American politics, the most famous theoretical product of behaviouralism was a new version of pluralism, best illustrated by Dahl's classic *A Preface to Democratic Theory* (1956). But it was in the subfield of comparative politics that positivist hopes were most ambitious. Comparative politics underwent a dramatic expansion in size, scope, prestige, and funding as America became a superpower engaged in the Cold War, competing for the allegiance of the new nations that emerged from decolonization in Africa and Asia. When Friedrich and Finer crafted new analytic frameworks for comparative study in the interwar decades, they grounded their categories in the historical experiences of Europe and America. Their categories had a restricted scope. In contrast, the SSRC's

Committee on Comparative Politics brought young scholars together in the 1950s in a bid to remake the subfield. The positivism of these scholars led them to take abstraction to a whole new level. They sought a general set of concepts that could bring comparative studies of all countries within a single framework. This quest for a general theory was pitched at the macro-societal level, drawing on functionalism and systems theory (see, e.g. Almond 1960). The members of the Committee on Comparative Politics were influenced by Parsons and his systems approach. They also owed a debt to Easton and British social anthropologists, which meant they adopted 'political system', rather than Parsons' 'social system', as their core concept. When crafting a general theoretical scheme for analysing changes in political systems, they made 'political development' their key concept rather than the more sociological and reductionist 'modernization' (see, e.g. Almond 1965).

If the behaviouralists brought anything new to the critique of the state, it derived precisely from their positivist concept of general theory based on observable phenomena. The behaviouralists argued that the core life of a society should not be sought in the empirically mysterious and dubiously intelligible entity called the state. They thought the social sciences should study empirically observable activities and behaviour. Easton (1953, 108), a doyen of the movement, argued that the state is dispensable in political science since it is empirically unknowable. Similarly, Lasswell and Kaplan (1950, 184) claimed that 'every proposition about the abstraction "state" can be replaced by a set of propositions referring only to the concrete acts of certain persons and groups'.

Behavioural theory, especially in its most aggressively positivist forms, barely appeared in Britain. To the contrary, even when British political scientists adopted techniques such as survey research or cross-national aggregate analysis, they remained tied to the older modernist-empiricism. The possible exceptions include Rose and Blondel, but they concentrated on empirical work, writing little about theory. Ironically, therefore, the main impact of positivist theory on British political scientists was that they began to define themselves against it. The biggest clichés about British political science define it in contrast to American positivism. This contrast enables British scholars to forget their modernist-empiricist inheritance, including the extent to which their search for formal explanations based on classifications and correlations among types of institutions embodied a modernist revolt against historicism. They define themselves instead as peculiarly sensitive to history, context, and agency. As Bogdanor (1999, 150) writes, typically unaware of the historical context of the contrast he is making, 'if there is a central tendency to the discipline as it has developed in Britain in the twentieth century, it lies in aversion to positivism'. This position does not distinguish British political science. It just aligns the mainstream of the British discipline on one side of the conflict between modernist-empiricism and behaviouralism that defines the mainstream of the American discipline.

Historicism and interpretation

Modernist-empiricism, positivism, and neo-Marxism dominated political science for much of the twentieth century.[3] However, they were by no means the only responses to the collapse of developmental historicism. One alternative was an emphasis on historical understanding and the interpretive nature of social science.

Hermeneutics

Hermeneutic theorists continued to conceive of action as meaningful even as they retreated from idealist notions of the absolute. They also began to craft a more radical historicism, replacing assumptions about a unified and rational progress with an emphasis on diversity, contingency, and ruptures. At the turn of the nineteenth century, German philosophers drew on the rich traditions of idealism and hermeneutics to discuss the philosophical foundations of the social sciences and their relationship to the natural sciences. These discussions produced some of the classic statements on historical understanding (*verstehen*). Dilthey's work had a profound impact on approaches to the social sciences within the hermeneutic tradition. Moreover, the German discussions helped to inspire similar ones throughout Europe, including, through the Italian Croce, the work of the British philosopher Collingwood.

Historical understanding has to do with grasping the intentional content attached to human actions. It is a distinctive approach to the social sciences, typically based on the idea that the meaningful nature of human action requires a distinct epistemology in the form of historical understanding. Philosophers who study historical understanding focus on three interwoven but analytically distinct concerns. The first concern is to lay out the ontological conditions for the possibility and grounds of historical understanding: what features of human nature support interpretation? The second is to clarify the epistemological nature of historical understanding itself: what does it mean to interpret actions that took place in the past? The final concern is to specify the role of understanding in historical explanation: how and to what extent does interpretation explain social phenomena? In stressing these issues, we challenge two myths about historical understanding. The first myth is that historical understanding is just a method for producing historical facts. The second myth is that it is inherently an intuitive, quasi-mystical act that resembles the work of an artist more than that of a scientist. In place of these myths, we highlight the philosophical content of historical understanding seen as an analysis of what it means to base the social sciences on the meaningful character of human action.

DILTHEY

Given that historical understanding concerns the intentionality of human action, it is not surprising that discussions of its philosophical principles arose against the background of idealism and hermeneutics. The idealists stressed the primacy of mind over matter in human existence including efforts to understand that existence. Hermeneutics was preoccupied with questions of understanding linguistic utterances by grasping the mental content expressed within them.

Dilthey was the first major thinker in both the idealist and hermeneutic traditions to attempt a systematic theory of historical understanding. Dilthey anchors both the possibility and the necessity of historical understanding in ontological arguments. According to his ontology, human life differs from the rest of the natural world in that it consists of an inner world expressed in outer manifestations such as gestures, words, music, poetry, churches, and universities. Understanding is the process of grasping the inner content to which outer expressions refer. It is only by such understanding that humans are able to live, act, and communicate in a society. Understanding is a fundamental presupposition of individual and social life. This ontology leads Dilthey to define the social sciences as dependent on historical understanding. The social sciences, like human life, are about understanding expressions. The social sciences grasp the inner content of outer manifestations.

How does Dilthey see the process of historical understanding? At times Dilthey (1996, 229) identifies understanding with an intuitive and imaginative re-creation of inner contents in one's psyche. He based this re-creation on an analogy with one's own lived experiences and enhanced by 'sympathy with everything human'. Scholars should 'transfer' themselves 'into a given complex of manifestations of life' in a way that enables them to experience the temporal flow of historical events within their own psyche (Dilthey 2002*b*, 235). In his later writings, however, Dilthey downplayed the importance of individual psychic processes. Instead he placed 'objective spirit' at the centre of historical understanding. Objective spirit refers to the ensemble of objectifications (outer manifestations) that comprise a society at a certain epoch. For Dilthey (2002*a*, 229), all these objectifications share 'a common stock of ideas, attitudes, and ideals', which 'even the work of a genius will reflect'. Our everyday understanding of the objectifications that surround us needs these common conventions. So, historical understanding can only be grasped by using these social commonalities; that is, by 'locating the individual manifestation of life within a common context' (Dilthey 2002*a*, 230).

The process of understanding is important for Dilthey's epistemology. It leads him to raise a question that remains prominent in many later discussions of historical understanding. How can empathetic historical understanding have a 'universally valid' objectivity (Dilthey 1996, 253)? On what grounds can a mental process occurring in the subjective experience of the historian be recognized as a valid interpretation of a given historical phenomenon? Dilthey treats the question of objectivity as one not of methodology but of philosophy. He does not answer it by offering a procedure that if followed by historians would secure the validity of their interpretations. He answers it by an ontological argument that, in his view, guarantees the validity of the re-created experiences in a historian's mind. Dilthey (2002*a*, 298) posits the identity of the subject and object of knowledge:

> The primary condition for the possibility of historical science is contained in the fact that I am myself a historical being and that the one who investigates history is the same as the one who makes history.... Lived experience contains the totality of our being. It is this that we re-create in understanding.

While this response to the problem of the validity of historical understanding may seem vague, underdeveloped, even quasi-mystical, Dilthey's work did much to raise issues that still concern philosophers interested in historical understanding.

COLLINGWOOD

Late in life Collingwood (1946; 1978) suggested that any statement or action was an answer to a question, where questions are posed in particular contexts that consist of historically specific webs of beliefs. History is a series of particular ideas and epochs uninformed by any real continuity let alone any concept of the universal. However, Collingwood did not see history purely as the particular. To the contrary, much of his philosophy retains idealist echoes. In particular, his famous concept of re-enactment keeps a form of historical continuity and arguably drifts towards some of the religious and mystical ideas he held in his youth.

Collingwood argued that historians know past thoughts when they re-enact them; that is, when they have the same thoughts but in the present (see Van der Dussen 1995; Bates 1996). At times, Collingwood treats re-enactment as a method or formal requirement of understanding. At other times, he leans towards a more metaphysical understanding of re-enactment. Re-enactment here involves a mind becoming directly aware of another that existed in the past in a way that suggests thought has the transcendent quality of persisting through time and across contexts. Collingwood's claim of a transcendent link with past thought is most clear in his early writings where he relates it to a mystical and immediate insight into the unity of the whole. He wrote:

> The necessity of the mystical experience lies in the principle that we discover new truths by an act of the mind which reaches out beyond the given, grasps new thought as it were in the dark, and only after that consolidates its new conquest. (Bates 1996, 36)

Although Collingwood (1946, 287) later dropped the reference to mystical experience, he still argued that historians can have thoughts identical with those of their subjects. He argued that, although 'acts of thought happen at definite times . . . thought itself is not involved in the flow of immediate consciousness', but rather 'stands outside time'. Thought has the peculiar property of not only 'occurring here and now in this context', but of being able 'to sustain itself through a change in context and revive in a different one' (Collingwood 1946, 297).

According to Collingwood (1946, 306), thought alone has some existence outside time: it 'is not merely immediate'. The transcendent quality of thought is what makes re-enactment possible. Because thought can reappear in different contexts while still keeping its identity, historians can re-enact it as it was in the past. Things other than thought are immediate, which means they cannot be re-enacted. Therefore, they are not amenable to historical study. As Collingwood (1946, 304) explained, 'of everything other than thought, there can be no history'.

An alternative to positivism

Between the world wars, Collingwood was almost a lone voice in Oxford drawing on an older idealism to address hermeneutic themes. But in the 1950s hermeneutic themes and the idea of historical understanding became a prominent alternative to positivism in anglophone philosophy. By the 1960s, a distinctive anglophone approach to historical understanding appears, especially in Britain and Canada. Philosophers such as Dray, Winch, and Taylor drew on Collingwood, Wittgenstein, and a range of hermeneutic and phenomenological thinkers to counter influential attempts to develop a positivist analysis of the social sciences. Instead, they insisted on the interpretive nature of social science.

The positivist challenge

A second wave of *verstehen* theory emerged in reaction to the positivist attempt to reunify the natural and social sciences on a naturalist basis. The positivist project, which had middle European roots, consisted of an attack, led by Hempel and Abel, on the idea that historical understanding could be a legitimate form of explanation.[4] Hempel (1965, 1966) claimed that empathy is not a basis for explanation in the social sciences but at most a source of hunches. He argued that historical explanations are always implicitly nomological in that they involve a deduction from premises that include at least one natural law. Explanations that appeal to the motives of actors presuppose psychological generalizations.

Abel's approach (1974, 85) is more complex than Hempel's. On the one hand, he claims that historical understanding is 'necessary and indispensable' for the 'study of social behaviour'. But, on the other, he restricts the role of historical understanding to the generation of hypotheses in which meanings are reduced to intervening variables. He writes, '*verstehen* . . . consists of the act of bringing to the foreground the inner-organic sequence intervening between a stimulus and a response' (Abel 1948, 214). Abel reduces historical understanding from a philosophy to a method. He makes historical understanding an 'operation' within a positivist philosophy.

Historical understanding

The positivist challenge provoked a lively debate about historical understanding in anglophone social sciences, and a number of scholars rose to defend its importance (see Truzzi 1974). However, the most systematic defence of historical understanding came not from social scientists, but from philosophers such as Dray, Winch, and Taylor.

DRAY

Dray (1995), following Collingwood, insisted that historical explanation depends on making sense of the inner world of actors. Dray departs from Collingwood's perspective, however, in his attempt to integrate causal explanation and historical understanding. In particular, Dray argues that the causal explanation of any action requires an understanding of the purposive reasoning, whether conscious or unconscious, spoken or latent, that caused the actor to perform that action.

Dray (1957, 125) describes interpretive explanation as follows:

> Rational explanation may be regarded as an attempt to reach a kind of logical equilibrium at which point an action is *matched* with a calculation [attributed to the actor]. A demand for explanation arises when the equilibrium is upset – when from the 'considerations' obvious to the investigator it is impossible to see the point of what was done. The function of the historian's explanatory story will in many cases be to sketch in the corrections to these 'obvious' considerations which require to be made if the reader is to be able to say: 'now I understand what he was about'.

The historian has an initial expectation about what a 'normal' course of events would look like in a given situation. A deviation from that expectation prompts the historian to piece together those elements of the actor's reasoning 'which are different from those we might have assumed in absence of evidence to the contrary' (Dray 1957, 125). The investigation is completed once the amassed knowledge of the actor's reasoning is enough to account for the 'deviant' course of action. Reconstructing the inner reasoning of historical actors is not an arbitrary, intuitive product of pure empathy. Rather, it is built up 'from the evidence' (Dray 1957, 129).

WINCH

Winch (1958, 23, 123) argues that social life is fundamentally different from the rest of the natural world in that social relations are 'internal relations'. Social relations exist through ideas held in people's minds rather than through the external, physical aspects of human interaction. Thus, all 'specifically human behaviour' is meaningful (Winch 1958, 52). Winch then adds that all meaningful behaviour is a matter of applying intersubjective, socially established rules in specific social contexts. For Winch, this view of human society is 'logically incompatible with the kinds of explanation offered in the natural sciences' (1958, 72). 'Historical explanation', writes Winch, 'is not the application of generalizations and theories to particular instances: it is the tracing of internal relations' (1958, 133). Explanation is a matter of understanding the social actors' own understanding of their reality.

Winch, like Dray, restores the constitutive role of meaning in social life and in our knowledge of it. But, unlike Dray, he rejects any association of historical inquiry with causal analysis. He attacks Weber's view that to get scientific validity, historical understanding needs to be supplemented by a probabilistic or statistical causal analysis. Statistical analysis, according to Winch, can never get us closer to understanding social action. For example, '[a] man who understands Chinese... is not a man who has a firm grasp of the statistical probabilities for the occurrence of the various words in the Chinese language' (Winch 1958, 115). Winch also rejects psychological forms of understanding directed at grasping internal mental processes. In his view, all understanding (of oneself, of one's reality, of the objects of historical inquiry) is mediated by socially established concepts. All understanding occurs within an intersubjective linguistic medium, rather than in a private unarticulated experience.

TAYLOR

Taylor studied at Balliol – the birthplace and stronghold of British idealism. After that, he was appointed successively a Fellow of All Souls College, Oxford, and Chichele Professor of Social and Political Theory at Oxford, before he later returned to his native Canada. His doctoral thesis reworked the idealist concern to defend a vitalist analysis of human behaviour against the formalist and positivist approach of behaviouralists. It drew on the emerging analytic and linguistic philosophy in Oxford to rewrite this concern as a conceptual and empirical issue. This issue could not be decided by an appeal to metaphysical categories such as absolute mind (Taylor 1961, 1964). After completing his doctorate, Taylor wrote a series of essays explicitly challenging behaviouralism and its core beliefs. He argued, in 'Interpretation and the Sciences of Man', that beliefs, meanings, and language were constitutive of human actions and practices. The social sciences were unavoidably hermeneutical. His argument entailed a break with 'mainstream social science' and its empiricist and positivist epistemology. In particular, 'we cannot measure such sciences against the requirements of a science of verification; we cannot judge them by their predictive capacity' (Taylor 1971, 51).

In 'Neutrality in Political Science', Taylor extended his argument to take direct aim at 'the cult of neutrality' (Taylor 1967, 48, 27, 46). Behaviouralists defended the superiority of their approach by arguing that older approaches were always permeated by value positions, so their frameworks were never scientific. They always served the interests of a normative or ideological theory. Behaviouralists proposed to turn the study of politics into a technocratic 'policy science', akin to engineering or medicine, which would 'show us how to attain our goals'. However, Taylor pointed out that when behaviouralists constructed theoretical frameworks to delimit the proper area of scientific inquiry, they too made fundamental choices that entailed normative commitments. The work of Lasswell, Easton, and Almond hid their norms. Taylor suggested that conceptual frameworks always depended on theory, and theory cannot be constructed apart from values. The ties binding theoretical frameworks and values also opened the possibility of seeing some values as especially meaningful responses to particular empirical contexts.

Stivers (2008, 943) suggests our argument for an interpretive approach was 'weakened by the failure to include its philosophical roots. Nowhere is there a citation to any of those who constructed the foundations of interpretivism'. Hay (personal correspondence) urged us to take account of 'similarly minded figures in the literature' and to situate our views 'with respect to the existing literatures on the state'. Initially, we were reluctant to provide yet another critical review of the present-day political science literature. Engaging with the literature is one of those 'rules' of the political science community that can lead to endless citations and much tedium. It is also a rule suffused with notions of cumulating scientific knowledge. As should now be obvious, we do not draw on present-day political science to any significant degree. So, to the extent we draw on a literature unfamiliar to many political scientists, we have now spelt out intellectual forebears. When relevant, as in Chapter 5, we will use endnotes to identify where our concerns overlap with those of some of our contemporaries. Our primary task, however, is to spell out our preferred approach to studying the state, and Part I concentrates on the general theory of the state.

A summary of the argument

The theory of the state is the historical heart of political science. As we show briefly in this chapter, during the twentieth century, the main approach to the state was modernist-empiricism with its associated empirical topics.

Positivists, including many behaviouralists, tried to replace the concept of the state with other concepts more amenable to their general theories, but modernist-empiricists nonetheless ensured that the concept kept a key place in the lexicon of political science. We looked at present-day versions of modernist-empiricism, unpacking the distinctive philosophies, concepts, and empirical topics. We did so to identify the distinctiveness of our approach. Our aim is to define, defend, and illustrate an alternative theory of the state. It is not based on modernist-empiricism but on hermeneutics and historicism; on Dilthey and Collingwood rather than Weber or Marx.

Chapter 2 examines the leading present-day expression of modernist-empiricism: the new institutionalism. First, we challenge the belief of new institutionalists that they have a shared new paradigm. Instead, we suggest it is varied, containing strands that can scarcely be reconciled with one another. Second, we argue that historical institutionalism exists primarily as a counter to rational choice institutionalism but its inductive, modernist-empiricist logic lacks a micro-level theory for explaining historical change and awareness grows that it is not a distinctive approach. Third, we argue that ideational or constructivist institutionalism offers a promising way forward provided it develops a micro-theory that appeals to the beliefs and desires of actors and it breaks with the ahistorical forms of explanation of modernist-empiricism.

Chapter 3 explores what many observers suggest are the leading present-day forms of interpretive social science; postmodern theories of discourse. First, we challenge the belief these approaches have a shared paradigm stemming from anti-foundational philosophy. Instead, we suggest that anti-foundationalism is compatible with all kinds of approaches to political science, and these approaches arose out of distinctive socialist or radical traditions, not mainstream political science. Second, we argue that much discourse theory still relies on structuralist and occasionally even determinist forms of explanation associated with modernist-empiricism. There is a clear tension between this lingering structuralism and historicist genealogies. Third, we suggest that discourse introduces several new topics to the theory of the state. These topics include governmentality, collective identities, ideologies, and resistance in governance.

In Chapter 4, we present our own theory of the state and highlight its distinct and distinctive features. Our approach differs significantly from the ideational and interpretive approaches found respectively within the new institutionalism and discourse theory. In particular, we defend a historical approach to meaning as situated agency, explicitly opposing structural concepts of signifiers and regimes. From this perspective, the state appears as a differentiated cultural practice composed of all kinds of contingent and shifting beliefs and actions, where these beliefs and actions can be explained through a historical understanding. We then provide the set of aggregate concepts appropriate to historical studies of the state: situated agency, practice, power, narrative, tradition, and dilemma.

We explain our approach to studying the state as an introduction to our main concern in this book; empirical shifts in, and debates about, the changing nature of 'the state'. We want to show how our anti-foundationalism leads us to see both the state and the reforms that produce changes in the state differently. In Chapter 5, we take our aggregate concepts and decentre present-day approaches to the changing state. Such changes are typically described as a shift to governance. First-wave studies of governance typically describe changes in the state and its links to civil society as akin to a differentiated polity. This polity was characterized by a hollowed-out state, a core executive fumbling to pull rubber levers of control, and, most notably, a massive spread of networks. Second-wave studies of governance herald a return to the state with the idea of metagovernance. We pronounce the death of both narratives, because we argue there is no single account or theory of contemporary governance, only the differing constructions of several traditions. We counterpose these narratives with a third-wave of governance that announces the arrival of the stateless state. We argue the state arises out of the diverse actions and practices inspired by varied beliefs and traditions. The state, or pattern of rule, is the contingent product of diverse actions and political struggles informed by the beliefs of agents rooted in traditions. We identify new research topics suggested by our decentred analysis under the headings of the '3Rs' of rule, rationalities, and resistance, and we provide examples of each in Part II.

There is no one-to-one correspondence between the '3Rs' and the individual chapters, but there is a steady shift of emphasis from rule to rationalities to resistance. We start by looking at patterns of rule as they are understood by elite actors. Chapter 6 describes the everyday life of ministers through an account of their daily life in government. We provide our interpretation of their interpretation of what the world looks like through their eyes. We watched people in their everyday office life, reporting on what they said and did, and also on their reasons for their actions. We understand 'ruling' and, therefore, 'the state' through their eyes.

We then turn to the rationalities or technologies used by government, specifically the rationality associated with the new public management, or managerialism, with its emphasis on targets and performance measurement.

In Chapter 7, we decentre the Blair government's putative reforms of a central feature of the British state as understood by Westminster elites, notably the civil service. We tell *three* stories about the civil service and public service delivery. First, there is the centralization story, which claims the changes sought to increase the power of the Prime Minister at the expense of Cabinet and the Departments. Second, we tell the management story, which claims the reforms of the civil service foundered on Blair's lack of policy making and management skills. Finally, we recount the governance story, which argues that the Prime Minister was locked into webs of dependence that undermined his initiatives.

Chapter 8 looks at the way senior civil servants coped with managerial rationalities: the continuous reform of the public service. The rise of the new public management in the 1980s led to recurring challenges to the administrative traditions of the public service in Australia, Canada, and the United Kingdom. We analyse how the heads of the public service articulate the traditions of 'constitutional bureaucracy' found in Westminster systems of parliamentary government and selectively draw on past understandings to understand present-day changes. We describe living traditions under challenge that reshape reforms as reforms reshape them. We conclude that the heads of the public services have found 'space' or 'voice' to identify innovative ways of combining past traditions with new organizing principles of governance. In each case, it is not a question of 'in with the new, out with the old', but of 'in with the new alongside key parts of the old'. The myths and legends of yore remain germane to the modern public service.

So far our focus has been on elite narratives and elite understandings of the state and its rationalities. In Chapter 9, we turn to the question of how middle-level managers, employees, and citizens experience the state and its rationalities. Again, we employ ethnographic methods to understand the ways in which they construct 'the state' in their everyday beliefs and practices. We show there are significant differences in the way the rationality of managerialism is experienced and understood. These different narratives are stories of resistance and are central to understanding what elites term the 'implementation gap' in reform of the public services.

Finally, in Chapter 10, we summarize our core argument on the stateless state. We highlight our key findings. We reflect on what we have learnt from observation compared with more conventional methods. We discuss the strengths and the weaknesses of our methods. We answer the 'so what' question by enumerating the benefits of our approach, theoretical and methodological. Finally, we reflect on the normative implications of our analysis for the Westminster state and its tradition of representative democracy. We examine briefly the case for supplementing representative institutions with participatory democracy, collaborative forms of governance, and dialogic policy making.

Notes

1. There is an extensive literature on the idea of the state and its evolution: see Hall and Ikenberry (1989), Skinner (1978), and Tilly (1975).
2. In their history of the idea of the state in the social sciences, Hall and Ikenberry (1989, 1) claim there is 'a great deal of agreement' that the state is a set of institutions that monopolizes rule making for a bounded territory. Hay and Lister (2006, 8) also see the state as a sovereign authority, comprising 'a set of institutions with a dedicated personnel' that wields 'a monopoly of authoritative rule making within a bounded territory', as the dominant view.
3. We focus on the dominant intellectual traditions in American and British political science, a position never occupied by Marxism. However, where relevant, we do note and comment on contributions from the Marxist tradition; see, Chapter 2, especially note 1; Chapter 3 on post-Marxism and other radical approaches; and Chapter 5 on neo-Marxist theories of metagovernance.
4. There was also a second wave of German writing on *verstehen* in opposition to this neo-positivism. Indeed, to some extent, we might read Gadamer as reviving Dilthey's hermeneutic approach, and Habermas as reviving Weber's project of synthesizing historical and causal analysis. See respectively Gadamer (2002) and Habermas (1988).

Part I

State Theory

Chapter 2

The New Institutionalism

Introduction

In Chapters 2 and 3, we seek to situate our approach to the study of the state in the existing literature. In this chapter, we look at the new institutionalism because it is the dominant approach of the past twenty years.[1] It is said to have many varieties but, we will argue, all have a common epistemology in modernist-empiricism. In Chapter 3, we turn to approaches sharing an anti-foundational epistemology. However, these chapters are not just neutral accounts of the existing literature. They are genealogies inspired by our alternative approach. In this chapter, for example, we tell a story about the new institutionalism that highlights its persistent debt to positivism and modernist-empiricism, the way it mingles confused and incompatible strands, and the almost empty nature of its appeal to history. Our story undercuts the self-understanding of many new institutionalists.

Therefore, Chapters 2 and 3 serve a number of purposes. First, they highlight the places where our interpretive approach differs from alternatives. Second, they are critiques, revealing the debts of these alternatives to positions they sometimes disavow and highlighting the contingent and confused content of these alternatives. Finally, they provide evidence of how our interpretive approach can narrate both itself and the leading alternatives. The ability of a theory of politics to narrate itself deserves more emphasis that it usually receives. Because the theories claim to make sense of human life, and because political science is part of human life, the theories ought to be able to explain themselves. If they cannot, they are guilty of not adequately performing what they preach. In Chapters 2–4, we provide narratives of the new institutionalism, post-structuralism, and our interpretive theory. We use our theory to show how all these approaches to the state arose out of traditions responding to dilemmas.

We now look forward to reading a new institutionalist narrative that shows the new institutionalism to be a product of political scientists acting in accord with norms that lock them into path-dependent development. We look forward with even greater relish to the Foucauldian narrative that shows governmentality to be a form of power/knowledge that disciplines individual subjects.

The authorized biography

New institutionalists have spread their own version of the history of their approach. Their authorized history introduces the new institutionalism as a distinctive period in the development of American political science. An old institutionalism dominated from the late nineteenth century until the interwar years. Then, in the 1950s, behaviouralism developed, flourishing as the disciplinary mainstream through the 1960s. It waned in the 1970s, with the new institutionalism emerging in the 1980s as a broad new paradigm with a different research agenda (see, e.g. March and Olsen 1984). As is so often the case with trends in American political science, this new approach crossed the Atlantic and influenced the research agenda in Britain and the rest of northern Europe. France and the Mediterranean countries have a natural immunity to American political science!

This storyline captures some features of the discipline's past, but it misleads in two ways. First, the phrase 'new institutionalism' suggests there is a shared research agenda. In fact, there is much diversity of topics and techniques, and we should avoid any implication that there is a shared, single paradigm. The new institutionalism can be decentred to show it encompasses several intellectual traditions. Second, the claim that the approach is 'new' obscures the continuities between the several institutional traditions and behavioural scholarship. Of course, there are differences between the two, but the nature and extent of the differences vary between the several varieties of new institutionalism. Most important, each of the traditions in the new institutionalism remains firmly wedded to the modernist-empiricism and positivism that dominated much political science for most of the twentieth century.

New institutionalists have spread not only an authorized history but also an authorized typology. Hall and Taylor (1996) offer a widely accepted account of the 'schools of thought' or traditions in the new institutionalism. They distinguish between rational choice, historical, and sociological new institutionalisms.[2] Their typology was a late arrival on the scene.

In fact, none of their labels enjoyed wide currency before the 1990s, although each of the 'schools of thought' are said to originate in the late 1970s. This disparity poses the question of how well the labels capture the ideas and agendas of the earlier periods.

Sociological institutionalism has its roots in organizational studies. It developed from the work of Stanford sociologist Meyer, with his 1977 article on 'Institutionalized Organizations: Formal Structure as Myth and Ceremony' seen as the seminal, founding contribution (Meyer and Rowan 1977). Rational choice institutionalism is also a separate school located at the intersection of economics and political science. It developed from the work of two political scientists at Washington University in St. Louis, Shepsle and Weingast. The key text here is Shepsle (1979), 'Institutional Arrangements and Equilibrium in Multidimensional Voting Models'. It was later described by Riker (1980, 444) as the exemplar of what a 'new kind of study of institutions might typically look like'. Each of these schools corresponds to a distinct tradition with a clear lineage from the late 1970s to the present day.[3]

The case of historical institutionalism is different. It is a more amorphous school than the others, grouping works of scholarship-covering topics and research methods so diverse they border on incompatible. One can only make historical institutionalism map into a single tradition by a substantial, retrospective rewriting of intellectual history. Most of the work that people describe as historical institutionalism was defined at the time it was written in terms of substantive topics, notably the state. The phrase 'historical institutionalism' barely appears until the mid-1980s at the earliest and, as we will argue below, it is not until the 1990s that its proponents present themselves as a distinct school.

Whether this school is distinctive is questionable. The label 'historical institutionalism' is peculiarly unhelpful. It does not tell us what, if anything, sets it apart. If the label historical simply implies a minimal willingness to discuss the past, then historical studies are found in all three schools of thought. If the label is meant to pick out approaches that use historicist forms of explanation, then none of the three schools of the new institutionalism merit this label. All three schools view the past through modernist-empiricist and positivist spectacles.

In the first part of this chapter, we revisit the history of the new institutionalism. For the decade 1975 to 1985, we track the origins of the scholarly agenda focused on the state. Subsequently, this agenda would be retrospectively characterized as the new institutionalism. It became an integral part of the debate with the rational choice tradition, which had staked its own claim to embody a new institutionalism. In the second part of the chapter, we chart the spread of the new institutionalism between 1985 and 1996, and the dilemmas posed by rational choice institutionalism, before turning to two more recent developments. The first development is the emergence of historical institutionalism as a rallying label under which diverse political scientists in comparative and American politics located and defended their work from the challenge of rational choice. The second development is the 'constructivist turn', sometimes referred to as ideational institutionalism, in the sociological school. In conclusion, we highlight the common ground with and differences between the various traditions in the new institutionalism.

Before new institutionalism, 1975–85

In the late 1970s and early 1980s, there was an increase in use of the concept of the state across several literatures. This shift would later be seen as the early stage in a developing new institutionalism, but it was not so understood before the mid-1980s.

Bringing the state back In

During the 1950s and 1960s, the concept of the state was unfashionable in many parts of political science and political sociology. But in the mid-to-late 1970s the pendulum swung back as a new generation of scholars embraced the older concept (see, e.g. Tilly 1975; Katzenstein 1976; Krasner 1976). This shift was in some cases a minor event, a signal of engagement with perspectives that had never gone out of fashion. In other cases, it was a rallying cry of young scholars resisting prevailing orthodoxies, and engaged with one or more of the neo-Marxist perspectives that flourished in the prior decade.[4] The turn to the state by these authors occurred largely independently of one another, each with his or her own concerns. However, there were some overlapping interests; for example, the international contexts for domestic politics. So, there were efforts to bring the various strands of scholarship together. In February 1982, a conference was convened at Mount Kisco in New York to consider the 'Research Implications of Current Theories of the State'. This conference led to the formation, under the auspices of the Social Science Research Council, of a research committee – the Committee on States and Social Structures. Its remit was to promote the state as an orienting concept and as a subject matter of empirical research. The committee was chaired by two conference participants, Skocpol and Evans, who edited versions of papers from the conference to form most of the Committee's first publication, *Bringing the State Back In* (Evans, Rueschemeyer, and Skocpol 1985).

The title of the volume was taken from the paper that Skocpol presented at the 1982 conference, which appeared in revised form as the volume's introductory chapter. This phrase combines the broad, and necessarily vague, imagery needed to frame the various contributions as a single movement with the rhetorical charge needed to propound a programmatic agenda. It offers the image of a continuing 'intellectual sea change', with scholars turning away from 'society-centred ways of explaining politics and governmental activities'. Instead, they are converging 'on complementary arguments and strategies of analysis' that take seriously the role of states as actors (Skocpol 1985, 3–4).

Such images presuppose that political science was dominated in the 1950s and 1960s by reductionist theories that did not consider states to be potentially autonomous actors. Such a view involves major simplifications, even inaccuracies. By basing their claim to novelty on it, the 'neostatists' (Katznelson 1984) left themselves open to criticism, especially from advocates of the approaches they were claiming to transcend. Almond (1988) took advantage of the opening to launch a stinging criticism of the new agenda. He considered it as little more than a mere semantic shift passed off as a substantive intellectual transformation achieved only by caricaturing the disciplinary past and obscuring hard-won insights.

Neither the neostatist image of transformation nor Almond's counterattack captures well the new scholarship's intellectual lineage. Almond was right; recognizing the autonomy of the state was no great departure. The neostatists were right; their analytic concerns were a break with behaviouralism. They rejected the theory and the techniques associated with positivist strands of behaviouralism. They rejected structural-functional theorizing. They rejected the whole project of crafting general, universally applicable, law-like generalizations. They were also wary of large-*N* statistical, cross-national comparative work. However, they kept the ambition of developing theory that was empirical (in the sense of being independent of normative commitments). They also aimed to generate and test hypotheses about recurring relations between prior conditions and outcomes. They preferred small-*N* studies hedged by 'context' to large-*N* statistical analysis. They were still 'analytical'; the research logic was to generate and test 'mid-range theory'. *Bringing the State Back In* rejects the idea of a general theory of the state and advocates a modernist-empiricist strategy of 'analytical induction'.

Modernist-empiricists and positivists in political science had long found common ground in the use of analytic classification and empirical theory, and the rejection of normative pursuits. The neostatists were comfortable with this research method. The contrast with developmental historicism is sharp. Their respective views of the state are as different. There is not a hint of the nineteenth-century ethical notions of the state. Rather, neostatists draw on Weber for both the idea of the state holding 'a monopoly on the legitimate use of physical force' within a given territory, and the method which 'abstracts from the values of the present day'.

To some extent, our story accords with the authorized version in seeing the Committee on States and Social Structures as the founding event of the new institutionalism. But the seminal, founding text never describes their efforts to bring the state back in as either the new institutionalism or historical institutionalism. Also, the effort to weld together a single neostatist agenda did not eliminate differences among its scholars. Differences among them existed before the Committee on States and Social Structures came together, persisted through the Committee's lifespan (1983–90), and led to divergent positioning in the 1990s. Finally, the authorized account of the rise and diffusion of neostatism fails to recognize there were other, different intellectual tributaries that later got subsumed under historical institutionalism. For our purposes, we do not need to provide a detailed history but we do need to note the main contributions.

First, there is an extensive literature on American political development which pre-dates the rise of neostatism. This literature shows a clear debt to behaviouralism with its concern for such institutions as elections, interest groups, the Congress, and the administrative state. However, as the focus on development suggests, it presents itself as historical (see, e.g. Huntington 1981; Skowronek 1982; Sundquist 1983; and for an extended discussion and citations see Adcock, Bevir, and Stimson 2007).

Second, in international relations, there was the study of regimes. An early contributor was Krasner (1978) who expounded a state-centric realism that linked the state with the national interest understood as the international equivalent of the public interest. However, the constraints on states in pursuing their national interest led Krasner to explore the notion of international regimes. Regimes were seen as 'mutual expectations, generally agreed-to rules, regulations, and plans in accordance with which organizational energies and financial commitments are allocated' (Ruggie 1975). States still made decisions in pursuit of their national interests but subject to regime constraints (Krasner 1984; Keohane 1988; and for an extended discussion and citations see Adcock, Bevir, and Stimson 2007). From these disparate roots came the 'schools of thought' that preoccupy political scientists to this day.

The spread of new institutionalism, 1984–86

Talk of a new approach to institutions had been common among rational choice scholars in political science at least since 1980 when Riker hailed Shepsle and Weingast. It did not enter the conversation of most other political scientists until March and Olsen published 'The New Institutionalism: Organizational Factors in Political Life' in the *American Political Science Review* in 1984. Within a few years, the phrase swept the discipline. By the late 1980s, all manner of intellectual traditions claimed to embody the approach in one form or another. The resulting confusion and debate fed efforts to identify and defend several species of new institutionalism.

The origins of much of the confusion enveloping the new institutionalism lie in the article that popularized this phrase. March and Olsen lift the new approaches to institutions in organizational sociology and rational choice out of their specific intellectual contexts. Instead, they treat them as examples of a general shift towards a new institutionalism.[5] Their new institutionalism not only incorporates these two independent, divergent approaches, but also encompasses other recent agendas, such as neostatism. March and Olson were able to construct such a broad new institutionalism only by defining it in contrast to a caricature of behaviouralism (for an extended discussion see Adcock, Bevir, and Stimson 2007). The strands of work they describe as institutionalist have little in common other than that they do not resemble this caricature of behaviouralism. Once the reader questions that caricature, little remains of the allegedly common agenda – or the alleged novelty – of March and Olson's institutionalism. All that remains is a confused hodgepodge of incompatible intellectual positions.

A similar confusion appears when the notion of a general approach to institutions first appears among the neostatists. In a review article, 'Approaches to the State', Krasner (1984) maintains the contrast between statist and pluralist orientations, but he begins to describe the former less as focused on the state and more in terms of a concern with institutions. Krasner (1984, 224) here reinterprets several neostatist works in the language of institutions by asking: '[H]ow do institutional structures change in response to alterations in domestic and international environments and then in subsequent time periods influence these environments?' This question constructed parallels between young neostatists and an older tradition of institutional political science with a macro-qualitative bent long prominent at Harvard. Indeed, Krasner remarks that Skowronek's *Building a New American State* (1982) 'complements the work of other scholars, such as Huntington'. In seeking to flesh out the characteristics of a broad institutional approach, Krasner (1984, 240) emphasizes a shared concern with the contrast 'between periods of institutional creation and periods of institutional stasis'. He suggests that such historical patterns may be conceptualized as 'punctuated equilibrium'. Though his terminology is novel, the ease with which Krasner groups neostatists with exemplars of an older institutionalism sits rather awkwardly alongside his claim that neostatism sets 'a different agenda' for research by taking institutions seriously (Krasner 1984, 243).

Krasner's review article symbolizes a large intellectual shift. By the mid-to-late 1980s the initial excitement associated with the concept of the state was fading, and attention was moving to institutionalism. This shift reflected growing scepticism about the substantive pay-off of efforts to bring the state back in. Scholars questioned the amount of explanatory burden that could be carried by notions such as state autonomy. As the novelty of a statist agenda wore off, the relation between neostatism and other strands of scholarship was re-examined. The vague term 'institutionalism' acted as a broad umbrella under which to fuse – or confuse – the broadly structuralist thrust of the neostatists with the concern with ideas and institutions that had long characterized the work of figures such as Hartz (1955), Huntington (1981), and Beer (1963). Certainly Beer's student Hall (1986, 1989) brings a distinctive concern with ideas into neostatist discussions of comparative political economy.

Once the vague term 'institutionalism' eclipsed neostatism, Skocpol came to identify her approach with new institutionalism (Levi 1987). By 1988, new institutionalist language was prevalent in the study of American political development, public law, and international relations. The spread of the term 'new institutionalist' often remade intellectual alliances. In particular, the earlier tendency of neostatists to define themselves in contrast to behaviouralism and pluralism largely disappeared. Indeed, after the neostatists adopted the label 'new institutionalism', they often forged an alliance with strands of behaviouralism that engaged with historical topics. This alliance was facilitated by a shared modernist-empiricist concern to approach the past inductively so as to forge 'analytic' generalizations rather than historicist narratives. Equally, the alliance owed much to the growing menace of a common foe: rational choice with its deductive logic. Rational choice posed a direct challenge to the inductive logic that was common to both behaviouralism and the macro-qualitative tradition of the neostatists.

The challenge of rational choice

Multiple strands in rational choice scholarship converged by the late 1980s, presenting other traditions in political science with a dynamic, self-confident rival that was enriching its technical base while also expanding its substantive scope. First, there were developments in formalized theoretical work. In the early 1980s, this strand, exemplified in the work of such figures as Weingast, expanded its repertoire of concepts and tools to draw on the new economics of organization associated with such economists as Williamson (and for a review see Moe 1984). This work provides the rational choice tradition with proprietary claim to be the first self-conscious new institutionalism to emerge in political science. Further cross-disciplinary exchange followed when leading economic historian North joined Weingast and others at Washington University in St. Louis in 1983. The criticism that this developing positive theory of political institutions was concerned only with modern American institutions became increasingly less plausible towards the end of the decade. Weingast and North started to work on historical topics (see, e.g. Milgrom, North, and Weingast 1990).

There was a second, less formalized use of rational choice in comparative politics, which built on Olson's arguments about collective action. This perspective was pioneered in the late 1970s in Popkin's *The Rational Peasant* (1979), and further developed in the early 1980s in Bates' *Markets and States in Tropical Africa* and *Essays on the Political Economy of Rural Africa* (1981). Popkin and Bates were concerned with the state, peasants, and the conflict arising from great political and economic change. Analytically, they broke with the structural-functionalism, which was prominent in comparative politics during the behavioural era. Instead, they relied on micro-level, rational choice theory. Their 'collective-choice school of political economy' adopted institutional language, and by 1983 Bates was identifying institutions as the core concern of this school (Bates 1983, 134–47). However, although Popkin and Bates do engage the past, the historical ambition of this strand of scholarship only became evident a few years later, with the 1988 publication of Levi's *Of Rule and Revenue* (1988). Levi's broad temporal scope exceeds that of any neostatist, encompassing cases from Republican

Rome, Middle-Age Europe, and early modern Britain, as well as twentieth-century Australia.

By the late 1980s, multiple strands of rational choice scholarship were converging into a self-consciously new institutionalist approach that was increasingly confident in its ability to take on the historical topics claimed as home turf by the neostatists, who were, at the same time, busy reinventing themselves as new institutionalists. These tensions came out fully in Levi's 'Bringing People Back into the State' (1988), published as an appendix to *Of Rule and Revenue*. She criticizes neostatism for an excessive structuralism in which 'individuals become little more than the embodiment of the structures they represent', while also suggesting that Skocpol's modernist-empiricist strategy of 'stockpiling case studies' is 'not the solution'. Levi argues that the success of a 'new macro-comparative history' requires greater attention to 'micro-foundations' and points to rational choice theory as the best available tool for the job (Levi 1988, 197; see also Taylor 1989). From Levi's standpoint as a rational choice institutionalist, it seemed obvious that more rigorous attention to the micro-level was needed to make theoretical sense out of the macro-comparative studies that neostatists and their emerging successors produced.

The challenge from rational choice led scholars to distinguish among competing variants of new institutionalism. While earlier discussions among neostatists and their associates had spelled out attributes that would now come to be associated specifically with 'historical' institutionalism, they did so without employing that label or framing their approach in contrast to rational choice. The label 'historical' begins to appear only as part of a conscious effort to distinguish and defend inductive modernist-empiricist approaches from the challenge of rational choice. So, Thelen and Steinmo (1992) describe historical institutionalism in two ways. First, they provide an intellectual history in which old institutionalism is succeeded by behaviouralism, then new institutionalism. Second, they draw a contrast in new institutionalism between a rational choice and a historical institutionalism. The term 'historical institutionalism' is credited to Skocpol, and presented 'to distinguish this variant of institutionalism from the alternative, rational choice' (Thelen and Steinmo 1992, 28 n4).

Since, as we have seen, rational choice scholars were already confidently addressing the past, the 'historical' adjective here could only make historical institutionalism distinctive if it meant more than studying the past. Introducing the term appears as a pre-emptive attempt to draw the boundary of the historical to exclude rational choice with its universalizing micro-theory. The key to this boundary drawing is the belief that a historical approach treats people's motives and actions as dependent on particular institutional settings. Thus, in their effort to spell out the divergence between historical and rational choice institutionalisms, Thelen and Steinmo (1992, 7–10) stress the role of the 'institutional context' in shaping individuals' goals and preferences. This emphasis on the role of social and institutional contexts in structuring individuals' preferences and choices can, however, only be taken so far. Contexts are not conceived as inherently historical, particular, and contingent. To the contrary, the particular and contingent get short shrift before the abstraction and comparison required by the continuing commitment to the modernist-empiricist goal of using analytical induction to generate and test mid-range empirical theory. While rational choice institutionalism offered a distinctive micro-theory, historical institutionalism followed neostatism in simply evading the relevant theoretical issues.

In so far as historical institutionalism has any claim to be distinctive, this claim lies in the role it sometimes gives to ideas. Neostatism generally employed a structuralism that gave little weight to ideas, norms, or values as independent explanatory variables. Historical institutionalists often take a different approach that owes much to the way Hall drew inspiration from Hartz, Huntington, and Beer. Thelen and Steinmo (1992, 22–6) in their introductory essay, identify 'ideational innovation', though within 'institutional constraints', as a previously neglected area that offers a new 'frontier' for historical institutionalists. When Hall and Taylor (1996, 942) arrive on the scene, we find attention to the role of ideas is a key feature distinguishing this school from other institutionalisms. There is one other distinctive change, central to the emergence of historical institutionalism. Behaviouralism is no longer 'the other' against which historical institutionalism defines itself. Now the 'other' is played by a general image of rational choice scholarship that lacks any nuance.

Constructivism – a new trajectory?

Historical institutionalism was not alone in paying more attention to ideas than did neostatism. In international relations, Katzenstein and other neostatists drew on sociological institutionalism to develop a constructivism that showed much interest in ideas.

Few international relations scholars adopted the label 'historical institutionalist'. In the early 1990s, they turned instead to constructivism. Keohane (1988) early on identified two approaches in the international relations literature to institutions; the 'reflective' approach and the rational choice approach. The 'reflective' label was soon supplanted by the alternative term, constructivism. Thus, Wendt (1992, 399) uses constructivism to refer to a 'cognitive, intersubjective' tradition which he contrasts with a competing 'rationalist-behaviouralist' tradition (see also Kratochwil and Ruggie 1986). A constructivist conceives of institutions as 'fundamentally cognitive entities', and 'institutionalization' as 'a process of internalizing new identities and interests'. In these early essays, Keohane and Wendt combined a reflective or constructivist approach with Ruggie's emphasis on regimes and the older sociological work, especially by Mead.

Later, however, in the mid-1990s, international relations scholars began explicitly to relate their constructivism to the sociological institutionalism. Only then did this third variety of the new institutionalism come into play in political science. It was, then, in the mid-1990s that Katzenstein teamed up with Wendt and several other younger scholars to produce the edited volume *The Culture of National Security*. Katzenstein, in his introduction to this volume, spells out disagreements with the path-dependency approach of many historical institutionalists, and invokes sociological institutionalism as a key, third position in debates about institutionalism in political science. He showcases the perspectives on culture and identity associated with sociological institutionalism as crucial for understanding the causal processes that define interests and 'constitute the actors that shape national security politics and global insecurities' (Katzenstein 1996, 16). Finnemore (1996, 326–7) not only spells out the frameworks and terminology drawn from sociologists, but also argues that their use of the term 'institution' is 'very different' from that of rational choice and historical institutionalists. For her, 'incommensurable definitions mean that despite similarities in labelling, these approaches – all called institutionalist – have little in common'. Sociological institutionalism, with its treatment of cultural norms and rules as institutions, is welcomed by Finnemore as more than just a parallel to political science's home-grown constructivism. It is, she holds, compatible with that tradition, yet different enough to offer ways of improving it. In particular, Finnemore suggests that sociological institutionalism offers 'a much richer and more detailed theoretical framework than has constructivism'. However, Finnemore displays a concern characteristic of constructivists. She wants to highlight the context, but remains committed to analytic generalization, and in particular, to the notion that empirical theory is key to achieving this goal.

Hay (2002, chapter 6) ostensibly builds on constructivist international relations to provide a more thorough-going ideational version of historical institutionalism, although he also draws extensively on strategic-relational theory with its roots in neo-Marxist theories of the state (see, e.g. Hay 1996 and Jessop 1990). He argues that actors are strategic with complex, contingent, and changing goals. They live and work in contexts that favour some strategies over others. Their perceptions of the context, whether accurate or not, shape their choice of strategies. Moreover, these ideas are not determined by, for example, the material context. They are socially constructed. They are not given by the institutional settings. Institutions too are socially constructed out of contingent political struggles. Change arises out of the interaction between strategic conduct and strategic context. Thus, he seeks 'to identify, detail, and interrogate the extent to which... established ideas become codified, serving as cognitive filters through which actors come to interpret environmental signals' and understand their strategic conduct (Hay 2006, 65). However, there is an ever-present reluctance in Hay's account to abandon structural explanations manifested in his discussion of ideational and material factors. He talks of ideational factors as 'variables' and of the relative weight of ideational and material factors in causal analysis; of material determinants of crisis. He is not prepared to abandon the association between subjective desires and real interests. The phrase 'cognitive filters' treats ideas as intervening variables. There is a clear reluctance to adopt a through-going constructivist perspective. Rather, he sits outside of, and comments on, the contending approaches.

Constructivist institutionalism is a work in progress.[6] Obviously we welcome the greater interest shown in ideas. Equally, however, we note critically how reluctant its advocates are properly to break with modernist empiricism or a lingering structuralism. Constructivist institutionalists may sometimes pay lip service to interpretive and historicist modes of thinking. But their empirical work still characteristically relies on modernist-empiricist and even structuralist modes of explanation, appealing to variables and correlations and to emergent social structures and institutional settings. Moreover, their theoretical writings fail to address two important questions. First, are social practices or institutions akin to natural kinds in having clear boundaries and some kind of essence that defines at least some of their other properties and behaviour? If they are, constructivist institutionalism falls back on a modernist-empiricism or even positivism that relies on reification to make possible formal explanations couched in terms of variables, correlations, and classifications. If they are not, constructivist institutionalists will have to stop dressing their explanations in the formal clothes of variables and instead concentrate on historicist explanations of contingent practices. They will have to do empirical work to show us what beliefs and actions led people to make the world as they did, and what traditions inspired those beliefs. Second, do structures and institutional contexts force people to try to act in certain ways irrespective of their perception of them? If they do, constructivist institutionalism relies on the same kind of determinism as found in older structuralisms. If they do not, the constructivist institutionalists will have to stop appealing to such structures as if they were given and instead focus on the subjective and intersubjective dilemmas that people believe the world poses. They will have to do empirical work to show us how the relevant political actors understood their context.

Conclusions

We started with Hall and Taylor's distinction between rational, historical, and sociological institutionalism (1996), which identified the distinct and distinctive features of each type. We have decentred this account. We have approached the typology of rational choice, historical, and sociological institutionalism, not as a static grid applicable since the late 1970s, but as a mid-1990s perspective on debates among political scientists. Before the mid-1990s, sociological institutionalism was not a player in those debates. In the 1990s, the debates were framed as a rivalry between historical and rational choice institutionalism but not before, and many were not persuaded that this was a useful way of highlighting the issues. A typological perspective also downplays changes over time. Thus, the assertion that historical institutionalism is sensitive to the role of ideas is misleading if applied to the 1970s and 1980s because attentiveness to ideas marks a significant departure from the structuralist tendencies of this neostatist literature.

Decentring the contrasts between rational choice and historical institutionalism also provides a better understanding of where we are today. Rational choice institutionalism revolves around a well-articulated and developing body of micro-theory. This theory makes it possible to identify rational choice institutionalism as a distinctive approach that is, for better or worse, clearly novel compared to political science's longer-standing approaches to institutions. There is a notable contrast here with historical institutionalism, which lacks a coherent shared theoretical core. Indeed, it is hard to avoid the conclusion that the 'historical' label jumbles up an eclectic range of modernist-empiricist efforts.

These contrasts have continuing legacies. Rational choice asks questions about the motor of change in macro-historical studies. It challenges the conceptual vagueness of punctuated equilibrium, critical junctures, and path dependency. Awareness grows that historical institutionalism lacks micro-level purchase. For example, when Kathleen Thelen (1999) reconsidered historical institutionalism alongside rational choice, she raised doubts about aspects of her earlier characterizations. She placed new emphasis on the potential compatibility of rational choice with macro-qualitative work. So, it would seem the contrast between historical and rational choice institutionalisms is in decline as a way of understanding the new institutionalism. Other, new lines of inquiry come to prominence.

Perhaps the most promising new avenue is ideational or constructivist institutionalism. In the study of international relations, comparative politics, and sociological institutionalism there is already a growing body of research. We welcome this development and will discuss its links to our approach in Chapter 4, but we fear the endless search for the novel and claims about progress may obscure important continuity. A focus on the interplay of ideas and institutions is a long-standing part of political science. Constructivist institutionalism will be an important development only if it develops a micro-theory that appeals to the beliefs and desires of actors without duplicating the ideas of rational choice theory. It will be novel only if it breaks with the ahistorical forms of explanation around which modernist-empiricism and positivism have cohabited for half a century.

Alas, the commitment to modernist-empiricism is strong. For example, even Ruggie, in his *Constructing the World Polity* (1998), argues his approach to constructivism maintains 'a commitment to the idea of social science'. His approach is 'rooted in the classical tradition of Durkheim and Weber', and has an 'epistemological affinity' to pragmatism and speech act theory. He contrasts his approach with a postmodern constructivism – associated with Foucault and Derrida – in which 'little hope is held out for legitimate social science.' Even if the differences between rival ontologies and epistemologies are irreconcilable, it is still possible to show that one approach is better than another. That is our ambition. Claiming the different philosophies are irreconcilable is not a neutral statement in political science. Currently it serves to reinforce modernist-empiricism and avoids an openminded engagement with postmodernism. We will suggest that engaging with postmodernism is one way for an emergent constructivist institutionalism to adopt both the historicism absent from many of the new institutionalisms and to provide micro-level explanations. We fear constructivist institutionalism may become another variant of modernist-empiricism, rhetorically wrapped up as another break from a misremembered past. We argue for a break with this modernist-empiricist past in Chapter 3.

Notes

1. Especially in the United Kingdom and continental Europe, neo-Marxist approaches presented themselves as rivals to this political science mainstream. For a survey of the relevant literature, see Dunleavy and O'Leary (1987), Hay (1996), Hay, Lister, and Marsh (2006), and Jessop (2000, 2007*a*). Some varieties embodied modernist-empiricism. For example, Miliband (1969) built much of his Marxist critique of the British state on behavioural empirical data, prompting a vigorous debate (see Poulantzas 1969 and Miliband 1970). Other varieties of Marxist theory share some of our concerns, most notably post-Marxism (see Chapter 3) and the neo-Marxist critical realist analysis of metagovernance (see Chapter 5). Marsh (1999, 325–6, 332–3) argues, first, that most modern Marxists reject economism and structuralism, preferring to emphasize contingency and accepting a key role for agents; they no longer privilege class, acknowledging the crucial role of other bases of structured inequality. So far, so unremarkable. Second, and this is where such work differs from both post-Marxism (see Chapter 3) and our work – 'almost all Marxists broadly share a realist epistemological position'. He contradicts himself twice. First, 'almost all Marxists' excludes all the post-Marxists, none of whom would adopt a realist epistemology. Second, after rejecting structuralism, he adopts a realist epistemology to defend a realist ontology of social structures. Once socialists assign a causal role to structures, they can retain the causal role of material factors at the heart of the neo-Marxist approach, and argue that the capitalist economy, as one such material structure, constrains the development of society and the state. We discuss the contradictions of the Marxist critical realist analysis of the changing state and its continuing debt to modernist-empiricism in Chapter 5.
2. Typologies of the varieties of new institutionalism now abound; see, for example, Lowndes (1996), Peters (1999), and Rhodes *et al.* (2006).
3. On the sociological school, see DiMaggio and Powell (1991) and Hay (2006). On the rational choice school, see Shepsle (1995, 2006).
4. These theories included dependency theory, world-systems theory, and structural Marxist theories of the state; see, for example, Frank (1967), Poulantzas (1973), and Wallerstein (1974). The wave of books and articles about the state included Evans (1979), O'Donnell (1978), and Stepan (1978) writing on Latin America; Katzenstein (1978) and Krasner (1978) on international and comparative political economy; and Skocpol (1978) and Trimberger (1978) on revolution.

5. In fact, the 'new' institutionalism in organizational sociology was a reaction against the 'old' structural–functional approach taken by post-war sociologists such as Talcott Parsons. The 'new' institutionalism in rational choice was a corrective to earlier approaches to formal modelling that had not incorporated institutional structure. Neither was a reaction specifically against behaviouralist scholarship in political science.
6. For an introduction to, and citations on, this strand of constructivist institutionalism, see Blyth (2002*b*), and Hay (2002, chapter 6). See also Blyth (2002*a*), Campbell and Pederson (2001), and Hay, Lister, and Marsh (2006, chapters 5 and 8).

Chapter 3

Anti-foundationalism

Introduction

Let us get one point out of the way at the beginning: anti-foundationalism is an epistemological doctrine not a critical approach to politics. Anti-foundationalism is a doctrine in the philosophy of knowledge. In most versions it asserts that none of our knowledge is certain. In some versions it asserts more controversially that we cannot provide knowledge with secure foundations in either pure experiences or pure reason. We will argue, moreover, that it would be wrong, especially if one is an anti-foundationalist, to assume that epistemological doctrines ever lead directly to particular approaches to political science. Anti-foundationalism could be compatible with a wide range of political sciences – from rational choice to ethnography – and an equally wide range of ideologies – from conservatism to socialism.

There is something strange about using an epistemological concept to define an approach to political science. This sense of strangeness dissipates, however, if we allow that the connection between anti-foundationalism and critical approaches to politics is a historically contingent one. Thus, after briefly reviewing anti-foundational philosophy and its relation to political science, this chapter will provide a historical narrative of the contingent ways in which anti-foundationalism has been brought to political science from critical traditions.

What is anti-foundationalism?

To begin, we want to spell out the relationship of anti-foundationalism to political science. An anti-foundational epistemology has several implications for social philosophy. We will begin by briefly mentioning some of the less contentious implications, although even these might be subject to some debate. After that we will explain why anti-foundational philosophy is compatible with diverse approaches to political science, and, to end this section, we will consider the implications of our analysis of anti-foundationalism for its place in political science.

Anti-foundationalism and philosophy

The term 'anti-foundationalism' is of recent popularity. It is used to refer to any epistemology that rejects appeals to a basic ground or foundation of knowledge in either pure experience or pure reason. Anti-foundational epistemologies thus include many that pre-date the recent spread of the term itself. Examples of anti-foundationalism include not only post-modernists and post-structuralists but also many analytic philosophers who follow the pragmatists, Quine, or Wittgenstein. It has even been argued that the high positivists of the Vienna Circle were anti-foundationalists (Uebel 1996). So, contrary to what many political scientists believe, anti-foundationalism is not an obscure, outlandish doctrine to be easily dismissed as a ridiculous rejection of the idea of an external world. Anti-foundationalism is a commonplace among philosophers, and it is surely time political scientists developed enough philosophical literacy to understand it and consider its implications.

The most obvious implications of anti-foundationalism are perhaps meaning holism and anti-representationalism. Given that we cannot have pure experiences, our concepts and propositions cannot refer to the world in splendid isolation. Concepts cannot directly represent objects in the world since our experiences of those objects must in part be ones that we construct using our prior theories. So, anti-foundationalists conclude that concepts, meanings, and beliefs do not have a one-to-one correspondence with objects in the world, but rather form webs. Although anti-foundationalists have defended many different epistemologies, from pragmatism to radical scepticism, many of them conclude that we cannot justify isolated propositions. Rather, any justification of a knowledge-claim must be one that applies to a web of beliefs or research programme. It is these kinds of epistemological ideas that inspire anti-foundational critiques of the positivism and modernist-empiricism found in much political science.

Anti-foundationalism, with its meaning holism, has implications for social ontology. Meaning holism implies that our concepts are not simply given to us by the world as it is. Rather, we build them in part by drawing on our prior theories in an attempt to categorize, explain, and narrate our experiences. So, anti-foundationalists typically uphold social constructivism. They argue that we make the beliefs and concepts on which we act and thus the social world in which we live. This social constructivism asserts not only that we make the social world through our actions, but also that our actions reflect beliefs, concepts, languages, and discourses that themselves are social constructs. It is this constructivist ontology that inspires anti-foundational critiques of the reified and essentialist concepts found in much political science.

Meaning holism feeds into anti-foundational analyses of social explanation. It undermines reductionist attempts to explain actions by reference to allegedly objective social facts without reference to the relevant beliefs or meanings. The crucial argument here is that because people's beliefs form holistic webs, and because their experiences are laden with their prior beliefs, therefore we cannot assume that people in any given social location will come to hold certain beliefs or assume certain interests. To the contrary, their beliefs, including their view of their interests, will depend on their prior theories. So, anti-foundationalists conclude that social explanation consists not of reducing actions to social facts but of the interpretation of meanings as part of webs of belief, discourses, or cultural practices.

Social constructivism also feeds into anti-foundational analyses of social explanation. It undercuts a scientism in which social explanation appears as a search for ahistorical causal links. The crucial argument here is that because beliefs and concepts, and so actions and practices, are historically contingent social constructs, therefore we cannot adequately explain them by a correlation or mechanism across time. Human norms and practices are not natural or rational responses to given circumstances. Therefore, many anti-foundationalists conclude that social explanation contains an inherently historicist moment: even those concepts and practices that seem most natural to us need to be explained in part as products of a contingent history.

Anti-foundationalism and political science

Approaches to political science are peculiar entities. What political scientists identify as an approach is usually a jumble of philosophy, methods, and topics. So, for example, behaviouralism combined positivist philosophy with new statistical methods and the study of the political behaviour of individuals and groups. Yet, the philosophy, methods, and topics do not entail one another; they do not logically have to go together. So, for example, several political scientists study group and network behaviour without using any statistical techniques, and even political scientists who use statistical techniques to explore voting behaviour now often do so without adhering to a positivist philosophy.

To understand the implications of anti-foundationalism for political science, we should distinguish between philosophy, method, and topics. Anti-foundationalism supports a social philosophy characterized by holism, constructivism, interpretivism, and historicism. This social philosophy provides a stark contrast to the positivism and modernist-empiricism of much political science. Anti-foundationalism thus offers a major challenge to political scientists to clarify and defend the philosophical assumptions that inform their work. Yet, to challenge political scientists to rethink their philosophical assumptions is not necessarily to require them to reject their favoured methods or topics. Anti-foundationalism cautions political scientists to reflect on the data they produce. It does not tell them that they must or must not use particular techniques to create data on particular issues.

We are suggesting that an anti-foundational philosophy does not require or preclude particular methods or topics in political science. Anti-foundationalism itself should lead us to recognize that there is a conceptual gap between a social philosophy and an approach to political science. Meaning holism implies that our beliefs or concepts form a web. It is possible for political scientists to reconcile anti-foundational philosophy with any given method by suitably changing their other beliefs or concepts. Political scientists can make their favoured techniques of data collection compatible with anti-foundationalism by modifying their other beliefs. They need to accept that their data is not only saturated with their prior theories, but it is also data about holistic and constructed webs of meaning to be explained by interpretations. Foundationalists might insist on particular techniques because some techniques produce pure facts while others do not. Anti-foundationalists, in contrast, should allow that all kinds of techniques produce theory-laden data that we can accept or challenge in narratives.

Anti-foundationalists might choose to undertake critical studies that reveal the contingency and partiality of beliefs that present themselves as naturally given or inherently rational. Equally, one can imagine anti-foundationalists relying on large-scale surveys to collect data which they use to postulate certain beliefs for which they then offer a historicist explanation. Alternatively, one might imagine them using formal models to explore the outcomes that arise from actions based on particular beliefs and desires. They could postulate particular beliefs and desires because they explain certain observed outcomes. No doubt any anti-foundationalists who used behavioural or rational choice approaches to political science would have to allow that the stories they told were provisional ones that related actions and practices to constructed webs of meaning. But there is no reason why their provisional stories should not rely heavily on surveys, statistical analysis, or even formal models to produce data.

Varieties of anti-foundationalism

In principle, anti-foundationalism could be combined with all sorts of approaches to political science. We cannot explain the impact of anti-foundationalism on political science by appealing to intrinsic conceptual links between an anti-foundational epistemology and a particular approach to the study of politics. To the contrary, the links between anti-foundationalism and approaches to political science must themselves be contingent historical ones. To explain the impact of anti-foundationalism on political science, we have to explore the particular historical traditions which led political scientists to turn to anti-foundationalism. Indeed, anti-foundational approaches to political science owe as much to concepts, concerns, and topics that persist from various historical traditions as they do to logical consequences of an anti-foundationalist epistemology.

In principle, anti-foundationalism could be combined with all kinds of approaches to political science. In practice, it is associated more or less exclusively with political scientists inspired by critical traditions of inquiry. We can identify three types of anti-foundationalism in political science. Each arose against the background of a different critical tradition. Each absorbed a different version of anti-foundationalism. Table 3.1 provides an outline. Governmentality theory arose against the background of theories of social control, and focused on regimes of 'power/knowledge'. Post-Marxists combined Saussurean linguistics with a concept of hegemony. Social humanists infused post-analytic themes into the New Left's concern with culture, agency, and resistance.

Our aim in distinguishing these three traditions is to offer an admittedly simplified account of broad movements in political science. We have divided anti-foundational approaches according to intellectual background because our aim is to provide a historicist narrative of the contingent ways in which anti-foundationalism entered political science. These three traditions are not separate from one another. Themes flow from one to the

Table 3.1 Varieties of anti-foundationalism

	Governmentality	Post-Marxism	Social humanism
Historical background (i) Thinker(s) (ii) Key concept	(i) Louis Althusser (ii) Social control	(i) Antonio Gramsci (ii) Hegemony	(i) Raymond Williams and E. P. Thompson (ii) Radical traditions
Anti-foundational background (i) Theory (ii) Key idea	(i) Genealogy (ii) Power/knowledge	(i) Post-structuralism (ii) Semiotic code – relations among signifiers	(i) Cultural studies (ii) Agency situated in cultural practices
Prominent topics	Technical discourses as ways of making subjects through public policy	Collective identities – especially those of gender, race, and sexuality	Governance, with an emphasis on ideologies and resistance
Examples	(i) Foucault (1977) (ii) Barry, Osborne, and Rose (1996*a*)	(i) Laclau and Mouffe (1985) (ii) Smith (1994)	(i) Hall (1983) (ii) Bevir and Trentmann (2007)

other, and anti-foundationalists often combine themes from different traditions. To offer just one example, Hall's work combined the New Left's emphasis on the sociology of culture with a concept of hegemony, while Laclau and Mouffe combined the concept of hegemony with a post-structuralism linked to Saussurean linguistics (Hall, Lumley, and McLennan 1978; Laclau and Mouffe 1985). Bearing such cautions in mind, we look at the three anti-foundational approaches to political science. In each case, we trace a historical movement from an early radical background (of Althusser, Gramsci, and the New Left), through the emergent anti-foundational themes (of Foucault, Laclau and Mouffe, and Hall), to the studies of politics they inspired.

Governmentality

Governmentality theory stems from the writings of Foucault. It has been applied to political science mainly by the so-called Anglo-Foucauldians. The early Anglo-Foucauldians typically had been attracted to the work of Althusser, and, more generally, to Marxist theories of social control. Foucault's work reproduced many tropes from social control theory

(Resch 1992; Stedman-Jones 1996). He deployed structuralist and post-structuralist ideas to imply that distinctions such as those between madness and sanity or sickness and health were products of particular epistemes or discourses rather than neutral or rational ways of capturing reality (Foucault 1973, 1989). He suggested that the function of institutions such as asylums and clinics was not the scientific and humanitarian promotion of health, but social control and normalizing deviant individuals. Governmentality theory applies a similar approach to explore modern power.

Foucault on modern power

Foucault defines governmentality as the conduct of conduct (Foucault 1991). He traces it back to the emerging 'art of government' in the middle of the sixteenth century. Before that time, writers, notably Machiavelli in *The Prince*, had adopted a monarchical notion of sovereign power. Princes stood apart from their territory, having a fragile relationship to it, so ruling consisted of identifying and forestalling threats to their rule. Then, in the middle of the sixteenth century, anti-Machiavellian theorists of the art of government began to focus on the conduct of conduct. These theorists explored how to influence, limit, correct, and determine the behaviour of individuals whether as members of the state, the economy, the family, or the Church. They concerned themselves with the activities and relationships in a given society, not the one relationship between a prince and his territory. In doing so, Foucault argues, they set the conditions for the rise of modern governmentality.

In Foucault's broader account, modern governmentality combines sovereignty with biopower and pastoral power (Foucault 1977, 1978–1985). The anti-Machiavellian concept of conduct implied a downward continuity from the well-organized state to an efficient economy and well-run families. In the seventeenth century, this downward continuity was associated with a broad concept of 'police' that embraced all attempts to exert disciplinary political power over people and their activities, including schooling, work, family life, and consumption. In the eighteenth century, populations were constructed as a social object liable to death rates, epidemics, and patterns of growth. Extending policing to populations resulted in biopower, that is, new techniques of discipline that aimed to increase the health, longevity, and productivity of the population.

The final stream that feeds into Foucault's analysis of modern power is a pastoral one. Foucault traces pastoral techniques of government back to practices that developed in the Church. Pastoral power requires individuals to internalize various ideals and norms so they both regard an external body as concerned with their good, and strive to regulate themselves in accord with the dictates of that external body. For Foucault, secularizing pastoral power involved the state replacing the spiritual end of salvation with worldly ends such as health and well-being. When people accept such ends, they examine, confess, and transform their own behaviour in accord with the regime of biopower.

The Anglo-Foucauldians

Anglo-Foucauldians often deny that Foucault provided a theory that sets up the best way of understanding politics. Instead, they claim he sketched out a mode and field of inquiry. The mode of inquiry (or method) is genealogy. The aim is to provide cultural histories of discourses that inform current practices to reveal their contingency and undermine any suggestion of their being neutral, humanitarian, or scientific. Anglo-Foucauldians describe themselves as offering critical genealogies of problems set by the present. Rose (1999, 11) writes, 'rather than conceiving of our present as an epoch or a state of affairs, it is more useful, in my own view, to view the present as a series of problems and questions, an actuality to be acted upon and within by genealogical investigation, to be made amenable to action by the action of thought'. Typically, the Anglo-Foucauldians suggest the purpose of genealogy is to open new possibilities, and even new ways of being. They dismiss the idea of promoting a particular way of being as tarnished by the utopian dream of erasing all forms of 'power or knowledge'. They argue instead that through genealogies 'the received fixedness and inevitability of the present is destabilized, shown as just sufficiently fragile as to let in a little glimpse of freedom – as a practice of difference – through its fractures' (Barry, Osborne, and Rose 1996*a*, 5).

The Anglo-Foucauldians' field of inquiry (or empirical domain) directs us away from an excessive focus on the state towards a study of the diverse processes by which subjects are normalized to sustain a pattern of rule. This field of inquiry covers all the diffuse ways in which government and social power impact on individuals, groups, and populations. It shows us the ways in which conduct is shaped to certain ends by discourses and practices. As Rose (1999, 5) explains, 'the state now appears simply as one element – whose functionality is historically specific and contextually variable – in multiple circuits of power, connecting a diversity of authorities and forces, within a whole variety of complex assemblages'.

The concept of the state as just one part in circuits of power might sound similar to the literature on policy networks. Yet, the Anglo-Foucauldians depart significantly from this literature precisely because their interest lies not with the study of formal institutions but with genealogies of discourses that inform present-day practices. Anglo-Foucauldians are interested in how apparently neutral, scientific discourses serve to establish particular forms of subjectivity. They focus on the ways in which expert discourses about education, health, risk, and insurance feed into public policies and establish normal patterns of behaviour. They focus on the ways in which statistical analysis and formal modelling provide new ways of measuring and analysing populations and governing people.

Liberal governmentalities

Foucault's essay on governmentality was first published in English in 1978. It appeared in a collection of essays, *The Foucault Effect: Studies in Governmentality*, edited by Burchell, Gordon, and Miller. *The Foucault Effect* also includes essays exploring governmentality written by French and Italian scholars as well as some Anglo-Foucauldians. The essays define the mode and field of inquiry associated with governmentality. Nearly twenty years later, there appeared another collection of essays, *Foucault and Political Reason: Liberalism, Neoliberalism and Rationalities of Government*, edited by Barry, Osborne, and Rose. This collection, with its anglophone cast of contributors, further illustrates themes that characterize a governmentality approach to political science.

The subtitle of *Foucault and Political Reason* captures one such emphasis. Anglo-Foucauldians grasp liberalism as a series of political technologies that arose from the nineteenth century through the welfare state and on to the neo-liberalism of Reagan and Thatcher.[1] Governmentality theorists portray nineteenth-century liberalism as a political rationality that arose out of worries about extensive policing. In this view, liberalism appears less as a rejection of state intervention and more as a positive political rationality by which to manage complex interactions in society and the economy. Liberalism seeks to produce certain outcomes through dynamics in society and the economy themselves rather than by state activity.

Governmentality theorists discuss the rise of the welfare state as a response to the changing problems of liberalism. In their view, modern industrial society caused new social problems with which liberalism had to contend. Liberalism tried to guarantee the security of the economy and the state by addressing social problems through an array of new technologies that collectively made up the welfare state. For governmentality theorists, public housing, unemployment insurance, and public health are understood as technologies of power that serve to normalize subjects.

The governmentality theorists' account of liberalism anticipates their understanding of neo-liberalism and present-day politics. On the one hand, neo-liberalism appears as a critique of welfare state liberalism. It promotes rationalities in society and the economy, especially technologies of the market, because the welfare state, trade protection, state planning, and Keynesian intervention are unproductive interferences with market relations. On the other hand, neo-liberalism appears as a set of governmental technologies that actively foster competitive market relations. It shifts responsibility to the individual while increasing social efficiency. Under neo-liberalism, 'it was the responsibility of political government to *actively* create the conditions within which entrepreneurial and competitive conduct is possible' (Barry, Osborne, and Rose 1996*a*, 10).

Making subjects

The governmentality theorists also extended Foucault's concern with the ways in which scientific discourses that appeared neutral established particular forms of subjectivity. Indeed, they often think of liberalism, welfare state liberalism, and neo-liberalism as policies that seek to normalize subjects by drawing on technical discourses from disciplines such as medicine, social science, statistics, and public health. Rose's work on the self, freedom, and psychology (1999, 1989, and 1998) provides a more general exploration of present-day forms of subjectivity (see also Miller and Rose 2008). He argues the shift from liberalism through welfare liberalism to neo-liberalism saw the morals and psyche of the individual replace larger units such as the economy as the main objects of governing rationalities. In his account, early nineteenth-century liberalism, guided by classical political economy, did not seek to manage individual morality so much as to guarantee the security of economic relations. Yet, Rose adds, in the middle of the nineteenth century, liberal governments began to regulate the morals of certain segments of the population. The role of distinct institutions, such as the poorhouse, was to discipline and correct people who had particular pathologies of character.

For Rose, an even more dramatic change occurred with the rise of the welfare state. He argues that early in the twentieth century, the use of statistics expanded from calculating national incomes to analysing and governing characteristics of the population. In his view, an emerging discourse of 'social' issues focused on problems that afflicted large portions of the population, and a new governmentality arose to prevent these problems spreading further. The welfare state and Keynesianism appear as technologies which experts used to govern subjects to manage pathologies made visible by new social statistics.

Rose also suggests that neo-liberal governmentality constructs and enforces a particular subjectivity. He associates advanced liberalism with an individualization of responsibility. The welfare state embodies a collectivist ethos. Now individuals are constructed as responsible for their own conduct. Neo-liberalism promotes freedom, understood as personal choice, at the same time as it deploys psychology to create new forms of control. Psychological technologies increasingly affect how individuals think about almost every aspect of their lives, including sexual relations, work, health, and consumption choices. For Rose, then, advanced liberalism is a form of governmentality in which individuals discipline themselves to use their freedom to make responsible choices. Individuals are expected to analyse themselves and to improve all aspects of their lives in ways that benefit themselves, their community, and the state.

Post-Marxism

The post-Marxists, Laclau and Mouffe, are influenced less by the structuralist Marxism of Althusser than by Gramsci's concept of hegemony. They modify and arguably even overturn Gramsci's humanism by infusing it with the concepts of language and mind developed by structuralists such as Saussure and Levi-Strauss and then reworked by post-structuralists such as Derrida and Lacan. In *Hegemony and Socialist Strategy*, Laclau and Mouffe (1985) analyse discourses mainly as the quasi-structural properties of signs. They trace the relations and properties of signs and discourses not to class or other social conflicts but to a quasi-structural psychology associated with Lacan.

Laclau and Mouffe

Laclau and Mouffe set out to rework Marxism to dissociate it from foundationalism and essentialism. They reject theories that privilege the economic (rather than the ideological) and social class (rather than discursively constructed identities). In doing so, they redefine hegemony to reveal a submerged strand of left-wing thought that resisted essentialism. Gramsci used hegemony to refer to class domination through ideology. A class could establish an ideological hegemony so its dominance rested on moral consensus. Gramsci implied, in particular, that bourgeois hegemony explains why the workers consent to capitalism and so why there has not been a revolution. In contrast, Laclau and Mouffe use the concept of hegemony not only to think about the role of ideologies in a capitalist system defined by means and relations of production, but also actively to dismiss social theories based on economic and class analysis. In their view, 'the search for a "true" working class and its limits is a false problem, and as such lacks any theoretical or political relevance' (Laclau and Mouffe 1985, 84).

Once Laclau and Mouffe empty Gramsci's concept of hegemony of its Marxist content, they can suggest that historically it has acted as what Derrida calls a supplement. The idea of hegemony is used to deal with evidence that does not privilege the economic base over the ideological superstructure, that is, cases in which the identity of a class does not match its objective social location. Laclau and Mouffe's aim is to make their concept of hegemony central rather marginal.

Laclau and Mouffe hope that by rethinking Marxist theory, they will redefine the strategy of the left. They argue that reducing ideology to class consciousness and objective social facts inspires a totalitarianism associated with the belief that Marxist parties can act as a vanguard of the workers. Leninism, they explain, promotes 'political leadership within a class alliance' (Laclau and Mouffe 1985, 55). Leninism legitimates an authoritarian Party or state by suggesting that the Party or state pursues the objective class interests of the workers. In contrast, the post-Marxist concept of hegemony seeks to draw attention to the need to provide 'intellectual and moral' leadership to construct subject positions, identities, and discourses. Laclau and Mouffe even write, 'political subjects are not – strictly speaking – classes, but complex "collective wills"' (Laclau and Mouffe 1985, 67). They conclude that the Left should renounce Leninism as the vanguard for historically specific, grass-roots struggles.

Discourse theory

The debt Laclau and Mouffe owe structuralist theories of language is obvious from their use of the word discourse as an alternative for ideology. The concept 'discourse' is, after all, less tied to ideas of class and social location than is the concept 'ideology'. Post-Marxists approach a discursive formation as 'a configuration, which in certain contexts of exteriority can be *signified* as a totality' (Laclau and Mouffe 1985, 106). Their language and approach stem from Saussurean linguistics. Saussure (1966) argued that the relationship of a signified (or concept) to a signifier (or word) is arbitrary. Any signifier can evoke any signified provided only that it differs from other signifiers. The value of any signifier derives solely from relations of difference in a system of signs. Post-structuralists, such as Derrida, have argued that the relation between concepts and reality is similarly arbitrary. Our concepts too can be understood not as referring to the world but as relations of difference among concepts in a discourse.

A Saussurean legacy appears in three prominent features of Laclau and Mouffe's concept of discourse. First, Laclau and Mouffe dismiss concerns with the relationship of discourses to a supposed extra-discursive reality, such as that of class struggle. Sometimes they imply the world, including class antagonisms, is a product of discourses. At other times, they allow for an extra-discursive reality while contending that only signs in existing discourses can be known. Either way, they rule out attempts to understand discourses as either reflections of or responses to the world. Second, Laclau and Mouffe stress the constitutive role of relations of difference within and between discourses. For example, they imply that in any given discourse, a binary structure governs concepts of identity, so identities are necessarily defined as opposition to an excluded other. Third, Laclau and Mouffe are dismissive of human agency. They argue that discourses fix or limit what individuals say and do. They analyse discourses as the structural relations among the signs of which they are composed rather than the use of language by agents.

Laclau and Mouffe tie their concept of discourse not to pre-discursive social facts but to Lacan's psychoanalytic theory. In their account, the subject (or individual) desires 'fullness', conceived as psychological stability based on integrating the self with the other. Yet, this desire for fullness is thwarted structurally by a primordial 'lack', since there is always doubt about whether the 'other' has recognized the self. This 'lack' then leads to the other getting blamed for blocked identity. This psychoanalytic theory implies that a quasi-structural antagonism between self and other is integral to the process of identity formation. Laclau and Mouffe argue that this quasi-structural logic also applies to discourses. On the one hand, discourses display a logic of equivalence in that they try both to integrate many views into one worldview and to stress commonalities in contrast to an other. On the other hand, discourses display a logic of difference in that they are formed by an antagonism to the other. This antagonism always limits the extent to which they can achieve integration. The interplay between equivalence and difference in discourses frames hegemonic struggles. So, Laclau and Mouffe argue that a hegemonic discourse increases its bloc of control through the logic of equivalence but its ability to do so is limited by a logic of difference that precludes its achieving full closure. This creates a space for counter-hegemonic discourses to emerge.

Racial identities

After Laclau and Mouffe wrote *Hegemony and Socialist Strategy*, Laclau concentrated on redefining and defending their approach to discourse analysis (Laclau 1990; Butler, Laclau, and Zizek 2000). Mouffe (1993, 2000) attempted to link their approach to a normative theory of agonistic democracy. The job of applying their work to specific discourses has fallen mainly to students of Laclau from the University of Essex (Howarth, Norval, and Stavrakakis 2000; Howarth and Torfing 2005).[2]

Many attempts to apply post-Marxism have concentrated on discourses connected with identities of gender and race. Post-Marxists argue that subject positions are the constructs of contingent discourses, rather than natural or biological givens. In their view, the subject positions that a discourse creates derive not from pre-discursive social relations or biological facts, but from political strategies and the structural relations between concepts in discourses. The appearance of normality that attaches to some subject positions is merely an effect of the hegemonic status of the relevant discourse.

Smith's *New Right Discourse on Race and Sexuality* is a good example of how to apply post-Marxism, in her case to race and identity in British politics. In the 1950s, Enoch Powell opposed the retreat from imperial power because the Empire was integral to British identity. Then, once decolonization seemed inevitable, he promoted a new British identity distinct from Empire. Smith writes, 'by representing the Empire as accidental and external, Powell was able to claim that Britishness had remained essentially the same through the imperialist period and would not be significantly altered by decolonization' (Smith 1994, 132). Powellism arose as a discourse of a 'pure' British identity defined against a menacing alien identity. Race was its 'nodal point'. It needed to create an 'other' if it were to postulate some internal space destroyed by decolonization. Powellism reconceived black populations as aliens. Black immigrants represented a disorderly and dangerous 'other' threatening Britain. What is more, Smith adds, Powellism constructed black immigrants as predatory, masculine subjects. For example, in his famous 'rivers of blood' speech,

Powell read a letter from a 'white woman old-age pensioner', portraying her as the victim of a black invasion that was taking over the once 'respectable' street on which she lived. The influx of blacks had made her a prisoner in her own home. No one came to her aid.

In Smith's account, Powellism displays the logics of equivalence and difference that post-Marxists associate with hegemonic discourses. Powellism claimed inclusiveness – a centrist position against 'excessive' immigration – even as it excluded groups. In particular, Smith identifies several devices by which Powellism pursued equivalence. Powellism claimed to represent the interests of both whites and blacks: it 'invoked the image of black supporters . . . to de-racialize his consistently racist discourse.' Powellism also left a place for the 'good assimilable black' even as it railed against the 'dangerous black invader' (Smith 1994, 140). Powellism did not assert that blacks are inherently 'prone to wrong-doing' so much as claim that the immigration of unassimilated individuals leads to social problems, tensions, and violence.

Institutions and policy

Post-Marxists have focused on discursive identities associated with gender and race. There is less work addressed to topics such as parliament, political parties, policy networks, and local politics. One exception is Griggs and Howarth's analysis of the campaign against a second runway at Manchester Airport (Griggs and Howarth 2000). In exploring this case study, Griggs and Howarth ask: how did the local village residents and direct action protestors overcome their collective action problem? As post-Marxists, they take the problem of collective action to be less about individual rationality than creating a shared identity through discourse. In the Manchester case, they point to three bases for creating such a discourse. First, there was a group identity in that all were affected by the environmental costs of the runway. Second, there was a social network and political entrepreneurs. There was a strong conservationist movement in the villages and the leaders of the relevant associations had the support of professional people in meeting the costs of the campaign. Third, the campaign forged new political identities aligning 'the Vegans and the Volvos'. According to Griggs and Howarth, this alignment worked because the pro-runway campaign used heavy-handed tactics and stigmatized residents and protestors alike, and because the media linked residents and eco-warriors as fighting a common foe. But, Griggs and Howarth continue, the alignment of the Vegans and the Volvos proved temporary. The protestors lost. The eco-warriors, after being evicted, moved on to the next protest site. The residents split over whether to mount a national-level campaign or to concentrate on the public inquiry. The local authority offered an environmental mitigation package and pursued their case with 'ruthless efficiency'.

Social humanism

It is interesting to compare Smith's study of race in Britain with one written some ten years earlier – Gilroy's *There Ain't No Black in the Union Jack*.[3] Both studies concentrate on meanings, both are inspired by critical traditions, yet they are markedly different. Smith's title privileges 'discourse'. Gilroy's subtitle proclaims his study to be one of 'culture and politics'. Smith draws on Laclau and Mouffe with their quasi-structuralist theories of language and psychology. Gilroy adopts a more historicist approach and even a 'materialist theory of culture'. For Gilroy, culture is both a product of agency and the inherited life-world of agents. His extensive use of black music (reggae and hip hop) suggested that subaltern agents might forge cultures of resistance to a dominant ideology.

Gilroy's concerns with agency, culture, resistance, and history all reflect the influence of the New Left on another tradition of anti-foundationalism. Governmentality theory and post-Marxism draw on structuralism and post-structuralism with their dismissal of subjects, agency, and humanism. In contrast, the New Left, including Thompson and Williams, espoused a humanist Marxism that emphasized the processes by which agents and classes made cultures, especially cultures that resisted capitalism (Thompson 1978).

The New Left

The New Left preceded Laclau and Mouffe in seeking to liberate Marxism from authoritarian politics and economic determinism. Many members of the New Left responded to the Soviet invasion of Hungary, and knowledge of the brutalities of Stalinism, by leaving the Communist Party and championing an indigenous heritage of radical cultural and moral criticism (Kenny 1995; Dworkin 1997). Historians such as Thompson and Hill reconstructed a popular tradition of resistance, from the Peasant's Revolt through the London Corresponding Society to Chartism (Hill 1965; Thompson 1981; and more recently Stedman-Jones 1983). Literary critics such as Williams and Hoggart reconstructed working-class auto-didacticism, and a tradition of literature from the romantics to Orwell in which the concept of culture challenged capitalism (Williams 1958; Hoggart 1957).

Williams provided arguably the most influential theory of culture from within the New Left. He appealed to culture as a way of explaining aspects of social and political life that did not fit with economic reductionism. He suggested that post-war economic prosperity had dampened the class struggle in a way that made culture an even more relevant counter to capitalist values. In doing so, he transformed the concept of culture. Previously, culture had been associated almost exclusively with high culture. Williams saw mass culture as a site of political dissent and struggle. In *The Long Revolution* (1961), he argued that political battles were being fought out in the world of art and ideas. He rejected the idea that the economic base determines the cultural superstructure. In his view, the impossibility of dominant groups entirely controlling social processes means there is always space for subordinate groups to contest ruling ideologies.

Cultural studies

While Williams and Thompson made culture and agency prominent concepts in the New Left, the emergence of cultural studies owed much to Hall and his work from 1968 to 1979 as Director of the Centre for Contemporary Cultural Studies at the University of Birmingham. Indeed, the relationship of the New Left to cultural studies was sometimes problematic. On the one hand, there is no denying the importance of the New Left as personal and intellectual influences on a younger generation who pursued critical approaches to the study of culture. Thompson's approach to a history from below inspired many explorations of the lived experience of subordinated groups – women, racial minorities, gays and lesbians, and peasants, as well as the working class. On the other hand, however, the New Left often remained at least loosely tied to an orthodox socialist historiography that privileged the economy, production, and class relations (Bevir and Trentmann 2002*a*). Students of race, such as Hall, and students of gender, such as McRobbie, sometimes found themselves fighting against a privileged and idealized white, male, working-class culture from which racism and sexism had been written out.

Hall followed the New Left in seeing culture as a form of expression that is manifest not only in high art but also in the everyday life of subordinated groups. However, in the late 1960s, an encounter with anti-foundationalism and post-structuralism led him to modify the New Left's notion of lived experience.[4] Williams, and especially Thompson, tended to describe cultures of resistance as responses to experiences of the brutal realities of capitalism. In contrast, Hall now paid more attention to the way in which ideologies constructed people's experiences (Hall and Jefferson 1993). The point was not to return to the old view that ideologies represented a false consciousness that hid the reality of the class struggle. The point was, rather, to insist on the importance of ideology as a site of struggle for social change. Other authors have recently explored the ways in which even capitalism and markets have been constructed in part through cultures of resistance (Bevir and Trentmann 2002*b*; 2004).

To bridge the gap between culturalism and anti-foundationalism, Hall turned to Gramsci's concept of hegemony. For Hall, hegemony is a specific process of ideological struggle – a process that he understands as humanist historicism rather than the quasi-structural psychology adopted by Laclau and Mouffe (Hall 1986; 1988). Culture appears as a site of hegemonic control and struggle. It reinforces present power relations while allowing space for dissent and resistance. Popular culture can reinforce hegemonic ideas and identities, notably by representing them as natural, inexorable, or rational. But popular culture can also be a site of resistance by subordinated groups. Indeed, Hall's concern with agency and resistance spills over into an emphasis on consuming as well as producing culture. Subordinate groups can resist cultural discourses and symbols by consuming them in ways that draw on local patterns of dissent.

Thatcherism and after

Social humanists characteristically explore ruling ideologies and resistance to them. The most obvious examples have been studies of Thatcherism and New Labour. In the 1980s, Hall offered an account of Thatcherism as a hegemonic project characterized by 'authoritarian populism'. In his view, Labour tried to be both a working-class party and a responsible caretaker of a capitalist economy. When the economy declined, Labour tried to continue its caretaker role by adopting corporatist management strategies. By so doing, it weakened its connection with the workers. The failings of the Left thus set the conditions for Thatcherism. Thatcherism aligned the neglected workers with anti-collectivism as an alternative solution to the problems of the economy. It presented neo-liberal ideas as the common sense of the British people. Hall explains, 'the essence of the British people was identified with self-reliance and personal responsibility, against the image of the over-taxed individual, enervated by welfare state "coddling"' (Hall 1983, 29; and 1988). This right-wing populism combined themes from an 'organic Toryism – nation, family, duty, authority, standards, traditionalism – with the aggressive themes of a revived neo-liberalism – self-interest, competitive individualism, anti-statism' (Hall 1983, 29). However, Hall adds, Thatcherism governed through authoritarianism. It brought an 'intensification of state control over every sphere of economic life', the decline of democratic institutions, and even curtailing formal liberties. The tensions between Thatcherism's populism and its authoritarianism provided a space in which the Left might recoup its ideological losses.

No doubt New Labour likes to think it recouped these losses. Social humanists disagree. Hall portrays New Labour as continuing neo-liberalism. He argues that New Labour is a hybrid regime, combining a dominant neo-liberalism with a subordinate social democratic notion of active government, and able to hold these two discourses together only through the constant use of 'spin' (Hall 2003). Younger social humanists, in contrast, have been more attentive to the ways in which New Labour has transformed both social democratic and neo-liberal traditions. Some suggest that New Labour has given up on grand ideological visions of a transformed society, and turned instead to modernization in accord with social theories that purport to analyse inexorable changes in the world (Finlayson 2003). Others argue, in addition, that the social theories on which New Labour most relies are communitarianism and new institutionalism (Bevir 2005; also see Moss and O'Loughlin 2005). They suggest that New Labour's policies deploy these theories in an attempt to transform state and society.

Dissent and resistance

Social humanists have explored the ideologies associated with political parties. They have also studied cultures of resistance. Even when the state promotes policies inspired by a given discourse, designing and carrying out these policies involves diverse actors who recast the policies with different content against the background of other cultures. These actors, whether intentionally or not, draw on diverse cultures to resist the governing narratives.

Dissent and resistance are, of course, found far beyond Westminster and Whitehall. Social humanists such as Thompson and Williams argued, as we have seen, that citizens can and do draw on local cultures to express scepticism and resistance to governing discourses. More recently, social humanists have explored resistance among street-level bureaucrats and citizens. Clarke argues, for example, that the meanings of choice are contextually bounded not universal, and that service providers and citizens alike are sceptical about official discourses (Clarke 2007). His interviews in policy areas such as policing and health reveal a resistance to the appropriateness of 'consumer' and 'choice' as identities and activities. Service providers and service users alike believe that the idea of choice sits uneasily alongside values such as equity. Citizens resist the language of choice and shopping as inappropriate for policing and health care.

Social humanists stress the contingent, diverse, and contested nature of politics. They imply that governmentality theorists and post-Marxists adopt a too monolithic analysis of discourses such as neo-liberalism. Governmentality theorists, with their debt to ideas of social control, focus almost exclusively on official discourses and policies. They pay little attention to how these are enacted locally. In contrast, social humanists, with their debt to the idea of cultures of resistance, explore the diverse ways in which street-level bureaucrats and citizens articulate and practise consumption and citizenship in their everyday lives, often in ways that challenge government narratives. Their focus shifts from the discourse of policy makers to the fractured and diverse processes by which discourses and policies are translated into actions.

Conclusion

At the beginning of this chapter, we said that anti-foundationalism never led directly to particular approaches to political science. But it has implications for ontology and social explanation, and political scientists would do well to ponder the following four implications.

- A commitment to studying *meanings* (beliefs and traditions) as constitutive of social and political practices.
- A belief in the *contingency* and contestability of meanings, and opposition to any claims that a culture, web of beliefs, or practice is natural, inexorable, or inherently rational.
- A commitment to *historical narratives* to explain meanings, and a stress on historical contingency to undercut appeals to formal models, fixed institutions, or reified social forms.
- A use of historical critiques to reveal the contingency of webs of belief that otherwise present themselves as natural, inexorable, or inherently rational.

This emphasis on meanings, contingency, historical narratives, and critique challenges a lingering, lukewarm positivism in political science that tries to avoid questions of meaning and contingency by hiding behind appeals to social facts, institutions, structures, and correlations. It leads to accounts of British government that are historically specific and contestable. It leads to a focus on the changing meanings that constitute British economic, political, social, and cultural practices in a broader post-imperial, transnational setting. It also leads to the idea of the 'stateless state'; to the ways in which patterns of rule, including institutions and policies, are created, sustained, and modified by individuals. The next step to this stateless destination is to explain our interpretive or decentred approach to the state (Chapter 4). We then provide a decentred analysis of the changing state (or governance) and identify the new topics that spring from such a decentred account, which we summarize as the '3Rs' of rule, rationalities, and resistance (Chapter 5).

Notes

1. For Foucault's own discussion of liberalism, especially German post-war liberalism and the Chicago School, see Foucault (2004); and for comment Lemke (2001).
2. Laclau's students have also written books introducing his theory; see Howarth (2000), Smith (1998), and Torfing (1999).
3. It is well worth pointing out that one legacy of the New Left and cultural studies is an important literature on post-colonialism. The combination of an anti-foundational focus on meanings with a post-colonial focus on transnational flows seriously challenges the almost ubiquitous persistence of assumptions about the nation state in the study of politics. Examples of the studies of race and transnationalism associated with cultural studies include Centre for Contemporary Cultural Studies (1982) and Gilroy (1993).
4. Hall identifies with an 'eclecticism' that has little concern for coherence. Typically, he flirts with a range of fashionable Marxist terms – from the Althusserian 'articulation' to signification – inserting them into a broadly constructivist and yet sociological approach to ideologies and cultures of resistance. His lingering debt to the New Left appears in his constant return to agency, practice, resistance, and (in our view rather problematically) modernist sociological categories. Compare Proctor (2004).

Chapter 4

Interpretation

Introduction

Chapter 1 showed how interpretive approaches to the human sciences arose out of philosophical alternatives to positivism, notably hermeneutics, phenomenology, and post-analytic philosophers. These philosophies encouraged an emphasis on historical understanding, that is, the recovery of the intentionality embodied in actions, practices, and social life. They suggested that to understand social life, one had to grasp its mental content.

In this chapter, we specify our interpretive approach, contrasting it with constructivist institutionalism and post-structuralism. Institutionalism and post-structuralism display creeping forms of reification and formalism. Our interpretive approach resolutely abstains from reification and formalism in favour of humanism and historicism.

Varieties of interpretation

A philosophical emphasis on interpretation stands in marked contrast to the modernist-empiricism and positivism that dominated the social sciences for much of the twentieth century. Yet interpretive approaches come in many guises. Some owe a debt to the theories of historical understanding that we discussed in Chapter 1. But some try to subsume interpretation in a larger framework derived from modernist-empiricism, as did the constructivist institutionalism mentioned in Chapter 2. Others try to fuse an emphasis on interpretation with a formal linguistics arising out of structuralism, as did the post-structuralists explored in Chapter 3. Indeed, we would suggest that these modernist-empiricist and post-structuralist approaches to interpretation are dominant today. As far as we know, our interpretive approach stands more or less alone in drawing on post-analytic philosophers such as Wittgenstein, Quine, and Davidson to defend humanism and historicism (Bevir 1999). Like most post-analytic philosophers, we are anti-foundationalists because we believe statements can have semantic meanings only in wider webs of belief. This version of anti-foundationalism differs from that associated with post-structuralism, notably in being far more open to humanism. Again, like most of these post-analytic philosophers, we regard interpretation as ascribing intentional content to people to explain speech and other actions. This form of explanation differs from those associated with modernist-empiricism, including constructivist institutionalism, notably in being far more historicist.

Post-analytic philosophy

Wittgenstein (2008) evoked some of the implications of a contrast between modernist-empiricist social science and an interpretive approach in a letter he wrote on 31 January 1934 to Sraffa, an economist who had fled Mussolini's Italy for Cambridge:

> Dear Sraffa
>
> The following are some remarks I've put down on the topic of our last conversation. I hope they won't be too disconnected and that you'll read them to the end.
>
> You said, 'The Austrians can do most of the things the Germans did.' I say, How do you know? What circumstances are you taking into account if you say that they can? 'This man, Austria, can remove the wedding ring from his finger.' True, it's too heavy and doesn't stick to his finger. But he may be ashamed of doing it, his wife may not allow it, etc.
>
> You say, 'Learn from what happened in Italy.' Bur what should I learn? I don't know exactly how things happened in Italy. So the only lesson I can draw is that things one doesn't expect sometimes happen.
>
> I ask, How will this man whose face I can't imagine in a rage look when he gets into a rage? And can he get into a rage? What shall I say when I see him in a rage? Not only, 'Ah, so he can get into a rage after all', but also, 'So this is the way he can be in a rage, so this is how it connects up with his former appearance.'
>
> You say to me, 'If a man is in a rage, the muscles a, b, c of his face contract. This man has the muscles a, b, c, so why shouldn't they contract? If you, Wittgenstein, wish to know what he will look like in a rage, just imagine him with these muscles contracted. What will Austria look like

when it turns Nazi? There will be no Socialist Party, there won't be Jewish judges, etc., etc., etc. That's what it'll look like.'

I reply, This gives me no picture of a face; apart from the fact that I don't know enough about the workings of things to know whether all these changes that you point out will happen together. For I understand what it means to say that the muscles a, b, c will contract, but what will become of the many muscles, etc., between them? Can't the contraction of the one in this particular face prevent the contraction of the others? Do you know how in this particular case things interact?

You may say, 'Surely the only way to tell the future physiognomy is to know more and more exactly the contractions, etc., of all, not only the main, muscles.'

I say, I don't think this is the only way; there is another one, although the two ways may meet. I may ask a physiologist what the face will be like, but also a painter. The two will give different answers – the painter by drawing the angry face – although if they both are correct they will agree. Of course, I know that painters have to study anatomy. I want to know the painter's answer, and I also want to know what the physiologist can tell me to check the painter's answer.

I am interested to know what phrases the Austrians will use when they'll have turned Nazi. Supposing their patriotism is only talk, then I'm just interested in their future talk.

I wish to say one more thing. I think that your fault in a discussion is this: YOU ARE NOT HELPFUL! I am like a man inviting you to tea in my room, but my room is hardly furnished; one has to sit on boxes, and the teacups stand on the floor, and the cups have not handles, etc., etc. I hustle about fetching anything I can think of to make it possible that we should have tea together. You stand there with a sulky face, say that you can't sit down on a box and can't hold a cup without a handle, and generally make things difficult. At least that's how it seems to me.

Yours,
Ludwig Wittgenstein

Wittgenstein is a dense and epigrammatic writer. Many of an interpretive persuasion pick up on his ideas. In what follows, we want to highlight two positions that he shares with post-analytic philosophers. These two positions give clues about how our approach to interpretation differs respectively from the modernist-empiricist forms of constructivist institutionalism discussed in Chapter 2, and the post-structuralist forms of anti-foundationalism discussed in Chapter 3. First, post-analytic philosophers suggest that we make sense of behaviour using what is now called 'folk psychology'. The language of folk psychology is incompatible with the kinds of languages that are found in natural science. Davidson argued that primary reasons were causes, saying 'central to the relation between a reason and an action it explains is the idea that the agent performed the action because he had the reason' (Davidson 1980). Such arguments lead us to a more historicist position than constructivist institutionalism. Second, post-analytic philosophers suggest that meaning is use within a language in a way that contrasts with the differential view of meaning held by many post-structuralists. Wittgenstein himself wrote, 'we are inclined to forget that it is the particular use of a word only which gives the word its meaning... the use of the word *in practice* is its meaning' (Wittgenstein 1972*a*, 69). Such arguments lead us to a more humanist position than post-structuralism.

After modernism

Post-analytic philosophy challenges two features of modernist-empiricist social science that linger on in some varieties of interpretivism. First, post-analytic philosophy rejects the idea of pure facts, challenging the misconception that equates interpretive approaches with particular techniques of data generation, such as ethnography or textual analysis. Even Popper argued that observations and evidence never confirm a theory (Popper 1959). It is worth belabouring what his argument implies as a surprising number of political scientists think that Popper lends support for their uses of induction. In Popper's view (1972), it is impossible to confirm a theory to even the slightest degree irrespective of how many observations support it and irrespective of the number of observations it predicts successfully. For Popper, no matter what methods we use, we simply cannot create data or correlations that give us a valid reason even to increase the degree of faith that we place in a theory.

Since Popper, moreover, post-analytic philosophy has moved decisively towards the holism pioneered by Quine (1961) and Wittgenstein (1972*b*). Meaning holism asserts that the meaning of a proposition depends on the web of beliefs or language game in which it is located. Therefore, what would have to be the case for a proposition to be true (or false) depends on the other propositions that we hold true (see Fodor and LePore 1992). This meaning holism decisively undermines the earlier concepts of confirmation and refutation. It implies that no set of observations can verify or falsify a proposition. We can reject or keep any proposition in the face of any evidence provided only that we make suitable changes to the other propositions that we hold true. No proposition can ever confront the world in splendid isolation. We can only evaluate whole bundles of facts, theories, and assumptions. Holism implies that political scientists are wrong if they think methods – surveys, ethnography, and regression analyses – can justify the data they collect let alone causal claims. Methods merely create more data, and the validity of the data always remains open to debate.

Therefore, interpretive social science should not be equated with specific methods, such as ethnography, and it should not be taken as incompatible with other methods, such as survey research and large-*N* quantitative studies. To the contrary, most post-analytic philosophy implies that all experiences, and so data, are theory-laden, irrespective of whether they arise, for example, from ethnography or surveys. In our view, an interpretive approach does not prescribe a particular way of creating data, but rather a particular way of treating data of any type. An interpretive approach suggests that political scientists should treat data as evidence of the meanings or beliefs embedded in actions.

Post-analytic philosophy also challenges a second modernist-empiricist influence within some varieties of interpretivism: a commitment to formal, even naturalist explanations. This challenge too arises from holism. Meaning holism has led many post-analytic philosophers to champion contextual and historicist explanations. Holism pushes us to adopt contextual explanations because it implies that we can properly explain people's beliefs (and so their actions and the practices to which their actions give rise) only by locating them in a wider web of beliefs. Holism points to the importance of spelling out beliefs by showing how they are linked to one another, not by trying to reduce them to categories such as social class or institutional position. We explain beliefs – and so actions and practices – by unpacking the conceptual connections in a web of beliefs, rather than by treating beliefs as variables. Also, holism points to historicist explanation because it implies that people can grasp their experiences and adopt new beliefs only against the background of an inherited web of beliefs. We can explain why they hold the webs of belief they do only by reference to the historical influences on them.

A commitment to contextual and historical explanations undermines modernist-empiricist approaches that introduce meanings or beliefs but only as 'ideational variables' alongside other variables (Wendt 1999). Constructivist institutionalists treat beliefs as a variable necessary to identify what they think of as the precise links between meanings and causal analysis. In doing so, however, they implicitly adopt a modernist-empiricist approach to explanation, failing to recognize the consequences of the meaning holism associated with post-analytic philosophers such as

Davidson and Wittgenstein. Meaning holism points to a form of explanation in which to recover the beliefs that inform actions simply *is* to provide an explanation of those actions. Any variable other than the beliefs and desires of the relevant actor can do explanatory work only if it is unpacked as beliefs or desires. Constructivist institutionalists try to assimilate contextual and historical explanations to modernist-empiricist causal logics. In contrast, we believe that these contextual and historical explanations already are causal, and we reject the idea that other causal logics apply to human beliefs and actions.

After structuralism

Post-analytic philosophy suggests meaning is use. When we interpret speech and action, we specify the intentional content that it embodies. This view differs importantly from the linguistic formalism that many post-structuralists inherited from structuralism. In our view, post-structuralism fails because its lingering debt to structuralism often leads not only to linguistic formalism but also hostility to agency, and at times even an anti-realist constructivism. Let us discuss each of these failings in turn.

Post-structuralism typically draws on the linguistic formalism of Saussure. According to Saussure, signs combine a signifier (or sound) with a signified (or concept). These signifiers and signified are presumed to have content because of their difference from other units in a system of signs (Saussure 1966). Post-structuralists often use Saussurean linguistics to argue that meanings arise negatively from the relations of difference within the system of signs that make up a language. They conclude that meaning is purely differential. Meaning is formed by relations of difference in a system. Thus, to study meanings is not to ask how language is used by intentional agents but to study the synchronic relations between units in a system.

There are several reasons to reject this linguistic theory. First, Saussure argued for it only as a methodological gesture that would establish linguistics as a science (Saussure 1966, 13). It is a mistake to treat his methodological gesture as akin to a philosophical account of language. Second, linguists themselves have rejected formal and structural analyses of language for transformational grammars. Political scientists should be wary of touting outdated linguistic theories. Third, there are excellent philosophical arguments against the idea that language is purely differential.

The easiest way to introduce these philosophical arguments is to distinguish a contextual theory of meaning from a differential one. Many philosophers, including Quine and Ullian (1970) and Wittgenstein (1972*b*), accept that concepts gain meaning only in broader 'webs of belief' or 'language games'. Consider the case of malaria. Perhaps we cannot teach someone the meaning of malaria merely by pointing to examples and saying 'malaria'. But our inability to do so shows only that the meaning of malaria depends on our background theories about the word, not that the meaning of malaria derives from its difference from other concepts. Once we accept various theories about the cause of certain physical symptoms, we can still define malaria positively as, say, a fever caused by the presence in the body of the protozoan parasite of genus *Plasmodium*. We can bind a concept to its referent in the context of background theories. Many post-structuralists treat arguments against pure meanings as sufficient to establish a differential theory of the sign. They are wrong to do so. A contextual theory of meaning provides a clear alternative.

Post-structuralists reject humanist concepts of subjectivity. They argue the idea of individual agency is the construct of a particular historical discourse with no basis in reality or reason. Poster argues: 'historians... blind themselves to the great question of the historical construction of the modern ideology of individualism by reproducing in their texts and lectures the very figure of such an individual, as if it were a natural being or a given fact of life' (Poster 2007, 46). Such arguments are, alas, ambiguous. We need to distinguish between two claims. First, the claim that modern ideologies about individual agency are given facts of life. Second, the claim that individual agency is a given fact of life. The first claim is trite. If we define an idea as exclusively 'modern', then obviously it is historically situated. The second claim is undefended. Even if people came to believe in something (such as individual agency) at a moment in history, it still could have been true earlier (individuals could have been agents without people knowing). When post-structuralists try to defend their rejection of agency, they characteristically appeal to their formal linguistics. They argue that subjectivity and agency are products not of people's intentions but of a semiotic code. Our beliefs (and our actions) arise out of the differential relations between signs. Clearly, however, this argument falls with the analysis of language on which it rests.

Post-structuralists might argue that the absence of a discourse of modern individualism just is tantamount to the absence of agency, for we construct the social world through our concepts. In doing so, they would recast their hostility to agency as derivative of an anti-realist constructivism. Many post-structuralists gesture at just such anti-realism when they use loose phrases such as 'there is nothing outside of the text' (Derrida 1976, 158).

Their argument seems to be that if meanings are differential, then we make our concepts. Therefore, the objects and properties to which these concepts seem to refer are not true to a world independent of us but rather the arbitrary constructions of our particular language. As White (2007, 227) tries to argue, if 'language is a complex system of encoded signs, the elements of which bear no necessary (natural) relationship to the things in the world to which they refer, then the meanings ascribed to things and their relationships in discourses are more a function of codes used to indicate them than of any substance or essence of which the things are different kinds of manifestation'.

Yet this argument for anti-realism too falls with the differential theory of meaning. Once we allow that concepts can refer to objects, though only as part of webs of belief, then we allow that they might be true to a world independent of us. The qualification that they 'might' be true of the world arises here only because the historic arguments for scepticism still may trouble us. What need no longer trouble us is the distinctive anti-realism of some post-structuralists.

Confusion arises here because post-structuralists sometimes elide anti-realism with anti-essentialism as an account of all concepts. Surely, however, we should offer different analyses of different concepts. The natural sciences can offer us concepts that might have essences: for example, water is defined as H_2O. More interestingly, even concepts without essences might be pragmatic rather than anti-realist. If concepts do not have an essence, they do not have determinate content, so they are vague, but that does not mean they do not refer to things in the world.

Pragmatic concepts refer to groups of things where membership of the group is vague. Social factors determine pragmatic concepts because there are many ways in which we can classify things, and it is our histories and purposes that lead us to adopt some classifications and not others. Nonetheless, the role of social factors in determining pragmatic concepts does not mean that these concepts have no basis in the world. To the contrary, we might justify adopting particular pragmatic concepts by arguing that they best serve our purposes, whether these purposes are descriptive, explanatory, or normative. For example, a pragmatic analysis of 'new public management' might say it refers to family resemblances between recent reforms of the public sector.

An anti-realist view of a concept would insist there is no group of things, not even a vague one, to which it refers. In such cases, we can argue not only that the concept is determined by social factors but also that it has no referent. For example, we might reject the concept 'new public management' as unfounded, especially if it is meant to refer to a global trend. Instead we could argue that different states have introduced different reforms that resemble their distinctive administrative traditions far more than they do a common neo-liberal blueprint.

Rethinking the social sciences

Although interpretive approaches thrive, they often remain tied to modernist-empiricism or structuralist themes. Constructivist institutionalism and post-structuralism often remain tied in particular to reified concepts and formal explanations. Our aim is to defend a more humanist and historicist theory of interpretation, drawing on post-analytic philosophy. From this perspective, the problem with modernist-empiricism (including much constructivist institutionalism) and structuralism (including much post-structuralism) is that they remain at best vague and at worst mistaken about the logic of their explanations. Their refusal of general theories and micro-level analyses means they often reify institutions or language, thus falling back on formal modernist-empiricist explanations. Political scientists can avoid reification only by breaking fully with modernist-empiricism and structuralism, adopting an interpretive approach characterized by decentred theory, new aggregate concepts, and historicist explanations.

New theory

Political scientists often use terms like 'state', 'institution', 'structure', or 'system' to elide questions about how their explanations work. These terms exercise a bewitching effect on political scientists, luring them intentionally or unintentionally to determinism, reification, and at times even foundationalism. This bewitching effect is pronounced in the new institutionalism. Consider, for example, the widespread claim that institutions possess an inertial tendency or stickiness (Pierson 2004). This claim leads to an unthinking determinism. It implies that there is a causal mechanism that fixes the content or development of an institution by fixing the agency of the relevant people. If agency was not fixed in this way, then the stickiness would appear only when the relevant people happened to act in a certain way. So, stickiness would be merely a descriptive term to be applied to such cases, not a term able to do explanatory work. What is more, when institutionalists try to make sense of the idea of institutional stickiness, they often fall into the trap of either reification or foundationalism. They commit to reification when they imply the mechanism or feedback process works independent of intentionality. But, when they conceive of the mechanism as a feedback process that operates through intentionality, they typically imply that the relevant people hold correct or rational beliefs about the nature of the institution, or about the costs of change, in a way that commits them to foundationalism.

Post-structuralists may be avowed anti-foundationalists, but their lingering debt to structuralism often leads them also to forms of reification and determinism. In particular, their linguistic formalism means that they characteristically treat language as a reified object, defined by the unstable relations among its internal units, rather than as product of use by human agents. Moreover, the post-structuralists' hostility to agency can lead to a variant of determinism. Barthes and Foucault famously argued, for example, that actors, authors, and their speech were defined not by their intentionality but by a social language that spoke through them. Barthes argued, 'it is language which speaks not the author' so they can now 'substitute language itself for the person who until then had been supposed to be its owner' (Barthes 1977, 145). These kinds of arguments look remarkably like a form of determinism. Of course, the post-structuralists themselves often criticize structuralists for exhibiting just such determinism while implying that as post-structuralists they have come to conceive of change, chance, and transformation as instabilities inherent in structures. These instabilities threaten the structure and put it into contradiction with itself. But the post-structuralists simply elide questions of whether we are to understand such instability, contradiction, and transformation as necessary qualities of a disembodied quasi-structure or as contingent properties and products of situated agents.

It is no accident that both modernist-empiricism and post-structuralism often lead to an implicit reification and determinism. These approaches neglect the micro-level of individual agency. They neglect the micro-level of beliefs and desires because they treat social facts and language as governed by norms, processes, structures, or the relations between signs. Likewise, modernist-empiricists typically neglect historical contingency because they appeal to atemporal correlations, classifications, and other such causal logics. No doubt appeals to institutions, quasi-structures, or discourses can be shorthand for appeals to clusters of contingent actions and beliefs. But the worry remains that modernist-empiricists and post-structuralists are bewitched by their shorthand. They forget to treat their metaphors as something that needs to be unpacked as the contingent actions and beliefs of particular individuals. Political scientists will fully break with reification, determinism, and even foundationalism only when they, first, analyse social life as human agency, and, second, explain beliefs and actions in historicist terms.

Our interpretive approach seeks to explain the state by reference to historical meanings understood as the beliefs of individual actors. It encourages political scientists to decentre concepts such as institution, norm, power, and language. To decentre is to focus on the social construction of a practice through the ability of individuals to create and act on meanings. It is to unpack a practice as the disparate and contingent beliefs and actions of individuals. It is to reveal the contingent and conflicting beliefs that inform the diverse actions that constitute the state. Thus, decentred theory involves challenging the idea that inexorable or impersonal forces, norms, or laws define patterns and regularities in politics. Instead, it implies the state is constructed differently by many actors inspired be different ideas and values.

Decentred theory arises from an anti-foundational perspective. Anti-foundationalists explicitly reject the idea of given truths whether based on pure reasons or pure experience. As a result, they emphasize the constructed nature of concepts, actions, and institutions. Constructivist theories suggest meanings are the stuff of all the social sciences where meanings are invented as much as found. Here anti-foundationalism has implications beyond the epistemological domain. The actors studied by social scientists do not have pure perceptions or pure reason. Thus, their reasoning, beliefs, desires, and actions cannot be simply read off from allegedly objective social facts about them. Rather, social scientists have to explore how people construct the world through acting on beliefs that they also construct. A decentred approach encourages us to examine the ways in which our social life, institutions, and policies are created, sustained, and modified by individuals.

New concepts

Decentred theory disaggregates concepts like the state by historical and micro-level analyses of individual actions based on an individual's beliefs. But, while such stories are interesting as cases, there are times when we want to tell more general stories. To do so, interpretivists will need new aggregate concepts that overtly refer to common meanings rather than to reified institutions, norms, discourses, or languages.

Perhaps it will help if we give examples of such aggregate concepts, analysing them as contingent meanings and actions, and indicating where institutionalists and post-structuralists might diverge from our analysis. In the next subsection, we will examine concepts whose main role is in explanations of the empirical nature of particular states: narrative, tradition, and dilemma. These concepts give detail to our analysis of a historicist form of explanation. To begin, however, we look at concepts that refer mainly to the ontological nature of the state: situated agency, practice, and power. These concepts give detail to our humanist analysis of the nature of the self, social life, and so the constituent objects of which the state is composed.

SITUATED AGENCY

A particular notion of the human agent is the bedrock and the micro-level of our theory. As anti-foundationalists, we reject the possibility of an autonomous self, which forms beliefs and acts on pure experiences or pure reason. All experiences and reasoning occur within a web of beliefs. Yet to reject autonomy is not necessarily to reject agency. To accept agency is to imply people have the capacity to adopt beliefs and actions, even novel ones, for reasons of their own, and in so doing they can transform the social background. So, agency is possible, but it is always situated in a particular context.

Some readers may mistake this talk of agency in context for the institutionalist claim that actors are rational within given institutional settings. Here we differ from the institutionalists in two respects. First, whereas they conceive of the context as external institutions, we think of it as the wider web of beliefs of the actor embedded in a historical tradition. Second, their concept of rationality is close to that associated with rational choice, our notion is of local reasoning.

Reasoning is always local in that it occurs against the backcloth of agents' existing webs of belief. The adjective 'local' refers, in other words, to reasoning that always takes place against the background of a particular subjective or intersubjective web of beliefs. While the content of the relevant web of beliefs varies from case to case, there is no possibility of reasoning outside any such background. To insist on the local nature of reasoning is thus to preclude the autonomous and universal concept of reasoning and subjectivity associated with much rational choice theory. Rational choice theory often gestures at a view from nowhere – as if people could adopt beliefs and decide in ways that do not depend on the prior views they hold. However, local reasoning occurs in the specific context of just such prior views. Similarly, whereas rational choice theory often gestures at an assumption of perfect information, local reasoning recognizes that agents can use only the information they possess, and they do just that even when the relevant information happens to be false.

While the adjective 'local' makes it clear that reasoning only takes place against the background of prior beliefs, it need not have a spatial content. Local here means 'local to a web of beliefs', not necessarily 'local to a geographical area'. Thus, local reasoning differs importantly from the cognate concept of local knowledge (Geertz 1983). Local knowledge refers to people's grasp of their own experiences, circumstances, and locality, and it is taken to be specific, concrete, and practical, rather than general, abstract, and theoretical. Usually local knowledge is contrasted less with an autonomous view from nowhere than with expert knowledge based on technical or professional training.

PRACTICE

Once we leave the micro-level for the macro-level, we think of social objects including the state as practices rather than institutions, structures, or systems. A practice is a set of actions, often a set of actions that exhibit a pattern, perhaps even a pattern that remains relatively stable across time. Practices often give us grounds for postulating beliefs, for we can ascribe beliefs to people only in interpreting their actions. Nonetheless, practices cannot explain actions because people act for reasons of their own. People sometimes act on their beliefs about a practice, but, when they do, we still explain their action by reference to their beliefs about the practice, and, of course, these beliefs need not be accurate.

There is a sense in which practices can constitute the consequences of actions. The effects of actions often depend on the responses of others. So, if we equate a practice with the set of actions by which others respond to an act, then, by definition, that practice constitutes the consequences of the act. Still, we should remember here that the practice is composed solely of the contingent actions of individuals. It is these actions in their diversity and contingency that constitute the consequences of the action. We explain these actions by reference to the beliefs and desires of the relevant actors, rather than by reference to the practice itself.

When political scientists appeal to the 'state' or 'institutions', they often evoke something akin to a practice, while ascribing to it a constraining power greater than our analysis allows. If they do want to ascribe such constraining power to practices, they need to specify what they mean by constraint and how exactly practices constrain actions. Clearly practices – or at least the actions of others – constrain the effects, and so effectiveness, of an action. But practices do not constrain the beliefs people might come to hold and so the actions they might attempt to perform.

POWER

An interpretive approach should avoid a concept of power that refers to social relations based on interests that people allegedly have outside the particular traditions by which they make sense of the world. It should do so because people always construct their understanding of their interests against the background of a tradition. Also, there are other ways of conceiving of power. For a start, power can refer to the way in which traditions impact on individuals' beliefs helping to define them, their actions, and the world. Power refers here to the constitutive role played by tradition in giving us our beliefs and actions, and in making our world. An interpretive approach is all about power so conceived, since it explains actions and practices by reference to contingent beliefs formed against the background of traditions. In addition, power can refer to the restrictive consequences of the actions of others in defining what we can and cannot do. Restrictive power works across intricate webs. Actors such as elected politicians, senior civil servants, doctors, police officers, and everyday citizens all find their possibilities for action restricted by what others do. In these terms, an interpretive approach shows how various actors restrict what others can do in ways that thwart the intentions of policy actors. Interpretive studies can show how local actors – Whitehall bureaucrats, doctors, and police officers – are able to draw on their own traditions to resist policies inspired by the narratives of others in the policy cascade.

Historicist explanations

One of the most distinctive features of our interpretive approach is its historicism. We want to replace modernist-empiricism and post-structuralist logics of explanation with avowedly historical ones. Confusion arises here because the historical institutionalists often mistake an interest in historical topics for a historicist form of explanation. Thus, while the new institutionalism has brought forth a chorus of 'history matters', the members of the choir rarely pause to explain why or how history is important. Sometimes their silence occurs alongside an implicit treatment of history as little more than a source of illustrative cases. The more historically minded evoke a sense of time with metaphors such as path dependency, critical juncture, event, and sequencing. The more theoretically minded even appeal to history because a satisfactory account of some aspect of social life must refer to temporal mechanisms and processes (Pierson 2004).

Unfortunately, however, institutionalists see mechanisms and processes in modernist-empiricist terms that are entangled, as one might expect, with determinism, reification, and foundationalism. Their temporal mechanisms and processes are generalizations that operate either irrespective of agency or, more usually, through an agency that is fixed by norms or a universal rationality.[1] Mechanisms and processes are treated as reifications that operate irrespective of contingent agency. They are treated as having an objective content divorced from specific times and places. Again, when institutionalists reify processes and mechanisms, then far from treating history as a mode of explanation, they provide us with explanations that rely on the abstract logic of the mechanism or process. The mechanisms and processes may be temporal in that they unfold over time. They are not historical because their operation is reduced to an abstract logic. It is not contingent on the particular beliefs and actions of people at a particular time (Pierson 2004).

If we are to avoid reifications and allow properly for agency, we need to treat history as a mode of explanation. Historical narratives explain social phenomena not by reference to a reified process, mechanism, or norm, but by describing contingent patterns of action in their specific contexts. Such narratives are not only temporal in that they move through time; they are also historical in that they locate the phenomena at a specific moment in time by using explanatory concepts such as tradition and dilemma.

NARRATIVE

It is often claimed that positivist political science provides causal explanations whereas interpretive approaches provide understanding of beliefs, motives, and actions. The problem with these definitions is they suggest political scientists using an interpretive approach try only to understand or reconstruct objects, not to explain them. Yet interpretive political scientists often write as if their narratives explained actions by pointing to their causes. Scholars from all sorts of disciplines use the word 'cause' to describe the explanatory relationship between people and events. When they do so, they typically use the word 'cause' to indicate the presence of a significant relationship that is characteristic of explanation in their discipline. Narrative is a form of explanation that works by relating actions to the beliefs and desires that produce them.

Narratives depend on the conditional connections between beliefs, desires, and actions. These conditional connections are neither necessary nor arbitrary. Because they are not necessary, political science differs from the natural sciences. Because they are not arbitrary, we can use them to explain actions and practices. Conditional connections exist when the nature of one object draws on the nature of another. They condition each other, so they do not have an arbitrary relationship. Equally, the one does not follow from the other, so they do not have a necessary relationship.

In narratives, pointing to conditional connections that relate people, events, and ideas to one another explains actions and practices without evoking the idea of necessity. Although these narrative structures also appear in works of fiction, we need not equate political science to fiction. Political scientists offer us narratives that strive, to the best of the narrator's ability, to capture the way in which events did happen in the past or are happening today, whereas writers of fiction need not do so. Political scientists cannot ignore the facts, although we must accept that no fact is simply given to them.

TRADITION

A tradition is the ideational background against which individuals come to adopt an initial web of beliefs. It influences (without determining or – in a strict philosophical sense – limiting) the beliefs they later go on to adopt. The philosophical justification for this definition of tradition derives from an anti-foundational rejection of autonomy with a defence of situated agency. Traditions help to explain why people hold the beliefs they do; and because beliefs are constitutive of actions, they also help to explain actions (see Chapter 8). They cannot fully explain actions partly because people act on desires as well as beliefs, and partly because people are agents capable of innovating against the background of a tradition. While a tradition explains why an agent adopted an initial web of beliefs, it consists solely of the beliefs of other actors. Because institutionalists have been relatively slow to concentrate on meanings, we are unsure how they would think of traditions. If they unpack them as systematic extra-individual level of meanings, then they need an analysis of how meanings can exist apart from individual subjects.

DILEMMA

A dilemma is any experience or idea that conflicts with someone's beliefs, and so forces them to alter the beliefs they inherit as a tradition. It combines with the tradition to explain (although not determine) the beliefs people go on to adopt and so the actions they go on to perform. Dilemmas and traditions cannot fully explain actions both because actions are informed by desires as well as beliefs and because people are agents who respond creatively to any given dilemma. Although dilemmas sometimes arise from experiences of the world, we cannot equate them with the world as it is because experiences are always theory-laden. Like meanings in general, dilemmas are always subjective or intersubjective. Institutionalists sometimes adopt concepts such as dilemma or pressure to refer to the sources of change. They then equate such pressures with objective facts about the world rather than the subjective beliefs of policy actors. If they are to define pressures in this way, they need an analysis of how these pressures lead people to change their beliefs and actions. They need to argue either that people are bound to experience a pressure as it is, or that a pressure leads to new actions (and presumably beliefs), even though the actor has no subjective awareness of it.

Conclusions

We have discussed the leading present-day expression of modernist-empiricism: the new institutionalism, criticizing both its lack of a micro-theory that appeals to the beliefs and desires of actors, and its ahistorical forms of explanation. We have reviewed the leading present-day form of interpretive social science – postmodern theories of discourse – arguing that it still relies on structuralist and occasionally even determinist forms of explanation associated with modernist-empiricism. We have defended a historical approach to meaning in which the state appears as a differentiated cultural practice composed of contingent and shifting beliefs and actions. We have provided a set of aggregate concepts appropriate to historical studies of the state: situated agency, practice, power, narrative, tradition and dilemma. The next step is to apply these aggregate concepts to understanding the empirical shifts in, and debates about, the changing nature of 'the state'. We want to show how our anti-foundationalism leads us to see both the state, and the reforms that seek to change it, in markedly different ways. That is the task of Chapter 5.

Note

1. The main analyses of path dependency of which we are aware rely on assumptions about rational action (Pierson 2000). These assumptions sustain a model of the way in which an initial choice *C* can create extra costs for later attempts to depart from *C* such that rational individuals stick with *C* even though, in the absence of these extra costs, *C* would no longer be the optimal outcome for them.

Chapter 5

Rethinking the State

Introduction

In this chapter, we offer our theory of the stateless state, building on the anti-foundational philosophy and the interpretive theory discussed in Chapters 3 and 4. We do not provide a historical survey of the extensive and varied literature on social science theories of the state, much of which is but a variation on the modernist-empiricism discussed at length in Chapter 2.[1] Rather, we focus on *recent* developments in the literature analysing the state; namely the various claims that there has been a change in the pattern and exercise of state authority from government to network governance; from a hierarchic or bureaucratic state to governance in and by networks. We identify three waves in this literature discussing the changing state; from government to network governance, metagovernance and bringing the state back in again, and decentred governance and its anti-foundational move to the stateless state.

The literature on governance focuses on the institutional legacy of neo-liberal reforms of the state. Governance is associated with the changing nature of the state following the public sector reforms of the 1980s. The reforms are said to have precipitated a shift from a hierarchic bureaucracy toward a greater use of markets, quasi-markets, and networks, especially in the delivery of public services. The effects of the reforms were intensified by global changes, including an increase in transnational economic flows and the rise of regional institutions such as the European Union. The resulting complexity and fragmentation are such that the state increasingly depends on other organizations to secure its intentions and deliver its policies. Governance evokes a world in which state power is dispersed among a vast array of spatially and functionally distinct networks made up of many public, voluntary, and private organizations with which the centre now interacts. The governance literature offers a compelling picture of the state; indeed Marsh (2008*b*, 738) is concerned it 'may be becoming the new orthodoxy' (see also Kerr and Kettell 2006, 13). We will decentre this first-wave approach to network governance, examining the work of the Anglo-governance school.

The second wave of metagovernance accepted the shift from bureaucracy to markets to networks but disputed it led to any significant dispersal of state authority. It focused on metagovernance or 'the governance of government and governance' (Jessop 2000, 23; 2007*b*). Metagovernance is an umbrella concept that describes the role of the state and its characteristic policy instruments in network governance. Given that governing is distributed among various private, voluntary, and public actors, and that power and authority are more decentralized and fragmented among a plurality of networks, the role of the state has shifted from the direct governance of society to the 'metagovernance' of the several modes of intervention and from command and control through bureaucracy to the indirect steering of relatively autonomous stakeholders. We also decentre this attempt at bringing the state back in (yet again) (Jessop 2007*a*, 54).

Third, we argue for a third-wave narrative of 'decentred governance' that challenges the idea there are inexorable, impersonal forces driving a shift from government to network governance. As we have seen, to decentre is to focus on the social construction of a practice through the ability of individuals to create, and act on, meanings. Thus, we argue that governance is constructed differently by many actors working against the background of diverse traditions. In effect, we pronounce the death of the Anglo-governance school, of metagovernance, and of the state. We argue, in their place, for the analysis of the various traditions that have informed the diverse policies and practices by which elite and other actors have sought to remake the state.

Finally, we explore the implication of this shift to a narrative of decentred governance. We challenge a craving for generality that characterizes the earlier waves of network and metagovernance and define governance as a series of family resemblances, none of which need be always present. There is no list of general features or essential properties that are supposed to characterize governance in every instance. Rather, there are diverse practices composed of multiple individuals acting on changing webs of beliefs rooted in overlapping traditions. Patterns of governance or state authority arise as the contingent products of diverse actions and political struggles informed by the beliefs of agents as they arise against a backcloth of traditions. We discuss the new research topics prompted by this conception of the stateless state.

The first wave of governance: the Anglo-governance school

Social scientists typically describe network governance as consisting of something akin to a differentiated polity characterized by a hollowed-out state, a core executive fumbling to pull rubber levers of control, and, most notably, a massive growth of networks. Of course, people define governance in all kinds of ways. Nonetheless, social scientists typically appeal to inexorable, impersonal forces, to logics of modernization, such as the functional differentiation of the modern state or the marketization of the public sector, to explain the shift from hierarchy to network governance by markets and especially networks. Indeed, neo-liberal reforms did not lead to markets but to the further differentiation of policy networks in an increasingly hollow state. Social scientists typically use a concept of differentiation here to evoke specialization based on function. They offer a modernist-empiricist account of network governance. They treat governance as self-organizing, inter-organizational networks; as a complex set of institutions and institutional linkages defined by their social role or function. They make any appeal to the contingent beliefs and preferences of agents largely irrelevant.[2]

The Anglo-governance school

In Britain, the first wave of governance narratives challenges the long-standing Westminster narrative, claiming to capture recent changes in British government in a way the Westminster narrative did not. They start with the notion of policy networks or sets of organizations clustered around a major government function or department. These organizations commonly include the professions, trade unions, and big business. So, the story continues, central departments need the cooperation of such groups to deliver services. They allegedly need their cooperation because British government rarely delivers services itself; it uses other bodies to do so. Also, there are supposed to be too many groups to consult so government must aggregate interests; it needs the legitimated spokespeople for that policy area. The groups in turn need the money and legislative authority that only government can provide.

Policy networks are a long-standing feature of British government; they are its silos or velvet drainpipes. The Conservative government of Margaret Thatcher sought to reduce their power by using markets to deliver public services, bypassing existing networks and curtailing the 'privileges' of professions, commonly by subjecting them to the rigorous financial and management controls of the new public management.

The new public management, or managerialism, is conventionally seen as a prime example of governmental control technologies or rationalities. The term encompasses managerialism and marketization. Managerialism refers to introducing private sector management methods to the public sector. It stresses hands-on professional management, explicit standards, and measures of performance; managing by results; value for money; and, more recently, closeness to the customer. Marketization refers to introducing incentive structures (such as market competition) into public service provision. It stresses disaggregating bureaucracies; greater competition through contracting-out and quasi-markets; and consumer choice. But these reforms had unintended consequences. They fragmented the systems for delivering public services, creating pressures for organizations to cooperate with one another to deliver services. In other words, marketization multiplied the networks it aimed to replace. Commonly, packages of organizations now deliver welfare state services. First-wave governance narratives thus concentrate on the spread of networks in British government. They tell us not only that fragmentation created new networks but it also increased the membership of existing networks, incorporating both the private and voluntary sectors. They also tell us that the government swapped direct for indirect controls so central departments are no longer either necessarily or invariably the fulcrum of a network. The government can set the limits to network actions: after all, it still funds the services. But it has also increased its dependence on multifarious networks.

The Anglo-governance school conceives of networks as a distinctive coordinating mechanism notably different from markets and hierarchies and not a hybrid of them. They associate networks with characteristics such as interdependence and trust. In their view, trust is essential because it is the basis of network coordination in the same way that commands and price competition are the key mechanisms for bureaucracies and markets respectively (see also Frances *et al.* 1991, 15; Powell 1991). Shared values and norms are the glue that holds the complex set of relationships in a network together. Trust and reciprocity are essential for cooperative behaviour and, therefore, the existence of the network (see, e.g. Kramer and Tyler 1996). With the spread of networks there has been a recurrent tension between contracts on the one hand, with their stress on competition to get the best price, and networks on the other, with their stress on cooperative behaviour.

According to the Anglo-governance school, multiplying networks means that core executive coordination is modest in practice. It is largely negative, based on persistent compartmentalization, mutual avoidance, and friction reduction between powerful bureaux or ministries. Even when cooperative, anchored at the lower levels of the state machine and organized by specific established networks, coordination is sustained by a culture of dialogue in vertical relations and by horizontal integration. In this view, coordination is rarely strategic, so almost all attempts to create proactive strategic capacity for long-term planning have failed (Wright and Hayward 2000). The Anglo-governance school explains New Labour's reforms as an attempt to promote coordination and strategic oversight and combat both Whitehall's departmentalism and the unintended consequences of managerialism.

Therefore, the Anglo-governance school tells us a story of fragmentation confounding centralization as a segmented executive seeks to improve horizontal coordination among departments and agencies and vertical coordination between departments and their networks of organizations. An unintended consequence of this search for central control has been a hollowing out of the state. The hollowing out of the state suggests the growth of governance has further undermined the ability of the core executive to act effectively, making it increasingly reliant on diplomacy. The state has been hollowed out from above by for example international interdependence, and from below by for example marketization and networks, and sideways by agencies. Internally, the British core executive was already characterized by baronies, policy networks, and intermittent and selective coordination. It has been further hollowed out internally by the unintended consequences of marketization, which fragmented service delivery, multiplied networks, and diversified the membership of those networks. Externally, the state is also being hollowed out by membership of the EU and other international commitments.

The second wave: metagovernance

Critics of the first wave characteristically focus on the argument the state has been hollowed out. For example, Pierre and Peters (2000, 78, 104–5, and 111) argue that the shift to network governance could 'increase public control over society' because governments 'rethink the mix of policy instruments'. As a result 'coercive or regulatory instruments become less important and..."softer" instruments gain importance', for example, steering through brokerage. In short, the state has not been hollowed out but reasserted its capacity to govern by regulating the mix of governing structures such as markets and networks and using indirect instruments of control.

Metagovernance refers to this role of the state in securing coordination in governance and its use of negotiation, diplomacy, and more informal modes of steering. It suggests the state now steers and regulates sets of organizations, governments, and networks rather than rowing by directly providing services through state bureaucracies. These other organizations undertake much of the work of governing: they implement policies, provide public services, and at times even regulate themselves. The state governs the organizations that govern civil society: the governance of governance. Moreover, the other organizations characteristically have a degree of autonomy from the state: they are often voluntary or private sector groups or they are governmental agencies or tiers of government separate from the core executive. So the state cannot govern them solely by the instruments that work in bureaucracies.

Nonetheless, there are several ways in which the state can steer the other actors involved in governance (see, e.g. Jessop 2000, 23–4; 2007*b*). First, the state can set *the rules of the game* for other actors and then leave them to do what they will within those rules; they work 'in the shadow of hierarchy'. So, it can redesign markets, re-regulate policy sectors, or introduce constitutional change. Second, the state can try to steer other actors using *storytelling*. It can organize dialogues; foster meanings, beliefs, and identities among the relevant actors; and influence what actors think and do. Third, the state can steer by the way in which it distributes *resources* such as money and authority. It can play a boundary-spanning role; alter the balance between actors in a network; act as a court of appeal when conflict arises; rebalance the mix of governing structures; and step in when network governance fails. Of course, the state need not adopt a single uniform approach to metagovernance. It can use different approaches, in different settings, at different times.

This summary implies much agreement about metagovernance. In fact, Sørensen and Torfing (2007, 170–80) identify four approaches to metagovernance: interdependence, governability, integration, and governmentality. Interdependence theory focuses on the state managing networks using a more sophisticated, indirect tool kit (Rhodes 1997*b*). Governability theory stresses that metagovernance and network management occur in the shadow of hierarchy (Scharpf 1997). Integration theory stresses the formation and management of identities (March and Olsen 1989). Governmentality theory focuses on the regulation of self-regulation: on the norms, standards, and targets that set the limits to networks (Barry, Osborne, and Rose 1996*a*). This categorization is odd. Proponents of integration theory and governmentality never talk of metagovernance, although some of their ideas are relevant, while integration theory lumps together strange bedfellows. Nonetheless, distinguishing these approaches helps to identify the differences over the extent and form of state intervention and control.

Proponents of interdependence theory would argue that manipulating the rules of the game allows the state to keep much control over governing without having to bear the costs of direct interference. Proponents of governability theory stress the resources the state has at its disposal for metagovernance. They argue that the state can easily deploy these resources to manage other policy actors. Proponents of integration theory argue the viewpoints and interests of different actors are so diverse that managing identities is the core task; for example – storytelling about best practice and successful cooperation and coordination. Storytelling can create coherent social and political meanings and identities that soften the tensions among competing viewpoints and interests. Proponents of governmentality theory identify the complex of rules, norms, standards, and regulatory practices that extend state rule more deeply into civil society by regulating the ways in which civil society self-regulates. Accountancy, performance management, and other management techniques are not just ways of achieving the '3Es' of economy, efficiency, and effectiveness. They are also ways of measuring, approving, appraising, and regulating the beliefs and practices of network actors (and for examples see McKinlay and Starkey 1998). Of course, the approaches are not mutually exclusive; state actors use a different mix of approaches in different contexts.

Common ground

For all their different emphases and the debate between the several proponents, the first two waves of governance share much common ground. First, proponents of metagovernance take for granted the characteristics of network governance. They accept that states are becoming increasingly fragmented into networks based on several different stakeholders; and the dividing line between the state and civil society is becoming more blurred because the relevant stakeholders are private or voluntary sector organizations. So, Jessop (2000, 24) concedes 'the state is no longer the sovereign authority . . . [it is] less hierarchical, less centralised, less *dirigiste*'. There is a shared modernist-empiricist description of the characteristics of network governance.

Second, the analysis of metagovernance not only recognizes non-state actors by granting them the power to self-regulate but also distinguishes them from the state so creating the space for the state to exert macro-control over their self-regulation. The state governs the other actors involved in governance. In other words, metagovernance heralds the return of the state by reinventing its governing role. This return to the state opens opportunities for policy advice on the practice of metagovernance. The two waves share a common concern with providing advice on network governance. Both assume the role of the state is to manage, directly and indirectly, the networks of service delivery. For example, Part III of Sørensen and Torfing (2007, chapters 10–12) on 'metagovernance' is devoted to such topics as governing the performance of networks, institutional design, and network management, and the possibilities for public authorities to shape network outputs. They are not alone.[3]

Third, both narratives rely on a reified notion of structure. The proponents of first-wave governance are self-confessed modernist-empiricists with a reified notion of structure rooted in an explicit social science theory of functional differentiation. The proponents of metagovernance also claim the state is a material object, a structure, or a social form. They draw on critical realist epistemology and such notions as 'emergence' and 'mechanisms' ostensibly to guard against the charge of reification (see, e.g. Jessop 2005, 2007*a*). Their position is flawed and has a closer affinity to modernist-empiricism than they realize or care to admit.

Modernist-empiricists rely on reified concepts such as institution, structure, state formation, and system to offer explanations that transcend time and space. They appeal to ideal types, institutions, and structures as if they are natural kinds. Rational choice theory challenges the reifications and raises the issue of micro-theory. Modernist-empiricists can respond in three ways. First, they could adopt the third-wave decentred approach. They could view social life solely as activity, reject reifications, and avoid rational choice theory by emphasizing contingency. They don't like this route because they have to give up their ideas about expertise, science, and some varieties of socialism (and often all three). Second, they can recast their reifications as if they were consequences of rational actors behaving more or less as rational choice theory suggests. This response is common in the United States but not with critical realists in the United Kingdom. They prefer to appeal to structure, emergence, and mechanism. They claim these concepts do not involve reification but they avoid the micro-level questions that would show how they avoid reification. Thus, they often shift back and forth between using the old reifications of modernist-empiricism and paying lip service to the micro-theories associated with rational choice or decentred analysis. For example, McAnulla (2006) argues that structures are emergent or temporal mechanisms rather than reifications, but never explains how these structures differ from practices, or how they determine individual actions without passing through intentional consciousness. He provides no clear account of why agents can't change emergent structures. The structure emerges from actions, so presumably, if all the relevant people change their actions, they will stop producing that structure, so changing it. The emergent structures are better understood as practices. They consist simply of what a bundle of people do and the unintended consequences of these actions. Of course, structure can be used as a metaphor for the way activity coalesces into patterns and practices. But the metaphors have a bewitching effect. People treat them as real, reified entities; the fate of Marsh (2008*a*) in his analysis of the British political tradition. In short, critical realism and the analysis of metagovernance all too often rely on the reifications of modernist-empiricism and of first-wave governance.

The idea of the state as a structure is useful only if we unpack it into the specific notions of tradition, dilemma, practice, and unintended consequence. First, the state might refer to traditions; that is, inherited webs of belief that influence what people do. Second, the state might refer to a subset of dilemmas; that is, to intersubjective views about the way the nature of the world precludes or impels certain actions. Third, the state might refer to cultural practices, where although these practices arise from people's actions, they then confront other people as if objective social facts. Finally, the state might refer to the intended and unintended consequences of meaningful actions, although, of course, to explain such consequences, we would have to refer to the actions and the meanings (or intentionality) they embodied.

Finally, both waves seek to provide *comprehensive* accounts of network and metagovernance. Social scientists typically aim to provide a general account of what governance looks like, and why it does so. For example, network governance is often characterized by the shift from bureaucratic hierarchies to multiplying networks. This defining feature is then said to explain other characteristics of network governance such as the need for indirect 'diplomatic' styles of management, and the search for better coordination through joint ventures, partnerships, and holistic governance.

Defining network and metagovernance by one or more essential properties, such as multiplying networks, implies these properties are general and characterize all cases of governance. So, we will find governance in its new guise if and only if we find a spread of networks. Moreover, these essential properties explain the most significant features of network and metagovernance.

A comprehensive account of governance makes sense, even as a mere aspiration, only if it has some essence. We should seek a comprehensive account only if the way to define and explain network and metagovernance is to find a social logic or essential property that is at least common to all its manifestations and ideally even explains them. But why would we assume that network and metagovernance has one or more essential feature?

The search for comprehensive accounts arises from a preoccupation with the natural sciences. However, even if appropriate in the natural sciences, it is counterproductive in the human sciences. Human practices are not governed by social logics or law-like regularities associated with their allegedly essential properties. They arise instead out of the contingent activity of individuals. Therefore, when we seek to explain particular cases of governance, we should do so by reference to the contingent activity of the relevant individuals, not to a social logic or law-like regularity. We should explain practices, including cases of governance, using narratives that unpack the contingent actions that embody beliefs informed by contested traditions and dilemmas. The contingent nature of the links between traditions and their development undermines the possibility of a comprehensive account that could relate any one practice to a specific set of social conditions as opposed to a historical process. If we explore these possibilities, we will adopt a decentred approach that refutes the narratives of previous waves.

The third wave: decentring the changing state[4]

Decentred theory

As we explained in Chapter 4, decentred theory explores the institutions of the state as the contingent meanings that inform the actions of the individuals involved in all kinds of practices of rule. It is a humanist and historicist theory of the state. It refuses to treat the state as uniform. The state contains diverse practices. In rejecting uniform concepts of the state, we echo those pluralists and behaviouralists who developed the twentieth-century critique of the state. The state has no defined or metaphysical nature fixed by the common good of its people or any other essence. It needs, instead, to be differentiated into its constituents.

First-wave narratives of the changing state focus on issues such as the objective characteristics of policy networks and the oligopoly of the political market place. They stress power dependency, the relationship of the size of networks to policy outcomes, and the strategies by which the centre might steer networks. The second wave of narratives about the changing state focus on the mix of governing structures such as markets and networks and using various instruments of control such as changing the rules of the game, storytelling, and changing the distribution of resources. In contrast to these comprehensive, reified views of governance, a third-wave decentred narrative focuses on the social construction of patterns of rule through the ability of individuals to create meanings in action. It encourages us to examine the ways in which patterns of rule, including institutions and policies, are created, sustained, and varied by individuals. It encourages us to recognize that the actions of these individuals are not fixed by institutional norms or a social logic of modernization. To the contrary, actions arise from the beliefs individuals adopt against the background of traditions and in response to dilemmas.

Any existing pattern of rule will have some failings. Different people will have different views about these failings since they are not simply given by experience but rather constructed from interpretations of experience infused with traditions. When people's perceptions of the failings of governance conflict with their existing beliefs, the resulting dilemmas lead them to reconsider beliefs and traditions. Because people confront these dilemmas against the background of diverse traditions, there arises a political contest over what constitutes the nature of the failings and what should be done about them. This contest leads to a reform of governance. The reformed pattern of rule poses new dilemmas, leading to a further contest over meanings and policy agendas. All these contests are governed by laws and norms that prescribe how they should be conducted. Sometimes the relevant laws and norms have changed because of simultaneous contests over their content and relevance. Yet while we can distinguish analytically between a pattern of rule and a contest over its reform, we rarely can do so temporally. Rather, the activity of governing continues during most contests, and most contests occur partially in local practices of governing. What we have, therefore, is a complex and continuous process of interpretation, conflict, and activity that produces ever-changing patterns of rule.

A decentred account of the changing state represents, therefore, a shift from institutions to meanings in action, and from social logics to narratives. The first-wave narrative of network governance reduces the diversity of governance to a social logic of modernization, institutional norms, or a set of classifications or correlations across networks. Its proponents tame an otherwise chaotic picture of multiple actors creating a contingent pattern of rule through their diverse understandings and conflicting actions. The second-wave of governance compounds this mistake by reinventing the state's capacity to control. The third-wave narrative decentres the changing state into governance practices. Thus, governance arises from the bottom-up because it arises from diverse practices, conflicting meanings and beliefs, competing traditions, and varied dilemmas. The third-wave narrative replaces aggregate concepts that refer to objectified social laws with ones that explain actions by relating them to the beliefs and desires that produce them.

What does this decentred approach tell us about governance? We have two answers. First, we offer a definition of governance as a series of family resemblances that does not crave generality and aspire to comprehensiveness because none of the resemblances need be always present. Second, we point to some of the distinctive research topics that spring from a decentred approach. Our concern with diverse and contingent meanings encourages a focus on such new empirical topics as rule, rationalities, and resistance.

Defining governance

A decentred approach to the changing state contrasts sharply with comprehensive accounts that seek to unpack the essential properties and social logic of network governance and metagovernance. Neither the intrinsic rationality of markets nor the path dependency of institutions decide patterns of governance. Rather, patterns of governance are explained as the contingent constructions of several actors inspired by competing webs of belief and associated traditions. A decentred approach explains shifting patterns of governance by focusing on the actors' own interpretations of their actions and practices. It explores the diverse ways in which situated agents are changing the boundaries of state and civil society by constantly remaking practices as their beliefs change. Because we cannot explain cases of network and metagovernance by reference to a comprehensive theory, we cannot define governance by its key features. Rather, we can define it only for particular cases. However, the absence of a comprehensive theory of governance also implies that there need be no feature common to all the cases to which we would apply the term. It is futile to search for the essential features of an abstract category that denotes a cluster of human practices. Worse still, the search for allegedly common features can lead political scientists to dismiss the particular cases which are essential to understanding the abstract category. When we provide a definition or general account of governance, it should be couched as a set of family resemblances.

Wittgenstein (1972*a*) famously suggested that general concepts such as 'game' should be defined by various traits that overlapped and criss-crossed in much the same way as do the resemblances between members of a family – their builds, eye colour, gait, or personalities. He considered various examples of games to challenge the idea that they all possessed a given property or set of properties – skill, enjoyment, victory, and defeat – by which we could define the concept. Instead, he suggested the examples exhibited a network of similarities, at various levels of detail, so they coalesced even though no one feature was common to them all.[5]

We do not master such family resemblance concepts by discovering a theory or rule that tells us precisely when we should and should not apply them. Our grasp of the concept consists in our ability to explain why it should be applied in one case but not another, our ability to draw analogies with other cases, and our ability to point to the criss-crossing similarities. Our knowledge of 'governance' is analogous to our knowledge of 'game' as described by Wittgenstein. It is 'completely expressed' by our describing various cases of governance, showing how other cases can be considered as analogous to these, and suggesting that we would be unlikely to describe yet other cases as ones of governance.

Some of the family resemblances that characterize governance derive from a focus on meaning in action and so apply to all patterns of rule. A decentred approach highlights, first, a more diverse view of state authority and its exercise. All patterns of rule arise as the contingent products of diverse actions and political struggles informed by the varied beliefs of situated agents. First-wave narratives of network governance suggest the New Right's reinvention of the minimal state and the more recent rediscovery of networks are attempts to find a substitute for the voluntaristic bonds weakened by state intervention (Harris 1990). A decentred approach suggests that the notion of a monolithic state in control of itself and civil society was always a myth. The myth obscured the reality of diverse state practices that escaped the control of the centre because they arose from the contingent beliefs and actions of diverse actors at the boundary of state and civil society. The state is never monolithic and it always negotiates with others.

Policy always arises from interactions within networks of organizations and individuals. Patterns of rule always traverse the public, private, and voluntary sectors. The boundaries between state and civil society are always blurred. Transnational and international links and flows always disrupt national borders. In short, state authority is constantly remade, negotiated, and contested in widely different ways within widely varying everyday practices.

A decentred approach suggests, second, these everyday practices arise from situated agents whose beliefs and actions are informed by traditions and expressed in stories. In every government department, we can identify departmental traditions, often embodied in rituals and routines. They might range from specific notions of accountability to the ritual of the tea lady. Actors pass on these traditions in large part by telling one another stories about 'how we do things around here', and about what does and does not work. For example, British civil servants are socialized into the broad notions of the Westminster tradition, such as ministerial responsibility, as well as the specific ways of doing things around here. They are 'socialized into the idea of a profession', and learn 'the framework of the acceptable' (Bevir and Rhodes 2006, chapter 7). Governance is not any given set of characteristics. It is the stories people use to construct, convey, and explain traditions, dilemmas, beliefs, and practices.

A decentred approach also might help to highlight a third family resemblance that characterizes British governance, but might not be found in patterns of rule in other times or places. In Britain, the reforms of the New Right and New Labour have brought about a shift from hierarchy to markets to networks. While this shift is widely recognized, a decentred approach suggests, crucially, that it takes many diverse forms. For the police, the shift from hierarchy to markets to networks poses specific dilemmas. They know how to rewrite the rulebook, manage a contract, or work with neighbourhood watch, but they struggle to reconcile these ways of working, believing they conflict and undermine one another (Bevir and Rhodes 2006, chapter 9). For doctors, the equivalent shift poses different dilemmas: the key issue is how to preserve the medical model of health and medical autonomy from managerial reforms that stress hierarchy and financial control (Bevir and Rhodes 2006, chapter 8).

A fourth family resemblance is that the central state has adopted a less hands-on role. Its actors are less commonly found within various local and sectoral bodies, and more commonly found in quangos concerned to steer, coordinate, and regulate such bodies. Once again, a decentred approach suggests, crucially, that such steering, coordination, and regulation take many diverse forms. In Britain, the pre-eminent recent example is 'joined-up' government as the Blair government sought to devise policy instruments that integrated both horizontally across central government departments and vertically between central and local government and the voluntary sector (Bevir 2005, 83–105).

A decentred approach highlights the resemblances that contribute to a general characterization of governance and a more specific characterization of governance at least in Britain. Nonetheless, it disavows any logic to the specific forms that governance takes in particular circumstances. So, a decentred approach resolves the theoretical difficulties that beset earlier waves or narratives of the changing state. It avoids the unacceptable suggestion that institutions fix the actions of individuals in them rather than being products of those actions. It replaces unhelpful phrases such as path dependency with an analysis of change rooted in the beliefs and practices of situated agents. Yet it allows political scientists to offer aggregate studies by using the concept of tradition to explain how people come to hold certain beliefs and perform certain actions.

New research topics

A decentred approach to the state rejects both comprehensive theory and the related idea that the state is a material object or emergent structure or social form. We reject the claim that the '*preexistence* [of social forms] implies their *autonomy* as possible objects of scientific investigation; and their *causal efficacy* confirms their *reality*' (Jessop 2005, 42). We offer a stateless theory in the sense that we reject the idea of the state as a pre-existing causal structure that can be understood independently of people's beliefs and practices. Studying the changing state is not about building formal theories; it is about telling stories about other people's meanings; it is about narratives of their narratives. As Finlayson and Martin (2006, 167) stress, the object of analysis is not the state but 'a diverse range of agencies, apparatuses and practices producing varied mechanisms of control and varied forms of knowledge that make areas or aspects of social life available for governmental action'. A decentred approach leads us to new narratives of such practices and knowledge, which we explore as rule, rationalities, and resistance.

RULE – ELITE NARRATIVES

Decentred theory suggests that political scientists should pay more attention to the traditions against the background of which elites construct their worldviews, including their views of their own interests. Moreover, the central elite need not be a uniform group, all the members of which see their interests in the same way, share a common culture, or speak a shared discourse. Our decentred approach suggests that political scientists should ask whether different sections of the elite draw on different traditions to construct different narratives about the world, their place within it, and their interests and values. In Britain, for example, the different members of the central elite are inspired by Tory, Whig, liberal, and socialist narratives. The dominant narratives in the central civil service used to be the Whig story of the generalist civil servant, spotting snags and muddling through. It has been challenged by a liberal managerial narrative that sees civil servants as hands-on, can-do managers, trained at business schools and not on the job. But the traditions coexist sometimes separately but sometimes bumping into one another to create dilemmas. Thus, civil servants continue to believe in the Westminster notions of ministerial accountability to parliament, a centralizing idea, even as they decentralize decision making in line with managerial notions.

Although Part II is structured around the ideas of rule, rationality, and resistance, there is no neat one-to-one correspondence between these ideas and our narratives; there are just differences of emphasis. So, Chapter 6 looks at a day in the life of a minister. We contrast the Westminster tradition's monarchical strand, and its deference to the Queen's minister, with the prosaic nature of much of his work. Rule equates to 'making a difference' and surviving the brickbats thrown by the media and political opponents at the goldfish bowl in which he lives. For the civil services, everyday life is about the protocols they use to domesticate everyday crises. For the minister, it is about the appearance of rule.

RATIONALITIES

Central elites may construct their world using diverse narratives but they also turn to forms of expertise for specific discourses. Nowadays different traditions of social science influence public policy. Our decentred approach draws attention to the varied rationalities that inform policies across different sectors and different geographical spaces. Rationalities refer here to the scientific beliefs and associated technologies that govern conduct; it captures the ways in which governments and other social actors draw on knowledge to construct policies and practices, especially those that regulate and create subjectivities. Britain, like much of the developed world, has witnessed the rise of neo-liberal managerial rationalities using a technology of performance measurement and targets that spread far beyond the central civil service to encompass the control of localities. Kelly (2006, 615 and 617) describes how the UK's Audit Commission acts as a meta-governor of local authorities for the New Labour government. It ensures that 'the regulatory regime is embedded in the everyday operations and actions of local government practitioners'. It espouses the notion of the well-run authority and it works 'with other inspectorates and professional auditing bodies to maintain professional standards and also to share best practice'. It sets auditors' fees and standards, and monitors the work of the auditors. It is one of those varied agencies employing indirect mechanisms of control and knowledge.[6]

In Chapters 7 and 8, we analyse the dilemmas posed when the Westminster tradition bumps into the performance measurement rationalities of the new public management, or managerialism. In Chapter 7, we provide an interpretive history of the managerial rationalities introduced by the New Labour government. We tell *three* stories about the civil service and managerialism; the centralization story, the management story, and the governance story. We seek to show that, even among the elite, there are contending stories about the reforms. State reform is variously constructed and civil servants confront the dilemmas posed by the contending Westminster and managerial traditions. In Chapter 8, we look at the ways in which senior civil servants coped with managerialism. We show how the heads of the public service articulate the living traditions of 'constitutional bureaucracy' found in the Westminster form of parliamentary government and selectively draw on past understandings to understand present-day changes. We describe traditions under challenge that reshape reforms as reforms reshape them. We show that the myths and legends of yore remain germane to the modern public service. In both case, we show that ruling has its long-standing myths and symbols but it is a fragile and fraught business remade 'by events, dear boy, events' filtered through Westminster, departmental and party political traditions.

RESISTANCE

When political scientists neglect agency, they can give the impression that politics and policies arise exclusively from the strategies and interactions of central and local elites. Yet other actors can resist, transform, and thwart the agendas of elites. Our decentred approach draws attention to the diverse traditions and narratives that inspire street-level bureaucrats and citizens. Policies are sites of struggles not just between strategic elites, but between all kinds of actors with different views and ideals reached against the background of different traditions. Subordinate actors can resist the intentions and policies of elites by consuming them in ways that draw on their local traditions and their local reasoning. For example, street-level police officers are often influenced by organizational traditions that encourage them to set priorities different from those of both their superior officers and elite policy makers. Combating crime is seen as the core of police work, not the 'touchy-feely' areas of community policing. The new police commissioner may want to set an example, cause a stir, or otherwise ginger up the troops. But the troops know he or she will be gone in a few years. There will be a new commissioner with new interests and priorities (see, e.g. on community policing, Fleming and Wood 2006; and on other street-level bureaucrats see Lipsky 1979 and Vinzant and Crothers 1998). In Chapter 9, we pursue such contrasts. We compare the different ways in which middle-level managers, employees, and citizens experience the managerial reforms of public services. We show there are significant differences in the way the rationality of managerialism is experienced and understood. We argue the different narratives are stories of resistance, and central to the 'implementation gap' in the reform of the public services.

Conclusions

In sum, network governance was the modernist-empiricist story of the changing state that described the shift from hierarchy to markets to networks. A decentred approach brings about the death of this first-wave narrative because, we argue, there is no single account or theory of governance, only the differing constructions of several traditions. We also announce the death of the second wave of metagovernance not only because it accepts the modernist-empiricist narrative but also because it argues for a top-down account of state regulation and control over a bottom-up one. There is no necessary logical or structural process determining the form of network governance or the role of the 'central state' in the governance of governance. Patterns of governance, and changes in such patterns, cannot be explained by any of the intrinsic rationality of markets, the path dependency of institutions, or the state's new tool kit for managing the mix of governing structures.

The third-wave analysis of governance announces the arrival of the stateless state. It argues that the state arises out of the diverse actions and practices inspired by varied beliefs and traditions. The state, or pattern of rule, is the contingent product of diverse actions and political struggles informed by the beliefs of agents rooted in traditions.

Our approach seeks to explain the state by reference to historical meanings infusing the beliefs and practices of individual actors. It encourages political scientists to decentre the state and governance and focus on the social construction of practices. We unpack the state into the disparate and contingent beliefs and actions of individuals. We reveal the contingent and conflicting beliefs that inform the diverse actions that constitute the state. We challenge the idea that inexorable or impersonal forces, norms, or laws define changing patterns of governance. Instead, we argue that the state is constructed differently by many actors inspired by different ideas and values. Our stories construct and reconstruct the stateless state and it is to these stories we turn in Part II.

Notes

1. Elitist, pluralist, and Marxist theories of the state have been described thoroughly and often by others. See Dunleavy and O'Leary (1987), Hay (1996), and Hay, Lister and Marsh (2006).
2. It would use too much space to provide supporting quotations but the point is well made in, for example, Marinetto's discussion (2003) of the 'Anglo-Governance School'. For specific examples, see Rhodes (1988, 1997*a*, 2000), Richards and Smith (2002), Smith (1999), and Stoker (2000, 2004).
3. There is an extensive literature on managing networks, collaborations, and partnerships including Agranoff (2007), Agranoff and McGuire (2004), Ferlie, Lynn, and Pollitt (2005), Goss (2001), Koppernjan and Klijn (2004), Perri 6 *et al.* (2002), Salamon (2002), and Stoker (1999; 2004).
4. Although they arrive at this point by a different route to ours, others also see the state as a mask hiding political practice (Abrams 1988, 1). Post-structuralism in the guises of governmentality and discourse analysis stresses the constructed nature of the state and governance. See, for example Barry, Osborne, and Rose (1996*a*), Burchell, Gordon, and Miller (1991), Dean (1998; 2007, chapter 2), Dean and Hindess (1998), Finlayson and Martin (2006, 2008), Howarth, Norval, and Stavrakakis (2000), and Miller and Rose (2008, chapter 3). They also favour research on rule, rationalities, and resistance, although they use a different terminology.

5. In his preliminary sketch of his discussion of games, Wittgenstein (1972*b*, 17–20) explicitly contrasts this position with a 'craving for generality' he ascribes to inappropriate attempts to model all knowledge on natural science.
6. For other examples of such rationalities see Dean and Hindess (1998), Jacobs and Manzi (2000), McKinlay and Starkey (1998), Miller and Rose (2008, chapter 2), and Power (1994).

Part II

Rule, Rationalities, and Resistance

Chapter 6
Ministerial Ruling

Introduction

This chapter attempts something markedly different from the existing literature on ministers.[1] We do not seek to engage with the academic literature but with our fieldwork observations. We aim to describe the changing world of permanent secretaries and ministers through an account of their daily life in government. We seek to provide our interpretation of their interpretation of what the world looks like through their eyes. So, we watched people in their everyday office life. We relied on what they said and did, on their reasons for their actions. We looked for patterns but we did not test hypotheses. We focused on meanings, not statistical frequencies. We did not break individual behaviour into specific roles, but looked at people in the round. We looked at the contingent, the improvised, the personal, and the subjective. We took everyday experience as the starting point. In a short phrase, we aimed at a 'thick description' of office life (Geertz 1973, chapter 1).

We provide a case study of what it means to a minister 'to rule'. It is an elite narrative of ruling. It is an exploration of situated agency. We locate the minister in both the larger Westminster tradition and the specific traditions of his department. We contrast the Westminster tradition's monarchical strand, and its deference to the Queen's minister, with the prosaic nature of much of his work. Rule equates to 'making a difference' and surviving the brickbats thrown by the media and political opponents at the goldfish bowl in which he lives. For the civil services, everyday life is about the protocols the ministers use to domesticate daily crises. We show that ruling has its long-standing myths and symbols, but it is a fragile and fraught business remade 'by events, dear boy, events' filtered through governmental and departmental traditions.

The first section of the chapter briefly outlines the research and our methods. The second and largest section of the chapter draws extensively on our fieldwork notebooks, supplemented by interviews with the ministers, to describe not only the everyday life of ministers but also our reaction to being with them for many days. Finally, we interrogate these data using the ideas in Part I of this book.

Observation

Observation is about 'thick descriptions'. What we call our data are really our own constructions of other people's constructions of what they and their compatriots are up to (Geertz 1973, 9). The everyday phrase is 'seeing things from the other's point of view'. The key point is that the ethnographer provides his or her own interpretation of what the informants believe they are up to, so his or her accounts are second- or even third-order interpretations. The task is to set down the meanings that particular actions have for social actors and say what these 'thick descriptions' tell us about the society in which they are found. And this analysis is always incomplete. Ethnography is a science 'marked less by a perfection of consensus than by a refinement of debate' – 'what gets better is the precision with which we vex each other'.[2]

To write a story that vexes the reader, we draw on three sources of information:

> [T]he pattern of practice, talk, and considered writing – the first is the most reliable, the second is the most copious and revealing and the third is the most difficult to interpret. (Oakeshott 1996, x)

Oakeshott will turn in his grave if we describe this approach as triangulation, but our account is based on these three sources of information. On 'practice', we observed the Private Office of two Ministers and three permanent secretaries for two days each, totalling some 120 hours. We also shadowed two Ministers and three permanent secretaries for five working days each, totalling some 300 hours of fieldwork. On 'talk', we had repeat interviews with nine permanent secretaries (2×2-hour taped and transcribed), three secretaries of state and three Ministers (1×2-hour taped and transcribed); and nineteen other officials (1×1-hour taped and transcribed), totalling 67 hours of interviews. On 'considered writing', we had copies of speeches and public lectures; committee and other papers relevant to the meetings we observed; and newspaper reports. We told everyone we would not write up the research during the life of the 2001–5 Parliament. One of the advantages of not publishing straight away is that we also had several insider accounts of the period to draw on. We also calculated that everyone would have a different job when we told the story, thus minimizing, if not removing, any political sensitivities surrounding the events.

The interviews and fieldwork observations were for citation but not for attribution without permission. We interviewed three female Ministers and two female permanent secretaries. There were so few women that if we give the person's gender, in effect, we identify them. Therefore, we use the male pronoun throughout. The Private Offices were more equally divided between males and females, and with 20 interviews it does not compromise a person's identity if we use the correct gender. We anticipated that at least some parts of the story would have to be anonymous. We chose three departments similar in size and status, so we could talk about the composite Minister, Department, or Permanent Secretary and remain plausible. Had we sought to draw a composite based on departments as unlike as the Treasury, the Foreign Office, and the Department for Work and Pensions, the result would have been implausible. We conducted the interviews in 2002. The fieldwork was carried out in 2003. There were several repeat interviews and short visits in 2004. It is an example of multisite or 'yo-yo fieldwork' (Wulff 2002).

When we cannot attribute a quote, and consistent with protecting the anonymity of the individual, we indicate the position held by the individual – minister, senior civil servant, member of a private office, and so on. All such information is from a taped interview. In every case, there will be at least three individuals who are possible sources for the quote.

We supplement this fieldwork with the usual primary sources and with the several insider accounts now available.[3] Also, nowadays, senior civil servants speak in public regularly. Moreover, the speeches are easily available from the Internet. We attended many lectures and seminars under the Chatham House rule,[4] which offered the opportunity to hear many senior public figures speaking, often frankly, and off the record. We found this combination of talk and considered writing a valuable primary source. Throughout, whether drawing on the fieldwork or other primary sources, we focus on the views of insiders because we are trying to describe their world through their eyes.

One of the more stubborn problems in writing up observational fieldwork is how to turn messy day-to-day experiences into a considered written account.[5] Van Maanen (1988, 35) declares that 'there is no way of seeing, hearing, or representing the world of others that is absolutely, universally valid or correct'. He identifies three ways of telling the fieldwork story: realist tales, confessional tales, and impressionist tales (Van Maanen 1988). Realist accounts are dispassionate, third-person documentary accounts of everyday life. A confessional story is autobiographical and told in the first person. Impressionist tales are episodic and complex, stressing contingency. We use the latter two ways of telling the chronological, personal story of the complex, episodic, ambivalent, and contingent everyday life of a Minister. In Chapter 9, we use 'factions' – or disguised accounts written by participants – and scenes – or story segments, as building blocks to develop specific themes. Throughout, we use dialogue, or reciprocal conversations, sometimes in the form of semi-structured interviews but also, during the observational fieldwork, they were part of everyday conversations at the office. The stories, factions, scenes, and dialogue are mainly in the offices of the public servants, written from the point of view, and sometimes in the words, of their inhabitants. Factions and scenes cover moments in time not days or weeks; there is no unfolding storyline or character development.

We present dialogue from the interviews in italics with the position of the interviewee and the date of the interviews. Observed practices from the fieldwork notebook (FWNB) are in roman font. Quotes from the FWNB are in inverted commas.[6] To show our stories are plausible, and to guard against the criticism that we have picked only juicy quotes from interviews and fieldwork notebooks, we cite other insider accounts. Most of these citations are in the endnotes and are illustrative, not comprehensive. Other quotations are attributed as usual. In this way, we can follow our own advice and compare observed practice (from FWNB), talk (from interviews and conversations), and considered writing (from autobiographies, memoirs, diaries, speeches, and lectures). Also, readers always know our sources. We triangulate these sources of information to increase confidence in our observation (Sanjek 2000, 281). We also reported earlier such details as the number and length of interviews and the total hours of observation for the same reason (Yanow 2006). Finally, we provide multiple quotes to demonstrate a point. Such detail is endemic in observational fieldwork; it is a defining characteristic of 'thick descriptions'.

Shadowing ministers, ministerial shadow

The stage

The main character in our tale is the elected politician who heads a central government department and is known as the Secretary of State. The top official in the department is known as the permanent secretary. Most are middle-aged, white, university-educated men, who have spent their working life in the senior civil service. They are a small elite group who work closely with the elected politicians.

The events we describe took place during the second parliamentary term of the UK's Labour Government, which began on 8 June 2001 and ended in May 2005. The prime minister and head of the government was Tony Blair and his official residence was 10 Downing Street. He appointed all Ministers, or Secretaries of State, who are in the Cabinet, and junior ministers, or Ministers of State, who are not, and the Parliamentary Under-Secretaries of State, who are the junior, third level and help more senior ministers. Most are drawn from the majority party in the elected House of Commons. Some junior ministers come from the non-elected House of Lords. The duties of Ministers are laid out in the *Ministerial Code* (Cabinet Office 2007*b*).

We call the main character 'the Minister', with a capital letter. Strictly speaking that is inaccurate. The correct title is 'Secretary of State' but the phrase is cumbersome. So, we use the everyday expression popularized by television 'Minister' and, where necessary, refer to the Ministers of State as junior ministers.

The Ministers are members of Cabinet, the fulcrum committee of British government, although its role and importance vary with the whims and wishes of each prime minister. The other key coordinating central bodies are the Treasury, which holds sway on all matters financial, and the Cabinet Office, which is home to a ragbag of central functions, and unkindly referred to as the rest home for the pet projects of past prime ministers.

Private Offices support both Ministers and permanent secretaries. Civil servants staff both offices. A principal private secretary (PPS), who will be a young, fast-stream civil servant expecting rapid promotion, heads each office and supervises several Private Secretaries (PS). For the Minister, 'the private office is the bridge between the minister and the department' (Jary 2004, 15; and see Chapter 9 for a more detailed account). There is always a member of the Private Office to open doors, steer the minister to the car, prompt in committee, and take notes of a meeting. They dress in suits. They carry notebooks. They speak but rarely, and never loudly. We accompanied the Minister as if part of the Private Office. We sought to become part of the furniture; to blend in with the wallpaper.[7]

The distinctive feature of any Minister's Private Office is the special or ministerial advisers (or SpAds). They are political appointments, not career civil servants. They are on tap but not on top.

Finally, most ministries are divided into functional directorates, headed by a Director-General (DG), although the terminology varies. Most have some form of Management Board comprising senior management of the Department and non-executive members appointed for their external experience and expertise. It advises on strategy.

Everyday life

Of course there is no such thing as a typical day. All days come with surprises, with stress, and with last-minute changes. If there is a typical day, it is long, with many meetings, few breaks, unexpected, and possibly unwelcome, changes, an evening engagement usually a speech or dinner, and a red box or two for late-night relaxation. A quick glance at the official engagement diary shows that the pace is unrelenting. It was tiring just reading it. How can anybody keep up this pace and remain at the top of their game? We think we know the answer. They cannot. Ministers have so many good intentions, so much to do, but finite energy and enthusiasm. So, there is anger, mistakes, defensive behaviour, and a sense of frustration. Our story is of people seeking to contain their complex and changing world within their diaries. We describe one day – see Table 6.1.

It is a commonplace day. It might even err on the side of easy because there is space for a sandwich lunch and there is no evening reception.

THE DEPARTMENTAL COCOON

On arriving at the Department, it is immediately clear that we are entering the land of the official and the powerful. There are security guards on every door and everyone has to check in at the front desk to get a security pass. The pass is issued provided you are already booked in by your host. There is a large board displaying today's security level – black, the lowest level. There is also a table with two more security guards who randomly check visitors and their bags. Once you have your pass, you are invited to sit down while your host comes to collect you. The process is not unfriendly but it is as impersonal as it is implacable, with social comments best kept to the formal 'good morning'. Flippancy is just ignored, cheeriness is tolerated, and

Table 6.1 The Minister's engagement diary

TIME	ACTIVITY – planned	ACTIVITY – unplanned
9.00–10.30	Ministers meeting	
10.30–12.30	Management Board Meeting	
12.30–13.30	Lunch with Management Board	Two phone calls with No. 10 Special Advisers, both booked while out
13.30–14.30	Departmental Special Advisers	
14.30–15.15	Meeting with interest group	
15.15–16.30	Meeting for the Prime Minister	
16.30–17.00	Meeting with DG	Telephone call with Cabinet colleague
17.00	Dental appointment, home, and the red box	

brevity and politeness are preferred. No matter how many times we went to one of the departments, and it was often enough to be recognized by surname, the process was the same, and we were not allowed to walk through the building unescorted. Our status as 'professional strangers' (Agar 1996) was all too clear. We were not one of them.

The Private Office was friendly. We had been in and around the Department on several occasions and for two lengthy stays. So, we are collected and taken to the PPS. He is a high-flying civil servant, marked as a potential Permanent Secretary, who heads the Minister's Private Office. Slim, dark, short hair, dressed in the inevitable dark grey suit, white shirt, and tie. He sits at a desk apart from everyone else in the open-plan office. The others sit at discrete groups of desks. The office is unrelentingly modern. Wherever governments shop, it is the office equivalent of Ikea. His desk is at the front of the office, with the front defined by closeness to the Minister's door. He faces everyone else and is the nodal point of communication, a constant point of reference for everyone else.

The internal management task of the PPS is burdensome (see Chapter 9) and the several constituent units of the Private Office have demanding roles. Few will have an interest in the Business Support Unit, essential though its financial tasks may be, but the Parliamentary Branch is another matter. It manages the Department's link with Parliament. The workload is often mundane routine, but it is always large; routinely, the Minister will get about twelve written parliamentary questions a night in the red box (see later). All too regularly it will be the locus of frenetic activity.

So, when we talk of the management responsibilities of the PPS and about the Private Office and its attendant units coordinating policy, resolving internal conflicts, and managing its external environment, we are talking about the heart of the Departmental machine; a mini-version of the core executive.

The PPS describes his job as the head of a team of some eighty people who support all the Ministers: 'The PPS's job is to make it "*a coherent whole*" and to make sure "*all of us have got one purpose here*", which is "*to serve the department and to serve the Minister and to act as that interface*" [PPS 14/4/04]. If that sounds prosaic, even boring, the job has its challenges because:

> *You're facing the Minister, you're facing the Department, you're facing the Permanent Secretary, and you're facing the other Ministers [of State]. And you are sort of caught between these different forces, and you know that there are going to be times when you can't please everybody. That's quite difficult but that's the job . . . It took me a while to realize that every time I spoke, everyone assumed I was the Minister. Now I'm careful.* [PPS 21/5/02]

We suggest that his key tasks are juggling several balls in the air while at the same time identifying priorities. He disagrees:

> *I think the core skill for a Principal Private Secretary, as opposed to a Private Secretary, is making sure that the relationships work at the top of the shop. I spend a lot of my time trying to make sure that these big powerful brains that are our senior colleagues on the Board and so on fit together seamlessly. I have to stitch it all together.* [PPS 14/4/04]

The PPS is described by the Permanent Secretary as 'the Minister's representative on earth'. It is said with a smile, but like many flippant remarks it is double-edged. The phrase recognizes his standing while reminding the PPS that he is the Permanent Secretary's subordinate. In turn, the PPS comments that the Permanent Secretary sometimes 'takes his frustrations with the Minister out on me'. An academic colleague commented that the PPS seemed like a 'ball bearing, caught between these different forces'. He is 'more subject than agent'. We prefer to describe him as a nodal point for information. Everything of importance goes through him to the minister. Information and selective attention bestow standing.

A former Minister, Richard Crossman (1975, 618), described the Private Office as both a 'Rolls Royce' and a 'cocoon'.[8] So, when the Permanent Secretary says his job is '*making sure that things run smoothly*', he is evoking these well-known metaphors. It is hard to overstate the dedication to making the Minister's life smooth or the Office's sensitivity to the Minister's moods. They know the Minister's mind before the Minister knows what he wants. Being the centre of so much attention must be addictive. One former Minister confessed that the withdrawal symptoms on leaving office were acute.

The Minister, like every other Minister irrespective of age, race, or gender, is waited on hand and foot. Privilege goes with the turf. He has the exclusive use of his own toilet, although there are two others within 20 metres. Water, coffee, tea, and sandwiches are offered and brought whenever the Minister wants them. A diary secretary controls when people can and cannot see him. A member of the Private Office escorts him everywhere, carrying bags and files. A car sits and waits on his every movement. Although the House of Commons is a mere five minutes walk away, he is driven there. When he leaves his coat in the car, the driver brings it to him. We often thought the short walk to Parliament and break from all the attention would be a welcome respite. We know one Permanent Secretary who insisted on a twenty minutes break at lunchtime to stretch his legs, and clear his mind, in a nearby park. We never saw a Minister forgo the perks of office for anything as ordinary as a walk. The Private Office is just as sensitive to moods. The comment that the Minister 'is not in a good mood today', evokes the comment 'Oh bollocks' and the epithet 'friggin' PQs', meaning the Minister's impending appearance in the House of Commons to answer parliamentary questions is the cause of his bad mood.

The first time we saw the Minister he walked into his cocoon remarking cheerily, 'Finally, a man in the office' because the Private Office is staffed mainly by women. He spots that a tile in the ceiling has been removed, so he continues, 'It's terrorists; there'll be men on ropes next'. The PPS immediately rings maintenance to get it fixed. There is a buzz around the office. We thought, 'Ladies and gentleman, Elvis Presley is in the building'. There is the same sense of celebrity. The Minister is the Queen's Minister; the office has a long history of grandeur. Everyone seems to change gear; they process their mails a little more quickly. Of course, the Minister's remarks establish he is a warm and amusing person to work for. Of course, we smile politely and thank him for his cooperation as he invites us to sit in his office of cream and oatmeal-coloured easy chairs and sofas, and pale-yellow walls with abstract paintings and modern bowls and vases. Tea arrives unbidden (and on the ritual of tea and coffee drinking, see Bevir and Rhodes 2006, 123).

The culture of the Private Office is one of long hours (see Chapter 9). There is always someone there when the Minister is there, and they have to prepare for his arrivals and departures as well as the briefings for that day's meetings and the boxes for that night's reading. Today was an early start because the Minister had a breakfast event with a speech. The PPS will not do such an event. There are three private secretaries and they will rotate who accompanies the Minister. The same is true of the Press Office, which also sends someone with the Minister. They are a put-on breed. The private secretary looks tired and finds the job hard going: 'the hours are awful. You can't arrange anything during the week.' They are young people, often newly married, some have a first child, they live miles out because they cannot afford Central London, and many look forward to their next posting. What is the compensation? They believe they are at the centre of things.

One academic colleague described this as an example of bureaucratic enchantment because they work long hours for low pay in offices that are at best undistinguished if not the clerical equivalent of a battery for hens. It matters not. Members of the private office know it is an essential posting for their career development. There is also the halo effect of being physically adjacent to, and being greeted by, the minister. So, they accept willingly that 'If you work 9 to 5, you wouldn't survive because you couldn't do the job'.

AT THE OFFICE

The department has a ministerial meeting every week and they refer to them as 'KiTs' or 'Keep in Touch' meetings. A junior minister describes the meetings as 'informal, sitting around, and the Minister talks to us about what's happening, what's going on across the Government, what his current priorities are'. The other ministers report on what they are doing but 'in pretty brief form'. The meetings alternate between ministers only and meetings at which also the Permanent Secretary is present with some senior officials.

At today's meeting there are no officials, only the several ministers with the SpAds, the PPS, and the Parliamentary Under-Secretaries. The latter are tolerated by officials but they are the lowest of the low and, even worse, they know it. Some self-knowledge is not good for self-esteem, but MPs have to start somewhere and, provided they show minimal competence, they will move on and up quickly. Most of the people attending are male in dark suits – grey or black – with white shirt and tie. In vain we look for the hand-painted silk tie or even the Paul Smith designer suit that is a hallmark of New Labour. The most distinctive outfit is a loud pinstripe that makes its wearer look like a spiv. And that is worn by an outsider, for today's meeting starts with a presentation by consultants on the Department's public image. Conventional wisdom has it that civil servants put together packages of advice from several sources for ministers to make policy, but we see more discussions about the presentation of policy than the substance.

Discussions start with a paper about the results of an opinion survey of stakeholders' views of the Department. There is a PowerPoint summary and, as is so often the case, the speaker hides behind it. Lights are dimmed, so you can't see him clearly. He drones on, in effect reading the slides. We think, 'you circulated the paper earlier and we've read it', only several of the ministers have not. Only the Minister with his Private Office and its succinct briefings are on top of the game. Interest is barely above zero. Tea is served during the presentation and the clatter of cups and the constant whispers about 'pass the sugar' and 'can I have a biscuit' drown out the speaker on occasion. This meeting is not a laugh a minute. The document reports that the Department 'lacks focus' and 'overall, stakeholders are critical'. Members of the audience wriggle in their seats, look around, scratch, whisper to their neighbour around the table, or doodle on pads. But the Minister is no mere mortal. He has to remain alert and look interested. And he does, with commendable aplomb. The meeting is boring, and the Minister is almost perky. After twenty minutes the audience can contain itself no longer and starts interrupting. The Press Office leaps to its own defence. The Minister intervenes to stop the meeting deteriorating. The report is 'a useful and timely reminder to keep the change process going' and although 'we are doing the right things we need to do more'. With that warning ringing in their ears, the ministerial team keeps their opinions to themselves. Questions and comments are desultory. Although the Minister's intervention was not meant to be a summing-up, it served that purpose and the consultants leave.

The tone of the meeting changes almost immediately. Everyone is paying attention because they are talking about what they want to talk about. First, there is a report on parliamentary business. Where is the bill in committee? How is it going? Any foreseeable problems? No, the meeting is reassured. All is going as well as can be expected. And that is what they want to hear. They need to know, but no one wants more problems. The conversation is that of familiars. There are no obvious undercurrents. It is businesslike, with little or no badinage. The Minister keeps things moving. 'Do we have enough speakers for the debate?' Each junior minister reports on her or his portfolio. The reports are brisk. What we are doing. The progress we have made since last week. The meeting expects to be alerted to any possible political problems. Interestingly, they pay as much attention to Parliament as the media. To outsiders, the purpose of the briefing seems not to give information but to reinforce their sense of being a team. They are in it together. If one minister is up to his or her eyeballs in a certain 'country commodity', it reflects on everyone. Their prospects hinge in part on the reputation of the Department.

The Minister reports last. He is pleased with the press coverage from yesterday but concerned about developments in the EU on which the Department will have to keep a weather eye. Here, he is less than forthcoming. He is not just concerned about specific EU policies but also about the Government's response. It is not clear whether the others latch on to this subtext. The SpAds know, but there is no reaction from the others. With his report, the meeting begins to wind down. One of the Ministers of State is going to Trinidad and Tobago and he asks for a briefing. There is much raucous laughter and various suggestions about what he could do, only some of which involve sunbathing and swimming in the sea. The Minister smiles but does not bother to call the meeting to order. The badinage continues, apparently a good point on which to draw matters to an end. He shuffles his papers and returns them to their red folder. The others take their cue and the meeting breaks up.

One minister's mannerisms suggest he is 'off message'. His report is excessively brief – two rather than the more usual five or ten minutes. When the others speak he is reading and highlighting a document, presumably a speech he will give later. In the lift, after the meeting, we ask the PPS about his standing. He is 'not a team player'. His poor reputation compared with other ministers is revealed in the way he is addressed by officials; his name is always prefixed by 'Mr.' Not so the others, who are often just called minister or, in the confines of the Private Office, referred to by their first name. Using this title speaks volumes. The PPS 'hopes' he will go in the next reshuffle, but that is a civil servant speaking. Ministerial posts are not always allocated by ability and for hard work. When we discussed this minister with one of his ministerial colleagues, we were told with much merriment that he would stay because 'he is harmless, a Brown-ite, and everybody has to have one'.

THE MANAGEMENT BOARD

The PPS is waiting with the folders for the next meeting. All such folders are colour coded. For example, parliamentary questions are coded orange meaning it is an 'ephemeral file. This file will be destroyed after ten years'.

Meeting files are red. First, there is a short briefing meeting with the Permanent Secretary before a meeting of the Management Board to consider the latest version of the Department's strategy or business plan. The Permanent Secretary comes to the Minister. He too is waiting. Their discussions continue as they walk to the meeting room. The PPS is not invited.

The briefing with the Permanent Secretary is the next step in a bureaucratic ambush. On the previous day, the Minister had met a stakeholder member of the Board to discuss their contribution to this meeting. There is a view shared by both the Minister and the PPS that the Permanent Secretary does not always follow through. After making it clear that he is talking 'off message', the PPS explains that he led the team that did the review. He comments that the Permanent Secretary didn't realize he needed 'to be constantly pushing'. He accepts 'he is pretty good at making people want to do things', and he ought to use these skills 'to keep things moving, to maintain the momentum on the Change Program'. He wants the Permanent Secretary 'to recognize his own leadership skills . . . to inspire people a bit more'. The Minister agrees: 'I could see it was getting bogged down'. It needed 'another mega injection of energy'. The Permanent Secretary 'says the right things' but 'he's actually not driving it'.

The PPS is of the view that he 'had to stiffen his resolve' over the internal reforms and the Minister is about to do the same. He tells the Management Board member that he wants him to challenge the business plan. He is happy to do so: 'It's a mixture of cliché and jargon with nothing to check progress on delivery'. 'Yes,' says the Minister 'I didn't realize we were getting bogged down in it'. He tells him he wants to 'sharpen up some of the objectives'. Also, 'how will we know if we are not making progress?' And now the crux: 'the Permanent Secretary is sensitive on this. I will heap praise on him but as a prelude to a discussion of lessons for next time. We must use the business plan to get people to make decisions.' The Board Member 'entirely agrees' with the Minister and he will address the issues of 'delivery' and 'outputs' at the meeting.

We suggest to the Minister that he is 'hands on' in managing the department. He says 'I am at the moment and I was to start with'. Privately, the PPS tells us the Minister does not do 'the really "nitty-gritty" stuff of managing because he's got plenty of other things to think about'.

This conversation introduces two pieces of managerial speak that are all too often heard inside and outside Whitehall. There is a fashion in such things. We were surprised to hear conversations about 'stakeholders' because that is one of yesterday's buzzwords for New Labour. Arguably, business plans declined shortly after. Service delivery was the fad on the rise.

The Management Board meeting begins *without* the preliminary tea ritual! In fact, the Board had tea in the anteroom to the meeting before we arrived. There is no interruption for tea and coffee during the meeting because there is a buffet lunch to follow. There is water but no ice as we are in England. The Minister starts the meeting by introducing the business plan. He praises the Permanent Secretary and suggests the meeting could sharpen up the objectives and try to identify the lessons for next time. The team leader talks the meeting through the plan with the ever-present PowerPoint presentation. The team leader identifies some weaknesses in the plan. It has too many objectives and not enough measures. When the Permanent Secretary speaks, it is clear that he had anticipated trouble or had been forewarned.

The Permanent Secretary is a large man of imposing presence. He often slumps in chairs as a way of taking the back seat at a meeting, but not today. He sits erect, leaning forward slightly. His tone is defensive but crisp. He does not invite discussion let alone contradiction. He suggests the plan is 'ground breaking'. It is 'business as usual while redirecting the tanker'. He makes several jibes about 'our friends at the Treasury', whose approval is required for budgetary and investment decisions. He dismisses their criticisms as 'niggling'. The plan may be 'weak on delivery'. However, it is the first of five years and next year delivery will be the priority. The FWNB records: 'He knows what's afoot. He's deflecting criticisms before they have been made.' The Permanent Secretary puts up a slide summarizing the major issues, which makes it clear he knew about the ambush. The slide could act as a summary of the Minister's meeting with the Board member. The Minister asks him to leave the slide on 'to guide discussion'. Why wouldn't he? It's a list of his concerns.

Has the Permanent Secretary captured the Minister's agenda? Or is he saving face by anticipating criticism? It is still his agenda that runs the meeting. It has no effect on the comments of the Board members on the business plan. They weigh in. Their several comments include: 'you don't have the metrics in place to measure progress'; 'detailed action plans are missing'; 'you are trying to be too clever'; 'get some measures and learn as you go along'; and 'there is too much waffle, too much woolliness, it needs to be crisp, more precise'. There is a general concession that the plan 'is going in the right direction' but the overall tone is critical, none more so than the Board member briefed by the Minister. He sides with the Treasury; 'they are clearly right about measurement' and he questions the skills of officials; 'do they have the skills and capacity for the job?' Also, he thinks the Board should have been involved earlier.

The Minister is taken aback by his trenchant critique and apologizes for not getting the Board involved earlier. He tries to steer the discussion back to refining objectives but is interrupted by another Board member who wants to know 'how you are going to achieve them'. After all, he continues 'you have been failing for a century'. If any useful lessons are being drawn beyond the Permanent Secretary's slide, they are not obvious. The discussion is not constructive or supportive.

The Permanent Secretary is impatient, commenting that most of these points have been discussed before, but the Minister, not the Permanent Secretary, is the focal point of the meeting. All the comments are directed to him. There are almost no cross-table exchanges. The meeting has moved on from the specific topic of the plan to a more general discussion of internal reform and trite phrases about the 'culture of the organization', 'the need for leadership' and 'the failure of innovation' abound. They are the day-to-day topics of the so-called new public management: the language of management consultants.

The Minister stops the chatter to allow the individual DGs in the department to provide a summary for the Board of what's going on in their area. We are subjected to a deluge of management speak: objectives, targets, trajectories, and evaluation are common currency. They are interspersed with some older language; one DG claims the title of his presentation fails 'the cocktail party test'. He means it is not witty and amusing. He doesn't seem to realize that the rest of us never go to cocktail parties and we don't know anybody who does. The presentations deliver boredom by the megaton. The Minister has the advantage. The Private Office has provided the usual succinct briefing on what everyone will say. So, even if his attention wanders, and it does, he still knows what's happening. Everybody uses PowerPoint. Nobody displays a gram of charisma. There is the occasional flicker of enthusiasm but zest is visibly absent. The meeting is 'a bore of grey suits' as the men live down to their reputation, and the women are right there with them.

The Minister is reading another document. When he is listening, he has his elbow on the arm of the chair and his chin resting on his hand. He does not fidget. He is not animated. He may adjust his spectacles. When he is talking he uses his hands. The Permanent Secretary is more obviously bored. He slumps, sits up, slumps again, or does some other work. He writes. The room is oppressive. The latest speaker drones on and on. Some people nod, probably to stay awake. Eyelids droop. The Permanent Secretary realizes it is drifting and makes some flippant remarks, but the drone wins. The meeting never recovers. There are a few moments of animation when the question of abolishing retirement age crops up. The Permanent Secretary cracks jokes about age.

LUNCH – ALMOST

When the Minister and the Permanent Secretary leave, they are chatting about 'keeping No. 10 in the loop' on the way to a buffet lunch. They turn to the implications of the discussion for the next round of business planning. They also discuss appointments. These appointments are patronage appointments to various government committees and agencies, not civil service ones. The Permanent Secretary tells the Minister he has 'deliberately put one of our best chaps onto this area'.

A government buffet is not normally something to welcome. Normally it is cold quiche with salads drenched in bottled dressing. But at this precise moment even cold quiche would look like manna from heaven. In fact, they have gorgeous hors d'oeuvres of lamb fillet *en croute*. So, Murphy's Law strikes. A private secretary arrives with a message for the Minister. He has two calls booked with SpAds at No. 10. So, with a handful of lamb fillet *en croute*, we traipse, dispiritedly, after him:

> 'Did he [the Permanent Secretary] really say chaps?'
> 'Almost certainly,' the Minister replies.

Traditionally, permanent secretaries are from 'Oxbridge', a term that refers to the universities of Oxford and Cambridge. There is a long-standing tradition of the civil service recruiting people from fee-paying schools and Oxbridge. It is a clear marker of a middle-class upbringing. It is associated with a specific accent, variously described as plummy or BBC. Words like 'chap' resonate of Oxbridge between the wars and an age we thought long gone. In England, accents and language are always reducible to class. As George Bernard Shaw famously commented, 'it is impossible for an Englishman to open his mouth without making some other Englishman hate him or despise him'. Such stigmata may be less acute today but there are still residues of the earlier era.

After the Management Board meeting, we asked the PPS if he had briefed the Permanent Secretary about the impending criticisms by the Board. He said not. Maybe we asked the wrong question. Perhaps he briefed the team leader who briefed the Permanent Secretary. However, in offices, information can not only move quickly but also seemingly by osmosis. The analogy with a village remains apt, although we doubt the Permanent Secretary sees himself as Miss Marple at the heart of St. Mary Mead's web of gossip.

The important point is that the top of a government department is a small world and everybody knows everybody else's business.

Back at the office, the telephone conversation with the No. 10 SpAds is unintelligible. The Minister just makes the conversational noises that usually betoken agreement or at least understanding. The conventions of such calls are, however, interesting. There is a hierarchy. When the Prime Minister announces his Cabinet, there is a public list. That list is the official hierarchy of ministers and ministries. So, the Prime Minister waits for nobody. His office gets the minister on the line and puts him or her through to Tony so he is not kept waiting. Whenever you hear the phrase 'Do you want to put your Minister on and I'll put him through', you know the protocol hierarchy has been invoked. On this occasion, 'our' Minister waits on the line until put through.

The Private Office has brought some sandwiches for the Minister from the buffet. The Minister has 'five minutes' – a phrase that signals a break of indeterminate length – so he is doing his e-mails as he eats his sandwiches. So, again, we have no idea what he is talking about. Instead, we watch the office at work.

OFFICE PROTOCOLS: THE RED BOX[9]

Administrative protocols, or the accepted codes of procedure and etiquette, are the tools of the trade for the office. They are often formalized and written down. Some exist as videos but the printed word remains the preferred medium of communication in the everyday life of the Minister's Private Office.[10] They know what they are:

> *I am a glorified postbox and I'm here for communication. I am just churning through the paper.* [PS 14/11/02]

The protocols cover the diary, the red box, correspondence, filing, the telephone, briefings, submissions, committees, travel, hospitality, and probity. They lie at the heart of managing the office. They are the tools by which departments domesticate their everyday life in the goldfish bowl that is modern politics. We give one example only: the red box (and for a more detailed account of the several protocols see Rhodes [2009*b*, 2010]).

Every day the Private Office prepares and collates the papers the Ministers and the Permanent Secretary must read for the next day's meeting and the letters that need to be signed. They are collected in a red, rectangular, box-shaped, brief case for the Minister to take home each night. The red box is a focal point of office activity. It is always battered. We never saw a new one.

In the spirit of Monty Python, we wondered if there was an office for battering boxes. The red box is governed by its own rules.

At the start of the day, the PPS will write a time such as 17.15 in the top right-hand corner of the red box. Everyone now knows the box must be ready by that time because that is when the Minister will leave the office. Everyone understands that it is '*best to get it all in one box. If there are two they get discouraged*' [PPS 10/4/03]. By 16.30 the box will be the focus of a flurry of activity. All the paperwork in the Private Office must come together at this point. After the diary, it is a key organizing device for managing the Minister. It is just a cardinal rule that it must be ready by the stated time.

The role of the PPS in preparing the box varies.

> *They [papers] come through me to check them off, just to check that they make sense. The same way that when I'm putting stuff in the box I just try and check things to make sure it looks reasonably okay.* [PPS 10/4/03]
>
> *[We used to have] some divisions that [the PPS] was first point of contact for and I have changed that because I think I can add best value by being able to look across the pitch. I see everything before [the Minister] sees it whereas [my predecessor] didn't. Stuff went in and [my predecessor] saw it on the way out. I felt very uncomfortable with that so I now see most things before they go in to [the Minister], certainly anything of importance will be shown to me. So the trade-off with the Private Secretaries is they might have more divisions to look after but they know that I'm going to help them take a proper view before it goes in to [the Minister].* [PPS 14/4/04]

These quotes don't capture the process; 'it's incredibly difficult to know what's important, what will cause controversy' [PPS FWNB Number 3 20/5/02]. A DG will have a quiet word to make sure his submission is in the box. The PPS has to exercise judgement about what the Minister needs to see. The sheer volume of material could overwhelm even the most committed Minister. Jary (2004, 18) claims a 'typical' box contains: twenty letters to sign, three draft speeches, four draft replies to PQs, ten briefings for meetings, six submissions for decision, three draft press releases, a question and answer brief for an interview and the minutes of last week's Cabinet meeting. This summary is not wrong but it errs on the side of understatement. For example, one department estimated there were on average twelve PQs in a box. Also, most had difficulty limiting the paperwork to one box.

To help the Minister, there are two folders at the top of the box: a priority folder of matters requiring immediate action, and the diary folder of engagements. In an ideal world of course the red box is returned next morning not only with the priority folders done but also with letters signed and decisions made. For obvious reasons, many Ministers will skim through much in the box. So if, for example, a letter really needs his attention, it had better be flagged. Some Ministers and Permanent Secretaries like to put their mark on letters and submissions (for example, David Blunkett). One DS announced with great glee that she had written the perfect letter; for once the Permanent Secretary had made no changes to it. Some are less assiduous:

> The first five letters have been signed, one speech and one submission has been read and agreed, one further submission has been lost behind the cooker, and the rest are untouched. (Private Secretary in Jary 2004, 18)

There is a world-weary cynicism to this quote that we did not meet. With most Ministers, most of the time, most of the box was done. And the Private Office becomes adept at judging what it can expect from the Minister and adjusting its demands.

THE MINISTER AND HIS MINDERS

If departmental committee meetings and office protocols can bore for the United Kingdom in the morning, matters improve in the afternoon. The Minister has a meeting with his 'cauldron of SpAds' – the officials' collective noun for them and the analogy is to the witches of Macbeth. There is no obvious difference in dress code between SpAds and civil servants but they are younger. Above all, they are enthusiastic and committed to 'their' minister. This meeting is almost family-like. They gossip furiously about the party and rival ministers. It is relaxed. People are sprawled out on settees, feet up. The Minister chats about his 'favourite' journalist and wonders 'if you can put poison in his breakfast for me'. Others doubt he will be there because the pubs are not open. It is staccato. People talk over one another. The formality, ever present when officials attend, is missing.

Everyone is bubbling. The Minister, not the Department, got friendly coverage from the media for a recent initiative. It 'has gone really well' with 'big ticks all round'. The Minister agrees, 'we should be really proud of this'. They start talking about more 'milestones' – jargon for newsworthy targets. They also discuss various photographs, including one of a smiling baby with only a few teeth. They wonder if they should airbrush the teeth out for the final version. And, dear reader, they did airbrush them out!

The features of such meetings are their informality and their unstructured nature. So, in a nanosecond we move from media coverage to Iraq. 'What are we doing to get our share of the contracts? The problem is American partiality in awarding contracts. The Minister wants a 'level playing field' at least in public. In private, he wants 'our share'. One SpAd observes, 'We should get credit because we're doing the killing.' Another replies, 'That's bloody stupid', not because it puts commerce before people, but because saying it 'will turn the Arabs against us'. The meeting is convinced we must do something, 'otherwise it will be the French and the Russians who'll get the business after we've done all the bloody work', said with no sense of irony. They agree the Department must talk to the Foreign Office and the Minister for International Development to get them to do more. 'And it mustn't be tied to aid'.

They mull over the Iraq War. Earlier in the week, the news came through of the 'victory'. The Minister remarks that 'it will leave a lot of bruises' and that 'for some people it is the last straw'. Even more are 'troubled'. 'It will be years before we know if we did the right thing.' Others comment 'it would help if we could find weapons of mass destruction'; prompting the reply 'it's why we went in'. The Minister closes the subject by asserting that 'Tony is handling it absolutely superbly' and conversation switches to the EU.

The subject does not involve any Departmental policy. Rather the focus is on internal Labour Party machinations and, in particular on Gordon Brown. The Minister wants a decision to join the Euro but Gordon Brown is a known opponent. The Minister wants data on the economic tests that Brown has set for entry so he can argue with him. 'We want Gordon's economic assessment and I want to reinterpret it.' He 'wants to keep bridges open to Europe'. He deputes a SpAd to prepare a brief for him. However, he is uncertain when to raise the matter in Cabinet. They discuss possible allies in Cabinet. They run through a list of names. They are uncertain of some Ministers' position. To find out the Minister could ring the relevant SpAd or he could use one of his SpAds. The SpAds agree to ring their counterparts in the relevant department. The Minister disagrees; 'do not ring around the advisers net, we don't want it leaking'. After the meeting he comments that he does 'have a different position on the Euro from Gordon' but 'until we get to the point of making a decision, there is absolutely no point constantly having headline stories saying 'The Minister has made another pro Euro intervention'.

The conversation moves from Europe to a possible Cabinet reshuffle. The Minister tells them it may not be at Cabinet level. So, they concentrate on junior ministers in other departments and backbench MPs who might be suitable recruits for the department. It is gossip about standing in the Party and in government. It is the lifeblood of such meetings. They love it. The Minister says, 'you didn't hear any of this'. They all laugh.

Gossip is the currency of both Westminster and Whitehall. Officials are also enthusiastic practitioners of the art. We said to the PPS that the

Permanent Secretary loved having a good gossip about what was going on. He replied: 'He gives the impression he's having a gossip but actually that's just his style, things do get done.' And that is the second use of gossip. It is not just reporting back on the informal political hierarchy, it is a way of greasing the wheels of conversation rather like the British and the weather. We don't care whether it is raining but the topic gets social interactions under way without embarrassment. And we all know the English, including civil servants, avoid embarrassment.

MORE VISITORS

The PPS announces that the parties for the Minister's next meeting have arrived. It is six officers from a major interest group. The Management Board was boring. This meeting is embarrassing. They begin by announcing they are 'good corporate citizens' and how much 'they welcome the opportunity' to meet the Minister. Their spokesperson talks of a 'true convergence' with the Department and describes their links as 'so exciting'. It's like listening to a sales pitch by a sleazy executive in a Hollywood movie. He is toadying up to the Minister and in turn the Minister is making them feel welcome at the top table. But the spokesperson is only just warming to his task. He describes the tenure of the Minister as 'stunning'. He offers the Minister a present, which he declines explaining it is against the rules, and it is. He tells him they should call any time; 'just pick up the phone'. There are smiles and laughter; they are bonding. The Minister feels he has to 'grant an audience to' a major interest group. But what is the point of the group's performance? There is no agenda. There is no possibility of a decision because they ask for nothing. It is a case of the Minister as celebrity. The private secretary comes in. The finishing time of this meeting is pre-arranged. Does the Minister expect such homage as his due?

TRAIPSING ABOUT

The Minister gets ready for the next meeting with a quick wash and brush up. Everybody tells you they avoid 'back-to-back meetings' – the Permanent Secretary, the Minister, their diary secretaries. Everybody has back-to-back meetings, regularly. The expression 'back-to-back meetings' is a mantra they chant to one another. Its meaning is not obvious. It is not a rule for limiting appointments. Rather it is a way of impressing on people that they are *so* busy they *have* to have back-to-back meetings even though they gave firm instructions to the contrary. It is a form of ministerial machismo.

We take the lift to the meeting and the Minister explains he is 'dreading' this meeting. It is a forum of sports representatives, which is not his normal area of responsibility but, in the era of joined-up government, his Department has to be there. The forum exists because a prominent sports personality, who is a friend of the Blairs, persuaded the Prime Minister to set it up. With some venom, the Minister describes the sportsperson as 'a lobby of one'. The Minister is the chair because Tony Blair asked him and he did not see how he could refuse. Its terms of reference are... there's the rub, and the reason he describes the meeting as dreadful. They are at 'loggerheads' over them. The topic of today's meeting is sponsorship and sport.

The Minister is a few minutes early. Tea is being taken – the essential lubricant of any meeting. He mingles, expertly recognizing faces, smiling, and seemingly relaxed and friendly. It is his public face. It is as if he has a case of 'faces' he can wear and he chooses the one most appropriate to his current task.

Throughout this discussion, the Minister does a good job of appearing interested. He nods in all the right places, looks at the speakers, turns his papers at the right time. He does not shuffle and organize his papers, check his diary, read and annotate a paper, or talk to his neighbour at the table. He speaks rarely but on the few occasions when he does he stresses setting priorities, limiting their interest to a manageable number of topics, and realistic costing. If anyone was listening carefully, they would know he is criticizing them and telling them what he wants if there is to be any progress. No one is listening.

What value was added by this meeting? The most obvious output is that the Minister has obliged the Prime Minister, normally a wise course of action. But for Blair's involvement, he would have sent a junior minister. A second outcome is that the Minister has discharged his representational or ambassadorial function in Whitehall and beyond. The Management Board was a bore but it was necessary. The main characteristic of this meeting is that it was unnecessary. It exists as an unquestioning reaction to prime ministerial whim. It has no clear agenda and if it has outputs, it has no obvious outcomes.

DEPARTMENTAL BUSINESS

We hasten back to the department where the next appointment is waiting. It is a DG who needs to discuss an appointment to a regulatory body. A Private Secretary attends. The DG talks the Minister through a list of possible candidates, commenting on their suitability – 'insufficient experience'; 'probably a first reserve'. After about ten minutes we get to the nub – 'the Treasury is briefing against us'. So, the department has a preferred candidate but the Treasury prefers someone else. The Minister is happy with the department's candidate. He is not happy about Treasury interference. He agrees he will ring the SpAd at Number 10 'and talk him through it'. In practice, that means the Minister's SpAd will do it. More important, the Minister will 'meet' Ed Balls (Chief Economic Adviser, Treasury, and Gordon Brown's *consigliore*) 'and tell him to stop it'.

There is just time for a quick telephone call. A Cabinet colleague called about an upcoming constituency visit. The Minister returns the call. They talk about travel arrangements, who will talk about what, and other details of the trip. When you hear only one side of a conversation, it is hard to know what you miss.

THE JOURNEY HOME

Our story of everyday life stops here. The rest of the day is taken up with the Minister's dental appointment. On the way to the hotel in his official car, there is no informative conversation about work. He is tired, so we talk about Australia. We agree Australian wine offers the best quality for price in the world. By London traffic standards we make good time, although we don't have far to travel. London itself may contribute to the air of rush and stress that surrounds the Minister. It is such a big, noisy, dirty, congested place. There must be corners of peace and quiet but they are few in the square mile of Westminster and Whitehall. There is no stillness here. The Minister will have his teeth seen to and go home to the red box. It will be finished in the kitchen tomorrow morning over breakfast.

The minister as situated agent

Observation delivers thick descriptions but how do we interpret our description? We see the Minister as a situated agent and we unpack our story as practices embedded in traditions (see Chapter 4).

Traditions

Ministers and officials talk to one another in ways that are striking to outsiders. There is no one set of ideas, no one vocabulary, which characterizes the culture of departments. Rather, there are overlapping and competing webs of beliefs. One set we have labelled simply traditional or Westminster beliefs.[11] The other set of beliefs originate in the public sector reforms of the 1980s and are commonly referred to as the new public management, or managerialism, although New Labour has given them a twist of its own. We can identify these beliefs through their separate languages. Each has its pet phrases and jargon. We were surprised to hear phrases like chaps, who are 'sound' and even echoes of a colonial heritage in 'elephant traps'. There were references to cocktail parties. They are archaisms, and not the dominant discourse. They are trace elements of an earlier time although some of them, such as probity and doing the right thing, are as relevant now as they ever were. Of such older traces, the most common surround homage to the Queen's Minister.

The Minister is called Minister or Secretary of State and rarely addressed by his first name by officials. Outsiders display equivalent verbal and physical deference. He is the centre of attention and this simple fact is displayed in language, beliefs, and practices. The monarchical tradition of hierarchy lives on as a central characteristic of the Westminster narrative and ministerial practice (see Rhodes, Wanna, and Weller 2009, chapter 3). There is the more magisterial Minister, with an eye for pomp and circumstance, who insists on formality. The expressions 'holding court' and 'granting an audience' remain all too fitting. This tradition is an example of power and the constitutive role played by tradition in giving us our beliefs and actions, and in making our world. The monarchical tradition helps to shape the world of the Minister and his civil servants. Ministers exercise the modern version of royal power, and that power extends beyond the Minister and his civil servants to encompass the larger public who treat the Minister as a celebrity if not quite royalty.

Other phrases survive from the era when civil servants were administrators, not managers, in itself a signifier of shifting beliefs. So, they 'clear lines' with ministers, worry about being 'off message', want to go 'with the grain', and avoid 'back-to-back meetings'. We found the best examples of this language in a video made for civil servants about working with ministers. It was made tongue-in-cheek but the key point is that everybody knew the phrases. The video presupposes familiarity with civil service beliefs about ministers. So, officials are told there 'is a bit of mystique around ministers and they make you feel inferior'. You have 'to put yourself in the minister's shoes'. Or, more formally, the Cabinet Office's booklet on working with ministers advises 'while it is helpful if ministers understand the needs of civil servants, it's essential that civil servants understand the needs of ministers (Jary 2004, 5). You must recognize that 'we are all on the same side'. This advice is mixed up with office folklore; 'get off the phone, you'll get it quicker' and 'everybody sticks their head down and ignores you'. The other feature of office folklore is the love of acronyms. It is all-pervasive. If you cannot talk acronym you are lost. On our first visit to the Department, we had to ask if there was a list of acronyms because the meeting we had attended was nearly incomprehensible. We had no idea who or what they were talking about. The Diary Secretary earned our undying gratitude by producing one. It was seven pages long! Afterwards we never went to any department without asking for one. They all found one, although it was not necessarily up-to-date. They had to have it. Even their own kith and kin, when they came from other departments, needed help. However, they need only the acronyms for other organizations. They knew about KiTs usually group meetings or '1:1s' usually a meeting with one other person. But to make matters even more confusing there was no consistency. So, a 1:1 could be a KiT in another department!

It is also common for civil servants to use indirect language to avoid conflict. So, we came across such phrases as: 'I am reluctant to support'; 'I haven't formed a view yet'; 'I am happy to discuss'; 'you might consider' and 'you should be aware'. All signify a lack of agreement. Depending on the context, they can suggest more than a mere lack of agreement. Indirect language goes along with understatement and distance (or lack of emotion). It also throws into relief the belief in *the proper way of doing things* [DS 25/4/02]. A common way of dealing with anger is to become cold. We came across variations of the phrase: *'He was one of those quietly icy men'* [DS 25/4/02]; *'It's a kind of withdrawal and coldness'* [PPS 21/5/02]. The following scene would be typical of the departments visited. The Permanent Secretary is 'mild'. It would be 'unacceptable' for him to swear. If something goes wrong, the PS will 'confess' that she lost the papers and the Permanent Secretary will 'sigh'. Then 'you know you've been ticked off' [FWNB Number 5 13/11/02]. Anger is managed by politeness; by detachment, not shouting or swearing.

Westminster language, beliefs, and practices are overlaid with the new public management or, as it is referred to by some, critically, 'New Labour-speak'. Managerial language abounds. It is unavoidable. The most common usages include customer, delivery, stakeholders, mission statement, partnership, strategic, vision, and value-added. Less common are scoped, champion, and trajectories. There are genuine oddities like 'grazing with the private sector'. We had to be careful to distinguish managerial language from today's buzzwords. For example, 'challenge' kept cropping up and we wondered if it too had managerial connotations. We decided not. It was just today's buzzword like 'nerdish', which was used regularly at one committee meeting about anyone who raised a detailed point. It was never so used again. Challenge also disappeared. New Labour added a distinctive layer with such words as joined-up government, delivery, and value-driven. Recent candidates for inclusion include 'innovation' and 'leadership'. Others mock managerial language. One PS talked about 'ventilating' and 'forward posture', inventing words and phrases in a parody of managerial language. He is mocking, but he knows the language is widely used otherwise there is nothing to mock. Others are 'off message' (see Jary 2004, 63–5) and fail to understand its core functions are to demonstrate that one is an 'insider' who is 'on-side'. David Blunkett (2006, 441) happily conceded, 'They talk the language' but, to his obvious irritation, 'they don't do anything'. That is not strictly accurate. There are strategic plans, visions, and glossy mission statements. It not clear what the consequences are, if any, of this linguistic shift for the everyday practices of civil servants. Even among sympathizers, there is uncertainty and ambivalence. So, one PPS suggests he has not seen *'a shift from policy to delivery, because I don't really understand that language, but... a growing awareness of the requirement for us to focus on outcomes'* [PPS 14/4/04].

The languages vie with each other. It is not clear to us that the language of management has become the dominant discourse. You have to be fluent in it but, at times, it seemed more like a veneer. Expressions like 'driving it down' suggest that reform has not penetrated far down the hierarchy. The world we visited was a world of process, of committees, not a world of output measurement. Officials talked the management talk with ease. But to use some of the more cringe-inducing phrases, it was not clear they 'walked the walk' and delivered 'more bang for the bucks'.

The problem with the Westminster and managerial categories is they squeeze the social world into artificial boxes. We discussed the language of the civil service with a PPS. His response is sophisticated. He believes that *'the sort of thing that sets senior people apart from not so senior people is their ability... to always have a story for something that's happening'*. So, he sees himself as *'in the middle of a web'* that *'is a bit like a language game'*:

> *[I]t only has meaning insofar as people use it and to ask for the meaning of it is to miss the point, rather ask for the use instead. We use words to go where we're going and that's what this web is. It's a web. Is it a web of words? I don't know, but it's a web of relationships.* [PPS 14/4/04]

Practices

Although the workload of both Ministers and top civil servants is not limited to running the department, it has been the focus of this chapter. We recognize that Ministers are part of networks that criss-cross Westminster and Whitehall and represent their department to the wider world. But here we focus on their everyday practices in running the department.

Management is not new. Replacing 'administration' with 'management' may signify a desire for change but it merely relabels much of the work of the department, which carries on as before. There are many examples of such continuing administrative activity in our account of the Minister's day, and the best example is the Private Office. It 'manages' the Minister in a hundred small ways. The several protocols are all long-standing, organizing devices for managing the minister. Committee work is another obvious and long-standing continuity. It may be obvious but, given twenty years of management reform, it is worth stressing that committees remain the main decision-making vehicle. The Minister's diary is made up of back-to-back committee meetings. They come in various forms and their purpose is not always to make decisions. They pose problems for the Minister who has to pay attention. Many of us who go to committees switch off at some point and fidget because we are bored. The Minister pays attention; a simple phrase for a hard task. He also has to keep up, switching from topic to topic. We know the Private Office is efficient because they provide the briefings for all these meetings and their multifarious agendas, and he moves through them without a hitch. The Minister knows his limitations; 'I'm not as on top of this as I need to be.' But he also knows it is possible to be fully informed on only a few subjects. Without his briefings he would quickly be lost. Even with them, he can struggle. If challenged by an expert, he does not have the detailed knowledge to sustain an argument. He escapes by agreeing to 'take it back for further consideration'. That phrase could be translated as 'oops'. As the PPS observes, 'he is pretty clever. He's pretty clear about what he wants. He's pretty decisive quite a lot of the time. So there aren't many times when I think he's completely lost.'

The primacy of committees, the boredom of endless meetings, the tyranny of the engagement diary, tea and coffee before meetings, and the routines of the Private Office are all examples of the rituals of the bureaucracy. They are routines that domesticate the turbulent working environment of the Minister. So, protestations of boredom miss the point. If issues are political and volatile, then emotions can run high. So, the Private Office sets up meetings, tea is drunk, matters are discussed through the Chair, the Private

Office synthesizes material for the red box, there is a further round of meetings, by which time there is an air of dispassionate consideration verging on boredom. Such routines also matter even when there is no big issue. The pace of events is unrelenting and the Private Office, the diary and the red box are the way of organizing, even disciplining, events. Political life is a constant flow of events, and they are coped with using bureaucratic routines.

These routines are sustained by more than the working practices of the office. As important are gossip, humour, and politeness. All serve to maintain the routines either by providing an outlet for conflict and aggression or by defusing it.

Gossip is 'the process of informally communicating value-laden information about members of a social setting' (Fox 2004, 42, citing Noon and Delbridge 1993). It is the currency of exchange in a culture of secrecy. A minister who went public with frank comments about his colleagues would damage his own reputation. So, David Blunkett's attributed comments on his colleagues in his biography were injudicious at best. For example, Alan Milburn (Health) had 'grown in competence and ability', Margaret Beckett (Environment and Agriculture) is 'just holding the ring', Charles Clarke (Education) 'has not developed as expected', Patricia Hewitt (Trade and Industry) does not think strategically, and Gordon Brown throws his weight around (Pollard 2005, 27–8). Of course his colleagues reciprocate. John Prescott, the deputy prime minister, is said to hold Blunkett in a mixture of contempt and suspicion while others grit their teeth at his 'idiotic indiscretion' (*The Observer* 12 December 2004). We have here a public example of a conversation that Westminster and Whitehall conduct all the time in private. Such gossip is the currency of court politics, and the judgements are markers in the endless ministerial jockeying for position and recognition. It is the accepted way of making loaded judgements about other people and some such outlet is necessary in the competitive world of ministerial advancement.

Politeness 'presupposes [the] potential for aggression as it seeks to disarm it, and makes possible communication between potentially aggressive parties' (Fox 2004, 97, quoting Brown and Levinson 2000). Politeness governs most workplace encounters. So, most meetings start with a discussion of the weather and general inquiries about one's health and journey to work, and, of course, cups of tea or coffee. And as Fox points out, this chit-chat includes 'the usual full complement of pleases and thank yous, appreciative murmurs from the visitors and humorously self-deprecating apologies from the host, and so on, and on' (Fox 2004, 185).

However, such practices have a serious purpose. They serve to relax committee members before stressful encounters and to diffuse potential aggression. In a meeting on internal budget cuts, one DG lost his temper and shouted at colleagues. The Permanent Secretary apologized for this behaviour all the way back to his office from the meeting. It simply wasn't done. Overt aggression was discouraged by the almost mandatory conventions of polite behaviour.

Humour does not refer to the jokes of a stand-up comic or the monologues of a Billy Connolly but to 'wit, irony, understatement, banter, teasing, pomposity-pricking – which are an integral part of almost all English social interactions' (Fox 2004, 179). Interaction in the ministerial team is oiled by badinage about trips to Trinidad and Tobago and references to a certain country commodity. The SpAds amuse one another at the expense of journalists. The Permanent Secretary seeks to enliven a dead meeting with quips about age. It is low key but ever present. Laughter releases tension and stress and sustains routines and the management of crisis.

If our account of the Minister's day does not include a Cabinet meeting or question time in the House of Commons, or passing a major bill, nonetheless politics is an everyday presence. It can be found in the gossip about ministerial standing in the cabinet pecking order. It can be found in the discussion of internal Labour Party politics and the Euro. Even the high politics of Iraq can invade the politics of a domestic service ministry with their discussions about how to win contracts after the war. They domesticate the Iraq War and turn it into a playing field on which Britain bids for reconstruction contracts.

We were struck with the centrality of the SpAds. Their importance is recognized in the language of officials in the joking references to 'a cauldron of SpAds'. They are part of a network that links departments but, more important, links the Department to Number 10. Lines can be cleared on this political network without the Minister's direct involvement. There is little or no antagonism between officials and SpAds inside the Department. They share loyalty to the Minister and have complementary tasks. In the department, each accepts that the other plays a necessary role. If officials can be 'stick in the mud', they also have expertise and information. If the zeal of SpAds can exceed judgement, their ability to manage the party and the media is seen as an essential complement to civil service skills. In any office there are raised voices, disagreements, even quarrels. We saw nothing other than a mild irritation. Thus, the PPS snapped, 'they think we are not up to the job but you'd have to be psychic to know what they want. Anyway they are too focused on spin.' If there is a recurrent tension, it is between the SpAds in the department and Number 10. John Prescott (2008, 256) 'railed' against Number 10's special advisers; he called them the 'Beautiful People'. With obvious irritation, he records:

> They used to ring up and say 'Number Ten here', and I would say, 'No you're not, you're just Jo Bloggs. Tony's Number Ten'. Then I'd hang up.

We understand why the Minister wants and likes his SpAds. They are noisy, boisterous, and committed – in short, fun. He also trusts them implicitly to put his interest first in both the party and the department. Officials are also trusted by most ministers most of the time but they do not operate in the party arena and there is always at least a touch of distance, of formality, with officials. We offer no criticism. It is, and they would agree, appropriate. But we can see that the Minister wants to relax in free-ranging discussions. He spends most of the day 'presenting' himself to others. Being a celebrity seems like a privilege, but you have to meet people's expectations and behave like a celebrity. In the privacy of his own office with the SpAds, he can forget for a moment, take off his public faces.

Conclusions

What does this everyday account tell us about the Minister and ruling? One conclusion is all too obvious. Ministers work long hours and are subject to great stress. One has only to compare the fresh-faced youth that was Tony Blair in 1997 with the drawn features of 2007 to realize that a high office exacts a high price. The relentless pace and pressure must adversely affect the quality of decision making. The Minister openly admits to it: 'Phew, I'm so tired. I didn't sleep well last night.' And our hearts go out to the Private Office, whose pay and status are not remotely acceptable for their hours. They are unflaggingly cheerful. Their rationale is simple: 'It's ever so difficult to give a bollocking to a cheerful person.' It isn't, but it makes them feel better.

There is also the challenge of wearing many faces. At various points in this story we have provided several examples of the contradictory roles the Minister plays. In the department he is all powerful, waited on hand and foot. Ceilings are mended without having to ask, coats are fetched from cars. But he is also dependent on prime ministerial whim, attending meetings of no great significance at his behest. He is a celebrity escorted everywhere in a chauffeur-driven car, greeted at doorways on red carpets by respectful hosts. He is a godfather, recipient of homage from expectant interests. He is all too human, banging tables because of delayed phone calls. He is a key decision maker driving through organizational change and automaton, chairing committees on autopilot because he has to be there. He has a public face of polite interest in the people he meets and the private face, tired and in need of dental care. We intend no criticism, no implication of insincerity when we describe him as an actor. Rather, we express admiration for his dexterity, for his skills. He is convincing in these several roles. We are impressed by the way the Minister slips between his roles. One minute he is chairing a committee, the next he is chatting away socially about breakfast at No. 10 with Tony, Cherie, and little Leo. Normally, being cynics, if we saw such transparent glad-handing on television, we would find it off-putting, but it is done with great skill and conviction.

There are also the dilemmas of the job. Most obvious is the incessant clamour for managerial change. Managerial reforms were anticipated by the Fulton Report in 1968 and successive governments have returned to the topic ever since. Yet the Westminster tradition's conception of the role of the administrative elite continues to be valued by both Ministers and their senior civil servants. The Private Office remains recognizably the same as in Harold Wilson's 1960s government. It is so for a reason. Ministers want the cocoon it offers. They use the generalist skills of the higher civil service even as they disparage them for delays in reform. Both Ministers and higher civil servants have to manage the dilemmas posed by the Westminster and managerial traditions bumping into each other. We explore the response of top civil servants to this dilemma in more detail in Chapter 7.

So, why does the Minister do it? On this occasion we were offered three reasons. First, he can make a difference: 'If I'm going to be here I'm going to damn well make a difference.' He expresses some amazement 'at the number of ministers who can't do that... who can't get their heads above grumbling about the amount of travel, or focusing on their office décor or whatever it is that gives them a sense of deep satisfaction... and... are desperately casting around for a role'.

Second, he just enjoys the work: 'to be honest the thing which I probably most like is knowing what's going on'. This sense of being at the centre of things is shared with many others at the top of the Department.

Finally, 'I am definitely an adrenalin junkie but I am not a workaholic. It's an adrenalin high. I love doing it, yes.'

This chapter provides a thick description of the complex, episodic, ambivalent, and contingent everyday life of a Minister. It is our interpretation of the Minister's interpretation of his everyday experiences and encounters. It is a story of power beset by contingency. He 'makes a difference', but spends much time and effort on the appearance of ruling. The job may be to make policy but much of the time it is about protocols that seek to domesticate chaos with routine. We tell a distinct and distinctive story about the British political and administrative elite at work. Our tale of a storytelling administrative and political elite with beliefs and practices rooted in the Westminster tradition, confronting the dilemmas posed by both marketization and managerialism, while using everyday rituals and routines to domesticate crises is not standard fare. J. G. Ballard (2006) talks of 'willed madness' in modern life. What we have in Whitehall is 'willed ordinariness'. The Minister is the heir to a royal tradition that is beset by managerial reforms the civil service both introduces and resists at the same time.

Notes

1. Little of note has been written about British ministers and their departments. For reviews of the relevant literature, see Bevir and Rhodes (2006, 109–10), Heady (1974), James (1999), Marsh *et al.* (2001), and Rhodes (1995).
2. This section is paraphrased from Geertz (1973, chapter 1). For the debate about Geertz and the literary turn in cultural anthropology see Inglis (2000), Clifford and Marcus (1984), and Geertz (1988). For a general introduction to ethnographic methods see Hammersley and Atkinson (1995, 134).
3. For the period 2001–5, Michael Barber (2007*a*), David Blunkett (2006), and Alastair Campbell (2007) were especially useful. Some historians and journalists should also be included in this list because of their impeccable off-the-record sources. The two-volume biography of Blair, written by Anthony Seldon (2004, 2007), has a staggering array of insider interviews. Peter Hennessy (various, but especially 2001) and Robert Peston (2005) are not far behind; the latter had the best access to Brown and his court. Less consistently useful contributions are Beckett and Hencke (2004) and Pollard (2005). Other memoirs, diaries, biographies, and autobiographies were of episodic use.
4. Although we usually say 'Chatham House Rules' (plural), in fact there is only one rule: 'participants are free to use the information received, but neither the identity nor the affiliation of the speaker(s), nor that of any other participant, may be revealed.'
5. On the problems of writing up fieldwork, see Clifford (1983), Clifford and Marcus (1984), Geertz (1988, chapter 6), and Van Maanen (1988).
6. All the material from the fieldwork notebooks is taken from FWNBs Nos. 9 and 10, dated 7/8 April and 9/10 April 2003 respectively unless shown to the contrary.
7. Initially, we used the usual term 'subject' to refer to ministers and permanent secretaries, treating them as objects of inquiry. Eventually we chose 'inhabitants' because we like the analogy with Westminster and Whitehall as a village.

8. For equivalent views see Blunkett (2006), Bruce-Gardyne (1986), Henderson (2001), Heseltine (2000), Howe (1994), and Walker (1970).
9. On the red box, see for example: Jary (2004, 18), Kaufman (1980, 37 and 40–1), Henderson (2001, 96–7 and 189–90), James (1999, 34–5), and Stanley (2008*a*, 5).
10. Many protocols are written down in induction packs and equivalent internal departmental documentation. Of the publicly available sources, Jary (2004) and Martin Stanley's web site 'How to be a civil servant' (http://www.civilservant.org.uk/ [last accessed 31 July 2009]) are useful. Martin Stanley is the Chief Executive of the Competition Commission who joined the civil service in 1971. His advice to aspiring civil servants codifies many a protocol with a welcome leavening of humour. Rhodes (2010) provides a detailed account of the protocols and rituals in the departments. Rituals are habitual practices or customs that, unlike protocols, are rarely written down. Indeed, people may not be aware of their habits until they are pointed out. They include for example 'coffee sipping amity' (Stothard 2003, 34 and 61). He also describes the messengers who deliver it as 'a source of continuity and a kind of comfort' (see also Stewart [2004, 21–2]). In fact, it was tea more often than coffee but the quality of ritual comfort remained (Bevir and Rhodes 2006, 123).
11. For summary statement of the traditional Westminster beliefs of civil servants see: Cm 2627 (1994), Jary (2004, chapter 7 and p. 85), and the several speeches of Sir Richard Wilson, former Head of the Home Civil Service. See, for example, Wilson (2003). The history of this constitutional bureaucracy is told in Parris (1969) and Chapman and Greenaway (1980).

Chapter 7

Managerial Rationalities

Introduction

Since 1968 there has been a constant stream of initiatives from Labour and Conservative governments aimed at strengthening central government and reforming the civil service. Many now belong to the dustbin of history, their labels redolent of times past. Who now remembers or cares about CPRS, MINIS, FMI, the '3Es', Next Steps agencies, and citizens' charters? A sceptic might remark that nothing persists except the persistent drive for reform.[1]

ven against this backcloth of frenetic activity, one word captures the New Labour Government's handling of state reform between 1997 and 2007 – hyperactive. However understood, whatever the results, nobody can deny there has been much activity. Our aim is to decentre this activity. The new public management, or managerialism and marketization (see Chapter 5), is conventionally seen as a prime example of governmental control technologies or rationalities. Yet this group of rationalities is both variously and severally constructed by elites, and these stories are acted out against a backcloth of core executive or court politics. So, again, ruling appears contingent because the changes in the state and its governance are contested.

This chapter tells three stories about changes in the central state and its governance. First, we tell the centralization story, which focuses on reforms aimed at increasing the power of the Prime Minister at the expense of Cabinet and the Departments. Second, we tell the management story, which focuses on the attempt to reform the civil service and the problems posed by civil service resistance along with a lack of policy-making and management skills at the heart of government. Finally, we tell the governance story, which argues that several of the reform initiatives were embedded in the contests of court politics and in webs of dependence that undermined changes in the state and its governance.

The centralization story

The trend to executive centralization is seen by many commentators as widespread in parliamentary government. For example, Poguntke and Webb (2005, 7) argue that executive presidentialism occurs when there is a shift of 'political power resources and autonomy to the benefit of individual leaders' and 'a concomitant loss of power and autonomy of collective actors like cabinets'. Such centralization was on New Labour's agenda before they came to power. For example, Peter Mandelson and Roger Liddle argued there was a need 'for a more formalised strengthening of the centre of government' that 'provides the means of formulating and driving forward strategy for the government as a whole' (Mandelson and Liddle 1996, 240). Journalists, academics, and insiders also agreed that Blair sought to centralize power in Number 10 (see Bevir and Rhodes 2006, chapter 6 for citations). For example, Jonathan Powell, Chief of Staff at the Prime Minister's Office, famously warned senior civil servants to expect 'a change from a feudal system of barons to a more Napoleonic system' (Seldon 2004, 437). Blair's Number 10 aides asserted that 'Cabinet died years ago', claiming they wanted 'to replace the Department barons with a Bonapartist system' (Kavanagh and Seldon 2000, 291). So, this section recounts the story of New Labour's search for a stronger, centralized executive.[2]

Structural changes to both the Prime Minister's Office and the Cabinet Office are the main ways in which policy making was centralized. These changes included an increase in special advisers, a strengthening of the Prime Minister's Office's role in managing the media and policy making, and the emergence of 'a Prime Minister's department that would not speak-its-name' (Hennessy 2000, 6).

Special advisers

There were six special advisers working in the Prime Minister's Office shortly before Labour came to power. After a sharp increase in the number of appointments following Labour's General Election victory, there was a more gradual rise, which finally levelled off in mid-December 1999 when 25 special advisers worked in Number 10. Most appointments were in the

Policy Directorate, which meant that it was staffed by non-civil servants, each shadowing a particular department or policy area.

Two special advisers had prominent roles: Jonathan Powell and Alistair Campbell, the Director of Communications and Strategy. Both were given line management powers over civil servants and, while the post of Chief of Staff was not new, the role that Jonathan Powell played as Head of the Prime Minister's Office was unprecedented in scope. The Prime Minister also appointed unpaid advisers who reported directly to him. The most notable example was John Birt. He was the Prime Minister's part-time Strategy Adviser, located in Number 10. His work was shrouded in some secrecy until freedom of information requests led to the publication of some sections of his reports.

Special advisers were also appointed across government, although concern over their growing numbers and cost led to a cap of two special advisers for each Minister. The only exception to that rule was the Treasury where Ministers were able to draw on the advice not only from their own appointments but also from the special advisers appointed to the Council of Economic Advisers. Although there were always several members of the Council, it was not the collective body its name implied. Members of the Council worked alongside the Treasury officials who were responsible for developing policy in their own area of expertise. The general growth in special advisers, especially in the Prime Minister's Office, led to charges of centralization and politicization of the civil service.

Politicians and civil servants consistently deny there is any politicization, associating that phrase with overt party political beliefs, but there are other interpretations. Advisers inject party politics into the advice process of Departments. So, the role of civil servants changed from providing advice to putting together packages of advice from several sources. As Gus O'Donnell recently commented, civil servants could no longer claim a 'monopoly on wisdom' but must instead earn their place 'as principal policy advisers' (O'Donnell 2006*b*).

Individual advisers also played a prominent role in departmental policy deliberations. For example, Andrew Adonis of the Prime Minister's Policy Directorate often intervened to influence education policy making, although some insiders opined acidly that 'if anyone knew Andrew was behind a policy, it immediately made people suspicious' (Seldon 2004, 642). The post became a springboard to high government office. The more prominent examples included Andrew Adonis, Ed Balls, and David Miliband.

Strengthening media management and policy making

Spin, or less pejoratively, news management and presenting government policy, are a long-standing part of the responsibilities of the Prime Minister's Office's, but this role was strengthened after May 1997. A change to the Ministerial Code required ministers to clear all major interviews, press releases, and policy statements with Number 10 before they were released to the media. The Office was also strengthened by creating a Strategic Communications Unit, which coordinated the release of departmental statements to avoid clashes. It was staffed by a mixture of special advisers and civil servants.

A few months after Labour's second electoral victory, the Prime Minister made more institutional changes to Number 10. The Prime Minister's Private Office was merged with the Policy Unit to form a new Policy Directorate. Its key functions were day-to-day liaison with Whitehall departments and writing briefs and speeches for the Prime Minister. It was also involved in developing short-term policy in the Prime Minister's priority areas, such as the Respect agenda, which was announced after the 2005 General Election. A new position of Director of Communications and Strategy was also created to oversee the work of the Strategic Communications Unit, the Press Office, and the Research and Information Unit. Its stature and influence weakened following the resignation of Alistair Campbell and the recommendations of the Interim Report of the Phillis Review of Government Communications.[3] Campbell's replacement was not given line management powers over civil servants, and overall responsibility for government media strategy and personnel was handed over to a new Permanent Secretary of Government Communications based in the Cabinet Office.

Supporting the prime minister

The Cabinet Office was always a ragbag of functions bequeathed to it by former prime ministers. Blair added to the ragbag, although he broke with tradition in the number of units created and the speed of change. Early efforts focused on tackling cross-cutting issues. Blair appointed an assortment of task forces, working parties, commissions, 'policy czars', policy forums, and policy action teams. Various cross-cutting units were also established or moved to the Cabinet Office, including the Social Exclusion Unit; the Women's Unit; the Anti-Drugs Coordination Unit; the Freedom of Information Unit; and, more recently, the Office of the Third Sector.

Most of these units changed their name to reflect changed priorities or responsibilities and many were transferred out of the Cabinet Office to other departments. For example, the Social Exclusion Unit started life in the Cabinet Office at the beginning of December 1997. It was transferred to the Office of the Deputy Prime Minister at the end of May 2002. It returned to the Cabinet Office in June 2006, with a revised name and remit. These changes show how Blair sought to control government functions without bothering himself with too many of the operational details. As Hennessy (1998, 15) noted, 'Number 10 is omnipresent'.

The second wave of initiatives sought to develop strategic policy for the Prime Minister. Initially, Blair set up the Performance and Innovation Unit (PIU; launched on 28 July 1998) and the Prime Minister's Forward Strategy Unit (PMFSU; launched on 22 June 2001). After the second General Election victory of June 2001, an Office of the Deputy Prime Minister was established in the Cabinet Office with several new units in the Department. The units included the Prime Minister's Strategy Unit (PMSU), the Prime Minister's Delivery Unit (PMDU), and the Office of Public Services Reform (OPSR).

The PMSU was formed from a merger of existing strategy units, including the PIU and the PMFSU. It had three roles: strategic reviews and policy advice on the Prime Minister's domestic policy priorities; helping departments develop effective strategies and policies; and identifying and disseminating thinking on emerging issues and challenges. It worked in project teams organized around five clusters: public service reform, home affairs, economy and infrastructure, welfare reform, and social justice and communities. It increasingly took on work formerly carried out by one of the policy-specific, cross-cutting units, yet it always remained relatively small. At its peak, there were no more than 90 people working in the Unit and by mid-May 2005 it contained some 55 people. The workforce was drawn from the civil service, the private or voluntary sectors, and the wider public sector.

It is difficult to assess the impact of the PMSU. It published some 90 reports between May 1999 and March 2007 but it also conducted many confidential projects. Despite the claim that its reports were not official statements of government policy, they often framed the public policy debate. Its work had direct effects on government policy and the delivery of services, for example the conclusions of the Energy Review (PMSU 2002). By the end, it had a central and growing role. It was responsible for developing reform of the public services. It was also heavily involved in the six Policy Reviews the Prime Minister launched in October 2006.

Its role was to develop big policy for the 'whole' of government, not just on a particular issue.[4] It also enjoyed broad support. It received a positive report from the House of Commons Public Administration Committee and the Conservative Party's Democracy Task Force (PASC 2007; Conservative Party 2007). By the prevailing standards for such units, its position was, and remains, secure. However, it is hard to judge its effectiveness because it was not the only strategic unit in the core executive undertaking such work. The Treasury always played an important role (see later).

Supporting the cabinet

The Cabinet Office under Blair had the usual secretariats: economic and domestic, European, defence and overseas, and intelligence. There has been a tendency to focus on the glamorous strategy units and ignore the long-standing, even dull, work of the Cabinet Office. That is a mistake. Contrary to assertions about the 'death of Cabinet', the Cabinet Office Secretariat continued to perform its traditional coordinating role. Of course, it was subject to the same pressures for change. Some of these changes were to meet the policy commitments of the Blair Government. For example, a Constitution Secretariat was created immediately after the General Election in May 1997 to coordinate the Government's wide-ranging programme of constitutional reform, notably the work on devolution, freedom of information, House of Lords reform, and human rights. Other changes were less significant examples of administrative evolution, such as the change in name of the Ceremonial Branch to the Ceremonial Secretariat in 2001.

The most notable reforms were in security, intelligence, and emergency-related matters. Two developments are noteworthy. First, a new post of Intelligence and Security Coordinator was created in June 2002. The Coordinator became the Prime Minister's principal adviser on security, intelligence, and emergency-related matters, assuming responsibility for functions previously discharged by the Cabinet Secretary. He was responsible for day-to-day oversight of the intelligence and security secretariat, providing the Prime Minister and other senior Ministers with timely, accurate, and objectively assessed intelligence from across government and the intelligence agencies. In November 2005, the newly appointed Permanent Secretary, Richard Mottram, also became Chair of the Joint Intelligence Committee and the title of the post was changed to Permanent Secretary, Intelligence, Security, and Resilience.

Second, the new permanent secretary was also responsible for overseeing the work of the civil contingencies secretariat which was created in

July 2001 when the Cabinet Office merged its existing emergency planning units with those from the Home Office. Its main role was to prepare for, and respond to, crises and major emergencies. It worked on incidents such as avian influenza as well as the London bombings of July 2005. In short, there was a major expansion of the Cabinet Office's work in both intelligence and security, and emergency planning. The new post of Permanent Secretary, Intelligence, Security, and Resilience, was created as a link between these two areas of work.[5]

So, this version of the rationalities story focuses on a government intent on centralizing policy making. The aim of the Cabinet Office and of Number 10, as a Prime Minister's Department in all but name, was to allow Blair to remain on top, if not in detailed touch. However, it was abundantly clear from the never-ending changes that the Prime Minister 'never [really] succeeded in finding a structure that suited him' (Seldon 2004, 694).

The management story

Improving public sector management was central to the New Labour reforms (see Bovaird and Russell 2007; Richards 2007). As with previous governments, the spate of initiatives continued unabated. As Antony Part, former Permanent Secretary at the Department of Industry testily asserted:

> Then, as now, the administrative class spent most of their time initiating or implementing changes. It was – and is – their characteristic function, a point that has been overlooked by a number of prominent people who ought to know better. (Part 1990, 20)

Managing change was to remain a characteristic function of the Administrative Class just as the search for management change was to remain a preoccupation of the political class. We now tell the story of the search for a civil service with better management skills. The reform process began with the *Modernising Government* White Paper (Cm 4310 1999), with joined-up government as its flagship innovation. This agenda mutated into the 'delivery agenda' by the General Election victory of 2001 and into the 'choice and voice' agenda after the 2005 election.

The Government presented these shifts as a naturally evolving process (see OPSR 2005, 6). In contrast, others protest that:

> It's a succession of knee jerks.... They are not standing back and defining what they mean. Phrases like 'joined-up government, and the 'Third Way' don't mean anything. (Hennessy 2000, 9)

The result was a frustrated civil service, seeking a clear sense of direction amid the plethora of detailed changes.

Modernizing government

The Modernising Government agenda was diffuse, although the theme given the greatest prominence was joined-up government (Cabinet Office 2000). The White Paper sought to develop a framework that government could use to coordinate its activity. Institutional fragmentation and the attendant problems of coordination had already been noted by Robin Butler, Blair's first Head of the Home Civil Service:

> It is essential that it [delegation] does not reach the point where individual Departments and their Agencies become simply different unconnected elements in the overall public sector, with ... no real working mechanisms for policy coordination. (Butler 1993, 404)

So, a new language gained currency and we talked about joined-up government, holistic governance, and partnerships (see Pollitt 2003; Richards and Smith 2003; Bevir 2005; and Bogdanor 2005). It was but a phase. As the House of Commons Public Administration Select Committee (2001, para 42) commented:

> The 'Modernising Government' programme as a whole is complex and has multiple elements. It is not always clear where the really key priorities are, with the resulting danger that civil servants will endeavour to work methodically on all of them at once. This is a great virtue; but it is also a considerable disability in terms of putting first things first. In our view the immense checklists contained within the 'Modernising Government' programme need to be converted into a much stronger definition of what the key priorities for action are, with clear responsibilities assigned for delivering them.

Delivery

Following Blair's second election victory, there was a clear shift in direction. The new focus was on 'delivery'. It was a policy shift that led to further institutional reform. Two new units were created in the Cabinet Office – the Office of Public Services Reform (OPSR) and the Prime Minister's Delivery

Unit (PMDU), which we discuss later. The OPSR developed and promulgated the 'philosophy' of the delivery agenda. It also advised the Prime Minister on the ways of implementing reform in the public services and the civil service. It covered all public services, including local government. It was at the heart of the delivery agenda. Nevertheless, the lack of a White Paper underpinning the delivery agenda means that its development has to be tracked through a series of policy papers, speeches, and statements (see, e.g. OPSR 2002). So, the principles of the delivery agenda were not always clear, mainly because they evolved over time. Even at the start, the Cabinet Office web site was less than specific in announcing the end of the Modernising Government programme and the arrival of the delivery agenda:

> Thus delivery of better, modern public service is the Government's **key** priority for its second term. This is not easy; one commentator has said, 'There is no drama in delivery . . . only a long, grinding haul punctuated by public frustration with the pace of change.' Failure will not be tolerated, nor will mediocrity.[6]

The clearest statements of the principles underpinning the early phase of the delivery agenda can be found in two separate documents. The first document, *Reforming our Public Services: Principles into Practice*, was published by the OPSR in March 2002. It outlined the 'Prime Minister's four principles of public sector reform'. They were national standards to ensure that people have the right to high-quality services wherever they live; devolution to give local leaders the means to deliver these standards to local people; more flexibility in service provision to meet people's rising expectations; and greater customer choice (OPSR 2002, 3). The second document, *Putting People at the Heart of Public Services*, contained much of the same rhetoric (OPSR 2005). In July 2004, each of the main delivery departments also published their own five-year strategies, which sought to identify how the Prime Minister's principles of public sector reform could be incorporated into the front-line delivery of services.

The general principles that informed the delivery agenda were also outlined in various speeches and interviews. Michael Barber (2007*b*), the Prime Minister's former Chief Adviser on Delivery, summarized what it meant for education in the following terms:

> Between 2001 and 2005 what Blair increasingly hankered after was a way of improving the education system that didn't need to be constantly driven by government. He wanted to develop self-sustaining, self-improving systems, and that led him to look into how to change not just the standards

> and the quality of teaching, but the structures and incentives. Essentially it's about creating different forms of a quasi-market in public services, exploiting the power of choice, competition, transparency and incentives, and that's really where the education debate is going now.... At the political level Blair really understands this challenge, but it is highly controversial – within the Labour Party and nationally.[7]

And in February 2004, the Prime Minister outlined what delivery meant for him:

> The principal challenge is to shift focus from policy advice to delivery. Delivery means outcomes. It means project management. It means adapting to new situations and altering rules and practice accordingly. It means working not in traditional departmental silos. It means working naturally with partners outside of Government. It's not that many individual civil servants aren't capable of this. It is that doing it requires a change of operation and of culture that goes to the core of the Civil Service.[8]

Blair also emphasized the principle of earned autonomy, which involved 'giving greater freedoms to high performing providers and focusing regulation, inspection and associated interventions on poor performers' (PMSU 2006, 41).

Choice and voice

Similar principles informed Blair's third term of public sector reform. The closure of the OPSR in January 2006 led to its functions being transferred to the PMSU. While the PMSU no longer described the government's overall approach to public sector reform as the 'delivery agenda', its 'self-improving' model of reform clearly encompassed many of the same principles (PMSU 2006, 23). The model sought to develop a more coherent narrative of public sector reform. It brought together several reform initiatives already being implemented and it returned to old favourites like joined-up government.

The PMSU model identified four components of public sector reform: top-down performance management pressure from government; greater competition and contestability in providing public services; greater pressure from citizens through choice; and measures to strengthen the capability and capacity of central and local government to deliver improved public services. There was a particular emphasis on choice and voice; of 'bottom-up pressures for choice, personalisation, voice and user engagement'. The aim was to ensure that 'public service users' needs, preferences and aspirations are transmitted directly to and acted upon' (PMSU 2006, chapters 4 and 7; see also PASC 2005). These principles were reaffirmed in the Prime Minister's policy review of public services. It restated the 'governing idea of the next phase of reform' that 'services need to be personalized according to the needs and preferences of users'. It also had a renewed emphasis on the role of the state as a commissioner of services. So the state would create

> self-improving institutions of public service, independent of centralised state control, drawing on the best of public, private and third sector provision. These institutions must be free to develop in the way they need to, responsive to the needs and preferences of citizens, and with a flexible workforce that is able to innovate and change. Out of this vision will come a new concept of modern public services: one built around the user of the service. (PMSU 2007, 30 and 7)

It is too early to comment on the significance of these ideas. Because so much changes, so often, with no evaluation, it is impossible to say whether any changes will, or could be, effective (see Hodgson, Farrell, and Connolly 2007).

Common ground

The modernizing, delivery, and choice agendas developed not only policy principles but also targets. For service deliverers and middle-level managers, the focus was on delivering against performance targets. As the Prime Minister's policy review stated: 'to drive up standards, and to tackle inequalities, the immediate focus was on stronger top-down performance management' (PMSU 2007, 23). The Prime Minister's primary institutional mechanism for doing this was the PMDU. It began life tracking how well departments were performing against their Public Service Agreement (PSA) targets in 'key delivery areas'. These included health (waiting times for in-patient treatment and accident and emergency), education (levels of secondary school performance, including General Certificate of Secondary Education [GCSE] results), transport (cutting train delays), and criminal justice (including street crime and the inflow of illegal asylum-seekers). It provided progress reports to the Prime Minister on each of these areas and intervened if it was felt that departments might fail to deliver (Barber 2007*a*). Over time, the Unit's remit extended to cover all PSAs, although it continued to focus on the Prime Minister's top priorities. The Cabinet Secretary also gave it oversight of the Capability Review programme, which assessed the capacity of departments to deliver their objectives (see later). The problem in assessing the PMDU is that it was only one of several mechanisms used by the core executive to track progress against PSAs.

Also running across the modernizing, delivery, and choice agendas was an ever-present desire to improve public sector management. All four of Blair's Cabinet Secretaries entered office with new ideas on the best way to reform the civil service. The Prime Minister delivered several speeches on the subject (see note 9) and there was a constant stream of individual reform initiatives clustered around five themes: leadership; skills training and employee secondments; individual performance management and reward; diversity; and better recruitment practices and career development.

Few of the initiatives stood the test of time. The reforms were not always seen as significant in the departments. As one official commented: 'the relatively subtle changes which have taken place in the reform agenda between 1999 and now don't seem worthy of close analysis from our end of the telescope' (Bovaird and Russell 2007, 319). However, the restless search for reform provided continued evidence of a floundering and directionless political and administrative class. As Richard Wilson, the former Head of the Home Civil Service, lamented:

> I would not want to claim that the manner in which we implemented all these reforms over the years was a model to emulate. There was not enough overall vision or strategic planning. Too often it was uncoordinated, with different parts of the centre of government launching similar initiatives simultaneously or at a pace which long-suffering managers in departments found difficult to handle. (Wilson 1999; see also Wilson 2006)

The Cabinet Office's Capability Review called for 'a clear operating framework running across the complex and varied business of the Department'. It concluded the absence of such a framework had 'seriously weakened – particularly in the area of Civil Service reform – its impact in delivering change through other departments, as departments are faced with a series of unprioritized, or sometimes competing, central Civil Service initiatives' (Cabinet Office 2006*a*, 22).

The governance story

The governance story highlights power dependency in the core executive. It stresses the horizontal networks of interdependence and resource exchange in which the core executive is embedded (see Rhodes 1995,

1997*a*). The core executive cannot be seen as a single decision centre focused on the Prime Minister and Cabinet. Rather, it is a set of overlapping networks and central institutions that are all too often confounded by central fragmentation. The New Labour reforms of the centre sought to impose the desired degree of coordination, but were confounded by the many interdependent networks that criss-cross Whitehall, Westminster, and beyond. So, now we tell the story of the rival courts of Brown and Blair.

If the Cabinet Office is all about using soft levers, such as influence, support, and partnerships, then the Treasury is its opposite, controlling, as it does, the hard levers, most notably the power of the purse. It was, and will remain, a prominent actor in the core executive. The court politics, personality clashes, and rivalry between Blair and Brown have been the subject of relentless commentary, culminating in Brown's declaration to Blair that '[t]here is nothing you could ever say to me now that I could ever believe' (Peston 2005, 349). By 2005, Brown was 'the official opposition to Blair within the very heart of the Cabinet' (Peston 2005, 13 and 353; but see Bower 2007, 475–6 for a more qualified view). There were also important institutional changes, which did not provoke the same media interest. The intertwining of court politics and institutional change meant there was not only a second centre of coordination but also a second wellspring of civil service reform.

As soon as he took up office, the Chancellor made it clear that he wanted the Treasury to extend its reach far beyond its traditional Ministry of Finance role. He outlined what he expected his department to do in a speech to the Institute of Fiscal Studies:

> A Labour Treasury would need to be not just a Ministry of Finance, but also a Ministry working with other departments to deliver long-term economic and social renewal. (Brown 1999)

The Department fleshed out these comments in a Memorandum that it submitted to the Treasury Select Committee (2000):

> With the macroeconomic framework now firmly established, more resources can be directed towards examining microeconomic issues. Evidence-based microeconomic and distributional analysis is essential to underpin the Treasury's output – from Budget tax measures through developments in competition policy and analysis of poverty issues to work on reform of the legal aid system and deciding transport priorities.

This theme became constant. The Treasury was 'not simply concerned with controlling spending, but also with achieving value for money and with using spending programmes to make the economy work better'.[9] More colloquially, the former Treasury Permanent Secretary, Terry Burns, explained the change of emphasis by saying that 'macro-economic policy is very boring... so... we are getting very interested in social policy' (Treasury Select Committee 2001, para 39).

This change of direction was given institutional expression. For example, the role of the Public Services and Growth (PSG) Directorate grew. It still comprised the spending teams shadowing departments, but it now combined that role with tracking performance against PSAs and efficiency targets. In brief, the Treasury took an interest in a much wider scope of issues and it relished this diversification.

The Brown Chancellorship was also notable for its reform of public expenditure control. He introduced Spending Reviews and a new performance management framework. PSAs were set for individual departments and for cross-cutting issues. Performance against them was monitored by several parts of the core executive: the PMDU in the Cabinet Office; the spending teams based in the PSG directorate; the Public Services and Expenditure (PSX) Cabinet Committee; and separate bilateral stocktakes between Ministers and the Prime Minister on specific areas, and the Chief Secretary to the Treasury on more general topics. As Paul Boateng, a former Chief Secretary to the Treasury, claimed, the Treasury has 'some responsibility, in some sense, for *all* PSA targets' (Treasury Select Committee 2005, Question 83).

Despite this admission, there remains a lack of clarity over how the Treasury and departments devise PSAs, as well as the incentive effects, especially when targets are either minimal or not met (James 2004). PSAs are best viewed as a tool providing the Treasury with a 'legitimate' reason for continued or extended intervention in departmental affairs. As a Senior Treasury official explained, the effect is that the Treasury 'plays a much more proactive and strategic role in the development of policy in Whitehall'. Of course, the Treasury would not be the Treasury without acerbic asides, so he added: 'This, of course, has had a positive impact on this enthusiasm for joined-up government' (private information). Given the increased spending on health and education, the Treasury saw this role as a natural extension of their powers and a necessary control on departments.

The Treasury was also heavily involved in public service reform through its efficiency programme. It was a different agenda from that of the PMSU but it was just as important. The efficiency programme can be traced to several reports commissioned by the Treasury (e.g. the Gershon Review (2004)). The overall aim was to achieve the headline target contained in the Gershon Review of £21.5 billion of efficiency savings by 2007–8. The scope of the efficiency programme was broad, so it had important consequences for all the public sector. In short, the PMSU and the Treasury public sector reforms ran concurrently. They coexisted. They were not coordinated, nor could they be, because one agenda was driven by Blair and the other by Brown.

To further complicate matters, the Brown Chancellorship also played a strategic policy role by conducting its own policy reviews. As one member of the Number 10 Strategy Unit put it, 'Gordon does have a strategy unit, it's called the Treasury'. First, there were internal reviews focusing on cross-cutting issues of government policy. Typically, there were six or seven reviews for each spending review. Typically, they concentrated on a few policy areas, such as for example, young children (seven reviews), the elderly (six reviews), and crime and drugs (six reviews). Second, there were independent reviews, usually headed by someone from outside government and typically produced with one or more departments, but with a secretariat drawn from, and based in, the Treasury.[10] As the former Cabinet Secretary Andrew Turnbull explained, the consequence was that the Treasury became a policy department:

> The reviews have varied a lot in quality. Some are actually quite good. But a lot of them are HMV – His Master's Voice – and are really written to order. The Wanless report on health spending was a good example of that. And that has changed the relationship between the Treasury and colleagues, and changed the way the Treasury works, making it a policy department. (Timmins 2007)

These changes were as much about the court politics of Blair and Brown as they were about public sector reform. In an unguarded moment, Andrew Turnbull also spoke of 'the more or less complete contempt' with which Brown and the Treasury treated ministerial colleagues. In his view, Treasury control had therefore come 'at the expense of any government cohesion and any assessment of strategy' (Timmins 2007). No matter how commentators interpret either the court politics of the two rivals or Brown's Treasury reforms, it is clear the Treasury's redefinition of its role altered the way central government worked. It also illustrated the limits of focusing on the Prime Minister and his machinery for coordination. If we do so, we miss the problem that central coordination was undermined by competing centres of policy making. It caused 'dilemmas and sometimes downright confusion' in the departments because ministers and officials had 'to pick their way across a minefield' (Barber 2007*c*).

Conclusion

The stories

New Labour built on the reforms of previous governments and the scale of its activity is as daunting as it is frenetic. What do our stories tell us about the attempt to introduce managerial rationalities to the British central state?

The centralization story tells us there is often a gulf between intervention and control. Central agencies intervened often, but rarely to great effect. For all the talk of a presidential Prime Minister, the most striking features of the attempt to reform the central state are the persistence of traditional practices and the elusiveness of coordination.

The claim that bilateral, or sofa decision making, was pre-eminent and cabinet government was in decline were premature. Cabinet, and especially its infrastructure of committees, thrived. As Rentoul (2001, 544) noted, 'a lot of the business of government continued to be done in cabinet committees'. The number of Cabinet committees grew. It was deliberate policy to give 'a more central role to cabinet committees in Government', particularly in dealing with 'cross-cutting, cross-departmental issues'.[11] In January 1998, there were twenty-seven committees but they gradually increased in number until November 2004 when there were fifty-nine. In 2006, there were between forty-four and forty-five Ministerial committees, excluding the five Policy Review Working Groups. Blair also chaired more committees the longer he was in office. He chaired five in January 1998, ten in November 2004, peaking at sixteen in December 2005, but only dropping by one to fifteen in December 2006. He also chaired the five Policy Review Groups. In short: 'there has been much more use of Cabinet as a sounding board' and Cabinet now 'regularly receives presentations on major new policy development' (Mulgan 2005). Blair's critics single out the decline of the Cabinet's policy-making and coordination functions for special criticism. Yet, it has been clear for over a half century that these functions have been carried out by several central agencies of the core executive, including but not limited to the Cabinet. The Cabinet persists in four forms: as the constitutional theory of ministerial and collective responsibility; as a set of rules and routines; as a political bargaining arena between central actors; and as a component of the core executive (Weller 2003, 74–8).

We also know that coordination of and by the state throughout Western Europe is episodically effective and rarely strategic (see Chapter 5). It is the 'philosopher's stone' of modern government, ever sought, but always just beyond reach, all too often because it assumes both agreement on goals and an effective central coordinator (Seidman 1975, 190).

The management story adds the lack of managerial capacity; there was a 'lack of clarity about both means and ends' and 'confusion about the role of central government' (Riddell 2001, 38–9; 2005, 41). As Richard Wilson observed in 1997: 'your problem is that neither you nor anyone in Number 10 has ever managed anything' (quoted in Seldon 2004, 629). The same point was made ten years later by Michael Barber (2007*c*):

> All Prime Ministers face their constraints, from their Cabinets, departments and the 'official view', but in Tony Blair's case there has been the major personal one that, prior to entering Downing Street, he had never run a government department, or even been a junior minister. As a consequence, he had a huge amount to learn about how organisations, especially large bureaucracies, work.

Blair's weaknesses included a lack of follow-through: 'He intervenes, persuades, and then forgets'. He lacks 'policy making and management skills' (Seldon 2004, 692). So, although he wants results 'he finds it hard to understand why things can't happen immediately' and he is frustrated when 'waiting for the pay-off and he doesn't have time' (Hennessy 2000, 10). Geoff Mulgan's assessment of Number 10 was that it had got bigger but less effective, it had lost authority, and its 'overall narrative was no longer clear' (Campbell 2007, 707).

The Cabinet Office is not exempt from this sweeping criticism. The Capability Review of the Cabinet Office (2006*a*, 14 and 17) commented that its

> overall performance, particularly as seen by its major partners in other government departments, is variable. Successes also tend to be attributed to particular units, not to the Cabinet Office as a department.

It added that this critical assessment

> reflects the gap between the current capability of the Cabinet Office and the task it faces in the future. For much of the Cabinet Office's work, there is either ambiguity over the scope of its role and powers, or overlap between

> the work of various units. Clearer remits and business models are essential if the Cabinet Office is to exert effective leverage over service delivery from its position in the centre.

In a similar vein, the Public Administration Select Committee (2001, para 42) commented on the 'difficulty in determining priorities' in the 'highly complex organization of the Cabinet Office itself, with a profusion of small units and divisions all exercising surveillance and issuing instructions from the centre of government'.

The governance story points to costs of dependence. A key characteristic of the period 1997–2007 is the vulnerability of the Prime Minister, like all Prime Ministers, to both national and international events. To compare Blair pre-Iraq and post-Iraq is to see that prime ministerial pre-eminence comes and goes. Add the court politics of the Brown–Blair rivalry and we have a picture of a government in which barons vie for favour in the court of a would-be president, as dependent on them for support as they are on him for favours. In addition, the greatest baron was Gordon Brown who constructed 'a command Chancellorship – not seen in Whitehall since Neville Chamberlain occupied Number 11 Downing Street, when Stanley Baldwin was at Number 10 in the 1920s and 1930s' (Hennessy 2005, 9).

Court politics and rationalities

The central state was characterized, not by prime ministerial centralization, or the new rationalities of managerialism but by two men each presiding over their territory, which was ever more jealously guarded. Brown was 'immovable', 'dominating his own territory' with 'jagged defences designed to repel any invader, including the Prime Minister'. So, 'they were not interested in submerging their differences in outlook, but in making an exhibition of them' (Naughtie 2002, 352). One result was a bifurcated centre. The Treasury set the strategic agenda across government, engaged in specific policy development, and monitored progress against targets to a previously unprecedented extent. There was significant overlap and competition with the Cabinet Office and the PMSU. But, there was one major difference. The Treasury had the hard levers, the Cabinet Office did not. 'He who pays the piper calls the tune', and Brown's reforms commanded the undivided attention of departments. Having witnessed visitations by both the Delivery Unit and the Treasury to the departments, it was clear whose views carried the greatest weight. The Treasury was greeted with a caution and care bordering on white-knuckle nerves. In all too sharp contrast, the

Delivery Unit was accorded a polite, urbane, reception. The Brown–Blair rivalry is not just about personalities and court politics. It is about control of the central state, and the Treasury won.

Politics, value clashes, interests, cultures, symbolic games, and accountability all limit the impact of managerial rationalities on the public sector. Civil servants are not venal, or even reluctant, when implementing such reforms. But the brute fact is that top civil servants in the Westminster tradition are political administrators, not managers. Their job is to take care of their minister. If there is failure, it is not a failure of leadership by Permanent Secretaries but a failure of political leadership because the Prime Minister and Ministers did not know what they wanted. There was no consistent vision and it led to muddling through rather than a thorough-going reform. That said, managerial rationalities were important because the contending beliefs and practices of Blair and Brown shared common ground. Both believed in the efficacy of specific technologies, especially targets, or performance indicators, and these technologies affected top civil servants, middle-level managers, and citizens. When they acted together, as they did over PSAs, the scope for passive let alone active resistance was reduced. We explore the effects of managerialism on top civil servants in Chapter 8 and of specific technologies on middle-level managers and citizens in Chapter 9.

Notes

1. On these several acronyms and a history of reform see Hennessy (2001), Massey and Pyper (2005), Rhodes (1997*a*, chapter 5; 2001), and Richards (2007). The first version of this chapter was written with Paul Fawcett. For his interpretation of managerialism as an exercise in metagovernance see Fawcett (2009).
2. We paraphrase some material from Bevir and Rhodes (2006, chapter 6) as we update the presidentialization story.
3. See: Government Communications Review Group web site at: http://archive.cabinetoffice.gov.uk/gcreview/news/FinalReport.pdf (last accessed on 30 July 2009).
4. For information on the Prime Minister's Policy Reviews see: http://archive.cabinetoffice.gov.uk/policy_review/ (last accessed 30 July 2009).
5. At the end of March 2007, the Prime Minister announced the creation of a new Ministry of Justice and a strengthening of the Home Office's role in security and counterterrorism. Most of the security and intelligence functions of the Permanent Secretary for Intelligence, Security, and Resilience will remain intact and the 'Cabinet Office will retain its role [in] supporting the Prime Minister on national

security and counter-terrorism'. But in the ever-changing world of strengthening central capability, it is wisest to conclude that observers should 'watch this space'.

6. Cabinet Office, 'The Second Phase of Public Sector Reform: the move to delivery', at: http://archive.cabinetoffice.gov.uk/eeg/secondphase.htm (last accessed 30 July 2009).
7. 'Education Reform Lessons from England'. An interview with Sir Michael Barber at: http://www.educationsector.org/analysis/analysis_show.htm?doc_id=344385 (last accessed 30 June 2009). See also Barber (2007*a*).
8. Speech by the Tony Blair to the Civil Service Reform, Delivery and Values event 24 February 2004, at: http://www.number-10.gov.uk/output/Page5399.asp (last accessed 30 July 2009).
9. See 'Guide to the Centre of Government' at: http://archive.cabinetoffice.gov.uk/roleofcentre/treasury.htm (last accessed 30 July 2009).
10. See, for example: the Wanless Review of Health Trends (HM Treasury 2002); the Leitch Review of Skills (HM Treasury and Department for Education and Skills 2006); the Barker Review of Land Use (HM Treasury with the Department of Communities and Local Government 2006).
11. Number 10 Downing Street, 'Cabinet Committees, Press Briefing at: http://www.number-10.gov.uk/output/Page7542.asp (last accessed 30 July 2009).

Chapter 8

Living Westminster Traditions

Introduction

Civil servants must constantly interpret their position. That does not mean there is no formal documentation about the proper roles of civil servants and their relationships with governments and clients. Australia, Canada, and the United Kingdom have both legislation and guidelines about how civil servants should work. They prescribe proper behaviour between senior officials and ministers. But these documents are often the rules of governments, handed down to suit their political purposes and even then they tend to be general.[1] Even within these boundaries, civil servants must still make sense of their position and their role in ruling their countries. They are professionals on government, and heirs to long traditions. They need to explain to themselves and their colleagues where they fit. As circumstances change, they need to rationalize how their circumstances may have altered and what expectations may now exist. Making sense is not a matter of law, but of identity.

Therefore, in this chapter, we do not ask about the formal position of civil servants, but about how they interpret and understand their place in the political firmament. Since such an enterprise could be enormous, we focus our discussion primarily on the way three senior civil servants, each head of the civil service in their countries at the time they spoke, explain their understanding of how they place themselves in the broad Westminster tradition that shapes their working life. We draw on various primary sources: speeches, writings, evidence to inquiries, and interviews. Of course, there are limits to this kind of evidence. Ideally, we would compare and contrast the pattern of practice, talk, and considered writing, as we did in Chapter 6. But these speeches are important data. They can be candid statements, expressions of self-interest, or exercises in myth making. There are always the questions of how to interpret the data, and the extent to which their expressed views shaped their own practices and the practices of others. Whatever the problems of interpretation, the position of their authors lends weight to the ideas and accords them influence. So, we consider the ways in which heads of the civil service, or former heads, articulate and proselytize about the Westminster traditions of 'constitutional bureaucracy' (Parris 1969). Their beliefs are important because they are essential data in any analysis of the public service, its traditions, and its reform. Each leader in his own way seeks to protect the eternal verities of his version of a 'constitutional bureaucracy'. They are rearticulating what they see as enduring traditions, selectively reinventing beliefs to equip themselves and the civil services they lead to make sense of the present. We read political rhetoric. We read about inherited myths. These arts are critical to making present-day myths influential. It is why we study them. So, we do not seek to show civil servants in action; to provide examples of where these principles may have been put into effect. Rather, we want to understand how they think and feel about their position; about the ways they perceive their world. We identify the arguments they use to justify and rationalize the relevance of the civil service in the new circumstances in which they must now work. We show how they look for continuities and consistency by appealing to the common themes and traditions despite different national circumstances.

We recognize that even in similar Westminster-derived countries with some shared heritage and common traditions of understanding government, there remain distinct differences. Their respective civil services are not identical, and have constructed interpretations depending on their different contexts and dilemmas. We are not claiming, therefore, that there is some comparative convergence. We seek to show how key actors across these Westminster jurisdictions engaged with their traditions and, in the process, helped to invent new versions.

Living traditions

Traditions are selective legacies passed down from generation to generation, and adapted to present-day use (see Chapter 4). Earlier traditions can be selectively reconstituted and reformed. Actors draw from memory and previous training to provide guides to their roles and responsibilities. So, practitioners reach for historical notions of governance and call into play antecedent notions to enable them better to manage or understand their present-day circumstances. Such antecedents may allow scope for reinventing governance principles or provide a suitable rhetoric that practitioners can wield as a defence mechanism to resist change. In this latter sense, governance legacies can be revisited and rehabilitated provided they have plausibility, believability, and authoritativeness. They provide a backdrop against which today's protagonists do not merely grasp their world but seek to guide its directions.

Traditions of governance are evolving, adaptable sets of beliefs that enable those acting in the political sphere to understand and make sense of their world. They are sometimes resilient and enduring, and at other times ambivalent or contradictory in their core beliefs. Some parts are codified and rule-bound; others exist as a loosely connected constellation of ideas variously constructed by participants or observers. Importantly, traditions of governance adapt and change with circumstances, events, and reinterpretations. This chapter explores how the leadership of the senior civil service reinvented its traditions when it confronted the dilemmas posed by managerialism and the call for greater responsiveness by politicians over the past two decades.

Westminster civil services evolved according to a hybrid set of traditions of governance that are partly inherited from the political and parliamentary realm and partly learnt through administrative practice. On the one hand, civil services are not the sole masters of their fates. They are not the autonomous inventors or creators of their own identifiable traditions. They exist in, and are subordinate to, a legitimate political authority. So, there is a derivative character to their traditions. They work in formalized traditions of governance that are dependent and contingent on the political process and notions of proper decision making and accountability. These *political traditions*, which we label the Westminster, or 'responsible government', tradition, frame the dominant narratives in which they construct and make sense of their roles and existence (see Rhodes, Wanna, and Weller 2009, chapter 3). There are distinct political variations in this broad church of ideas – Tory-conservatism, Whig-liberalism, labourist-socialism, and, especially in the former dominions, statist traditions of social liberalism and agrarian socialism.

The civil service enjoys some institutional continuity and both keeps and refracts these traditions of 'responsible government', while also remaining embedded in them. So, although the formative political legacies of 'responsible government' were created and moulded elsewhere – through parliament and cabinet government, by the electoral process, by constitutionalists and the judiciary, by interest groups, and by public consent or popular discourse – the civil service nevertheless is an active conduit, conductor, and disseminator of such traditions.

On the other hand, the civil service also embodies two related sets of *administrative traditions* – the generalist and specialist traditions – that are couched in the normative aspirations of a constitutional bureaucracy (Parris 1969). These, in turn, created professional administrative bureaucracies with strong norms, precepts, and values. Such administrative traditions have organic or discrete roots in the bureaucracy but must coexist with the political traditions. So, evolving conventions of responsible government are complemented by evolving notions of professionalism, degrees of independence, expertise and technical proficiency, management, and preferred patterns of recruitment and workforce composition.

In addition, bureaucratic organizations also develop distinctive agency traditions based on their inherited beliefs, their continuing relationships and collective memories, their discrete training and types of expertise, and their professional values and codes. Often these are agency-specific, insular, and self-referential. These departmental philosophies interact with the service-wide constitutional bureaucratic or administrative traditions in complex and iterative ways.

Civil service traditions represent a plurality of inherited beliefs – sometimes separate and distinct, sometimes coexisting but also competing. Such traditions are not merely passively picked up from the political framework of responsible government. Rather, the civil service is an active cultivator and preserver of its traditions. It functions as the repository of government history and institutional practice. Its political and administrative traditions are not mutually exclusive but are constantly intersecting together. They provide meaning not in the form of some abstract, external constitutional doctrine but in the intersection of daily practice and reflection – occasionally with tensions but often in harmony.

Civil servants construct their understandings of these complementary and competing traditions through two forms of socialization. First, they imbibe beliefs through on-the-job learning and practitioner mentoring. They work and operate in institutional settings and learn the transmitted beliefs. Career structures are learning apprenticeships. Second, they are informed by a literature that packages dominant ideas or beliefs in the traditions of responsible government. This literature has two strands – 'insiders' and 'outsiders'. The 'insiders' comprise former experienced public servants expounding normative frameworks or explaining changing conventional practice (e.g. Bridges 1950; 1956 is the *locus classicus* but more recently see Wilson 2003). The 'outsiders' comprise journalist, academic, and constitutional writers attempting to describe and make sense of evolving political systems to explain to others (see, e.g. Bagehot 1963 [1867]; Dicey 1914; and Hennessy 2001).

Dilemmas

Such socialization is not frozen in time. The civil service can be seen to be continually reinventing its traditions. It does so consciously, unconsciously, and episodically as it confronts new dilemmas. Intensive episodes of change can be interpreted as attempts to update traditional legacies and beliefs or as attempts to endorse and legitimize cherished traditions in changed circumstances. Living traditions evolve, but they can also be more comprehensively reinvented when they confront major challenges.

The main challenge faced by the Westminster-derived civil services over the past 20 years was the belief among governments that the civil service was impervious to political rule (see Caiden 1990; Lange 1992; Aucoin 1995; and Savoie 2003). There was a clear belief from the 1970s onwards shared across much of the Westminster democracies that the bureaucracy had become too powerful and obstructionist. It was accused of having invested too much in its own independence and permanency. It was accused of being insular, self-referential, and unresponsive; and also of being an 'entrenched aristocracy within a democracy' and seeking to be above governments (Savioe 2003, 12). In the United Kingdom, Prime Minister Margaret Thatcher (1979–90) was out of sympathy with the ethos of a 'permanent' civil service she thought too risk-averse. Prime Minister Tony Blair (1997–2007) extended, rather than reversed, this trend and sought to make the civil service more responsive, contestable, and focused on delivery (see Chapter 7). In Australia, successive governments eroded permanent appointments in the public service, expanded contractual employment, and introduced performance regimes. They also used various mechanisms for exerting political control over agencies and their agendas (such as the growth of political advisers as policy managers). The story is similar in Canada, where deputy ministers are personally exposed to public accountability, employed on short-term contracts, and more open to political pressure. Their ministries are run on results-based business lines.

Relationships at the centre of government between politicians and departmental heads have also changed. The civil service now deals with a different set of politicians. Compared with the nineteenth century, when much of the Westminster tradition came into being, politicians are now full-time career politicians, well educated, reflexive, and spin-conscious. Ministers are more interested in immediate impact and effectiveness. They invest in driving change, and intensive media exposure makes them more directly accountable in the community for the performance of their agencies. Many ministers are not prepared to accept conventional ways of doing things but are interested in choices, in alternative solutions, comparative experiences, and transforming the incentive structures within policy frameworks (for instance, greater citizen-choice models of delivery).

The roles and responsibilities of Westminster governments also changed (for a more detailed account, see Rhodes and Weller 2001). Initially, government played largely a regulatory role and had limited responsibilities. In the twentieth century, governments created the welfare state but that era of big government gave way to the new public management (NPM) and outsourced services. Today, managerialism stresses improving service delivery, which has become a key priority for government (see Chapter 7).

Most important for the civil service, there is far more contestability in policy advice, research, and information. Much of the contestable advice is from outside the public sector – from think tanks, consultancy firms, management consultants, academic centres, and peak bodies and their research arms. The civil services no longer hold a monopoly on advice to ministers. Mostly they play a smaller role in original policy formulation, but instead 'add value' by collating, arbitrating, and recommending between contestable options circulating the minister. The picture is further complicated by ministerial advisers and minders. They not only mediate and liaise between the department and the minister but also give the minister more capacity to become involved and have an impact.

One Australian minister summed up these changes as follows:

> There has been a transition over 25 years from the final days of an imperial public service to a public service which is focused on policy advice and service contracts, as an enterprise operating in a competitive environment where governments have alternative sources of advice and service provision . . . it was an institutional struggle between the democratically elected governments and the public service for control over the public service. And in that struggle the elected governments have won. (Cited in Weller 2001, 81)

Resistance

While core relationships at the top have changed over past decades, the key bureaucratic actors did not always welcome the changes. There remains nostalgia for the days when the civil servants were reputedly at their most effective, when they were regarded as 'statesmen in disguise'. Mostly, this golden era refers to the mid-twentieth century, and to such giants of the profession as Sir Warren Fisher (see O'Halpin 1989) and Sir Edward Bridges (see Chapman 1988). These cabinet secretaries in Britain were educated, urbane, effective, and regarded as the archetypal mandarins. In Canada, the senior officials of a similar era became the subject of a collective portrait, *The Ottawa Men* (Granatstein 1982), which charted their considerable impact on post-war Canada.[2] In Australia, a group known collectively as the 'Seven Dwarfs', men small of stature (at least some were) but of dominant intellect, ruled for decades at the top of the Australian public service. They were scarcely a united team, but they were able to monopolize the provision of advice in an environment where there was little intellectual or institutional challenge to their position. The most dominant, Sir Roland Wilson, was secretary of the Treasury for fifteen years and regularly participated at cabinet as if he were a senior minister.[3]

Why this particular era of civil servants attained such hallowed status is not difficult to determine. Mass mobilization of society to pursue total war, followed by Keynesian beliefs in the efficacy of welfare state and social democracy, gave them credibility in the decades before the decline of faith in state solutions in the late 1970s. Whether the giants of those periods deserve the plaudits is debatable and disputed as the files become available to historians. The other side of this nostalgic coin suggests that today's leading public executives are pale by comparison. But, as the current Australian Secretary of the Department of Prime Minister and Cabinet, Peter Shergold, observed:

> There is a growing tendency to look back to the Secretaries of the past with nostalgia, finding in them qualities that have failed to withstand the passage of time and which reflect badly on their contemporary incumbents. The past becomes legend, and those who occupy the present are portrayed as unworthy to stand in the shoes of those who have gone before. (Shergold 2004*a*, 3)

In a subsequent reflection, he invited his audience to:

> Call me cynical but I cannot help but notice that the perceived decline in the power and status of public service often seems to coincide with the departure of the perceiving public servant. There is a remarkable conjunction of personal and administrative history. Whether individually, or in collective groups... retired diplomats, military brass and mandarins have a disarming if understandable tendency to see their successors as failing to live up to their own high standards of truth, ethics and integrity. (Shergold 2005, 2)

So, we have a conundrum. The so-called golden era of the civil service was regarded by ministers as a period when officials were too powerful, and there was a need to reassert political leadership. Now, in a period of enhanced political control, the senior echelons of the civil service are regarded as 'lacking the fearlessness and courage' of their predecessors, open to politicization and partisanship, and ready to adopt a willingness-to-please mentality (Shergold 2004*a*, 4).

Reinventing traditions

The controversy is not an either–or debate. We focus here on three examples of how the present leadership of the civil service goes about appropriating and reinventing its traditions. In each case, the person was appointed head of the civil service by their prime minister and each was aware of the inherited responsibility that came with the position. We are concerned to identify which aspects of its traditions the leadership selects and embraces. Which elements of the broader traditions do they engage with and select for endorsement or dissemination?

Britain

In Britain the touchstone for many practitioners are the principles reflected in the Northcote–Trevelyan *Report on the Organisation of the Permanent Civil Service* (Cmnd 3638 1968 [1854]), still regarded as the main foundation for the modern civil service. It provides the source of the administrative tradition read against the accepted backdrop of the political tradition of responsible government.[4] It provides an 'ideal', a related set of ideas, and even a measuring stick against which to judge current practice. Even if not often read or understood by officials today, appeals to the supposed principles of Northcote–Trevelyan remain common features of debates about the progress and the behaviour of the modern civil services.

In his valedictory address, the British Cabinet Secretary and Head of the Civil Service, Sir Andrew Turnbull (2005, 1), concluded:

> The British Civil Service enjoys an excellent reputation and it is particularly admired abroad. . . . Yet it has its detractors and critics, particularly at home. I have reflected on this and have come to the conclusion that the Civil Service has been strongly shaped by the Northcote–Trevelyan report and the traditions which have developed from it, but that this has also given rise to many of the features which people find unsatisfactory.

Turnbull argued (2005, 1):

> The Northcote–Trevelyan report grew out of the clash between a growing state and an administration based on nepotism. It recommended a series of changes, which have shaped the organisation even to this day. These were:
>
> - A permanent and impartial civil service;
> - Accountable to Ministers who are in turn accountable to Parliament;
> - Recruitment and promotion on merit;
> - Based on self-sufficiency, i.e. largely developing its own talent with a presumption of one employer for a whole career;
> - Providing services from within with little outsourcing;
> - Highly federal, organised into departments each of whom [sic] has a Secretary of State accountable to Parliament.

Turnbull believed these principles were fundamental to Westminster civil services.

Turnbull also noted there was a price to pay. This constitutional bureaucracy produced a 'closed world' that was 'hierarchical and inflexible'. It was slow to change and draw on external talent or use outsourcing. It gave little priority to the development of leadership, and had few incentives to improve efficiency. The service was also 'too reliant on the skills of those recruited many years earlier, leaving it underpowered when requirements changed' (Turnbull 2005, 2–3).

His direct appeal to, and criticism of, Northcote–Trevelyan is interesting because the report was silent on many of the principles Turnbull itemizes. Myth becomes synonymous with tradition.[5] For example, apart from the term 'Permanent Civil Service' mentioned in the introduction, the report does not mention permanency or defend the case for it. Nor are key attributes such as anonymity or impartiality discussed. The civil service is valued for having 'sufficient independence', but this is not expressed as demonstrating apolitical values. There is no mention of self-sufficiency, although the report did allow for both recruitment from outside and for the dismissal of the indolent. Nor is the civil service's accountability to ministers mentioned or explored. The authors content themselves with the comment that officials occupy 'a position duly subordinate to that of the Ministers who are directly responsible to the Crown and to Parliament'.

Turnbull's appeal to Northcote–Trevelyan attempts to identify and preserve the virtues of the traditional civil service in the face of recent challenges. His message is code for continuity, rather than fundamental change. It represents a reinterpretation of administrative traditions by an administrative elite coping with present-day uncertainties and, in the process, defending *their* understanding of *their* administrative traditions. Put another way, Turnbull was projecting his version of the eternal verities of a constitutional bureaucracy. He was also critical of those inside government who did not share his view or his preferred ways of working. He described Chancellor Gordon Brown's operating style as 'sheer Stalinist ruthlessness' (Timmins 2007).[6] Brown was perceived as challenging the sanctity of the administrative tradition; Turnbull was defending it against such attacks.

The views expressed in Turnbull's reinterpretation are not idiosyncratic. Similar statements have been made by previous cabinet secretaries who were themselves coping with earlier bouts of reform. For example, the White Paper *The Civil Service. Continuity and Change* (Cm 2627 1994) claims that the Northcote–Trevelyan Report set out the principles that continue to underlie the civil service. According to the then head of the civil service, Sir Robin Butler, they were 'integrity, impartiality, objectivity, selection and promotion on merit and accountability through Ministers to Parliament' (cited in Cm 2627 1994, para 2.7, p. 8; see also Wilson 2003, 366–7). So, Northcote–Trevelyan is employed as a myth set up as an ideal and used as a defence of the civil service, less to resist change and more to select the parts that fit with existing departmental philosophies.

Australia

The Westminster notion of a non-partisan bureaucracy subordinate to ministers is a long-accepted feature of Australian government.[7] The Royal Commission on Australian Government Administration (RCAGA), headed by H. C. Coombs, a public servant who was nominated as Australian of the Century in 1988, starts by commenting:

> This system has traditionally been identified and described as an example of the Westminster system. The Commission has become increasingly aware of the degree to which the Australian system in fact differs from the Westminster model and of the significance for the administration of such differences. (RCAGA 1976, para 2.1.2)

Its definition was that:

> The Westminster model envisages a government chosen from elected representatives and responsible and accountable to them. It presents the bureaucracy as simply an extension of the minister's capacity; it exists to inform and advise him; to manage on his behalf programs for which he is responsible. Except where Parliament specifically legislated otherwise, its power to make decisions or to act derives entirely from the minister by his delegation and he remains responsible to his Cabinet colleagues and to Parliament for decisions made and actions performed under that delegation. (RCAGA 1976, para 2.1.4)

The Australian public service has long accepted this interpretation of their position. Ask departmental secretaries about their relations with ministers and they often say: 'I'm a traditionalist. I believe in the Westminster system'. They mean they are non-partisan and work solely for the minister (Weller and Grattan 1981, 69; see also Weller 2001). Ministerial supremacy was a given.

However, after a series of recent scandals[8] in which the professionalism of the public service was called into dispute, senior officials drew on interpretations of Westminster to defend their position and responsiveness to ministers. So, Peter Shergold, Andrew Turnbull's Australian counterpart, lamented in a speech, entitled *Once was Camelot in Canberra?*, that recent critics of public administration in Australia thought Westminster was now dead and no longer found in the administration. He summarized the critics' case thus:

> The current view is that 'accountability and responsibility Westminster-style no longer exist' and that the public service has been tarnished by 'politicisation, intimidation and demoralisation'. The public service, and particularly those who head it, now lack the fearlessness and courage of [their predecessors]. Instead, behind layers of secrecy, has been built a rotten edifice of 'plausible deniability', designed to protect Ministers from unpleasant or inconvenient truths. (Shergold 2004*a*, 4)

Shergold referred several times in his speech to the Westminster legacy. Most references were used as an anchor for his argument and to dispel contrary views:

> It is too often forgotten that a Westminster system depends on expectations of confidentiality. (Shergold 2004*a*, 4)

> Australia may be rightly proud of its Westminster tradition but Canberra is far more open to scrutiny than Whitehall. Over the last generation there has been a profound increase in the extent to which public decision-making can be accessed and examined. (Shergold 2004*a*, 5)

> I do not fear that the particular and distinctive role of the ministerial staffer will bring about the demise of an independent public service or destroy the Westminster tradition. (Shergold 2004*a*, 12)

To Shergold, Australia's Westminster system was less precisely defined and constantly adapting (Shergold 2004*b*). He talked of Westminster 'systems', 'traditions', and 'styles', all in the same speech. He argued that its past ideals, variously constructed, were still alive and well, and in some cases they were more robust now than previously. He not only recognized the imperative to accommodate and anticipate change, but also warned against distorting the picture by simplistic or idealized versions drawn from perceptions of previous eras. He disputed that only former heads were frank and fearless. His message was that there was never a 'Camelot' in Canberra.

His version of the administrative traditions stressed that Westminster was an evolving system involving relations of trust. It was based on balances and counterbalances of power and position, roles and responsibilities, and ideas and advice. To him, administrative law and new public management were enhancements to Westminster not threats to it. While he eschewed the term 'constitutional bureaucracy', his argument for an evolving continuity was a plea for 'the preservation of a shared tradition' (Shergold 2004*a*, 15).

Canada

In Canada, the Privy Council Office's (PCO) submission to the Royal Commission on Financial Management and Accountability explained the foundations of Canadian constitutional government.[9] Its submission, entitled *Responsibility in the Constitution*, commenced with the proposition: 'Our system of government, deriving from British and pre- and post-federation practice, is ministerial in character' (PCO 1993, 1.1). It traced precedents back to the earliest constitutional developments of the Middle Ages: 'The system faithfully reflects the evolution of constitutional responsibility stretching back to Magna Carta and beyond' (PCO 1993, 1.21). Many of the early references to precedent were to British writers. The PCO drew on British traditions, while delineating Canadian adaptation and practice.

More recently, a commission of inquiry held over 2004–6 into the 'Sponsorships Scandal',[10] led by Judge John Gomery, examined the behaviour of the civil service. Gomery criticized the lack of formal accountability in the system. He disagreed with officials on the meaning of conventions. He wrote in his final report that the 'government expresses the belief "that the public service has no independent identity, and hence no accountability apart from that of Ministers and the government of the day"' (Gomery 2006, 62). Instead, he agreed with one of his academic advisers, Lorne Sossin, who argued forcefully that

> [a] range of unwritten constitutional conventions and principles clearly give rise to obligations, responsibilities and constraints on decision-making by members of the public service which arguably together confer constitutional status on the public service as an organ of government. (Sossin 2006, 30)

Gomery's interpretation was a response to a host of senior Canadian public service executives appearing before the commission who used the opportunity to defend their record with a restatement of the traditional verities of their profession. They evoked the principles of Westminster to explain their behaviour and that of ministers in the scandal. Some used Westminster conventions to lay responsibility squarely on the shoulders of ministers, while others wielded their understandings of Westminster to shield themselves from direct accountability.

In contrast to Australia, key actors in the Canadian government do not often explicitly articulate traditions of Westminster – principally because it would imply English cultural dominance over French sensitivities. Canadians talk of 'responsible and representative government', derived from parliamentary practice (Jackson and Jackson 2006, 35–51). However, in the context of the inquiry, a number of senior officials described the Canadian variant of Westminster as they interpreted it. The former Clerk of the Privy Council, Jocelyne Bourgon, in her testimony to the Commission on 8 and 9 December 2004, spoke of the strength of the 'parliamentary accountability system' in which a minister 'assumes full ministerial responsibility' (cited in Gomery 2004*b*, 8162 and 8257). Ministers were accountable for every decision, while public servants were only accountable for the advice they gave or for 'personal responsibilities'. In her view, 'we're always responsible for advice we may have given, good or bad, for lack of courage in not giving any when it needed to be given. We're responsible for our personal actions' (cited in Gomery 2004*b*, 8257).

Alex Himelfarb, the Clerk of the Privy Council and Secretary to the Cabinet at the time of the inquiry, in his testimony before the Commission on 27 September 2004, stressed that the Canadian public service was one of the variety of 'Westminster systems' each with slight differences in convention and law:

> The public service has a long tradition of continuity. It precedes and often exists longer than a government of the day. So it brings all of that accumulative knowledge of the processes, of the procedures, of the conventions to bear on its advice. It provides a degree of continuity that political advice doesn't. It also has particular responsibilities by tradition. (Cited in Gomery 2004*a*, 1835–6)

He argued that the public service had to remain 'non-partisan' in its provision of advice and in implementing policies (cited in Gomery 2004*a*, 1833). Continuity gave the public service specific duties and responsibilities – to advise the minister as best they could independently. But elected officials 'are ultimately responsible for everything that happens in their portfolio or department under mandate' (cited in Gomery 2004*a*, 1905). He defended a precise definition of ministerial responsibility by stating:

> The principle of ministerial responsibility in the Westminster system is that a minister would be answerable in parliament for everything in their mandate even for things over which they have no authority; in fact, for decisions that they may be obligated not to interfere with. (Cited in Gomery 2004*a*, 1889)

Himelfarb contrasted legal responsibility ('to our superiors through the hierarchy of government and, ultimately, to parliament') with ethical responsibility ('to report wrongdoing even if you don't have the authority'). Although he commented that 'every public servant coming across wrongdoing has a larger responsibility', he reflected that there was a 'lacuna' in the system that left 'enormous space for judgment and courage' (cited in Gomery 2004*a*, 1934). However, when Gomery argued that the civil service should have constitutional independence when ministerial instructions were deemed illegal or unethical, several ministers and civil servants wrote to the prime minister disagreeing and restating the orthodox view. The prime minister agreed with them, so orthodoxy rules.

Again, the appeal to notions of Westminster serves more than its ostensible purpose of describing the system. Himelfarb and colleagues were answering from the dock under oath, emphasizing the inherent ambiguity of Westminster administrative traditions, but insisting that lines of responsibility still exist. They stressed the ambiguities because otherwise they could be accused of reneging on their professional responsibilities. Westminster is, therefore, variously an ideal, an explanation, and a defence all rolled into the same expressions of principle and convention. In the face of this barrage, which was also aimed at NPM's reinvention of the public service, it was an appropriate time to explain that not all had changed.

Conclusions

Such appeals to Westminster from the heads of the respective civil services do not imply that nothing has changed. Some academics have recently portrayed the systems as radically changed. Savoie (2003) writes about the fracturing of the implicit agreement or 'bargain' between politicians and civil servants. Campbell and Wilson (1995) write about the end of Whitehall. Mulgan (2006) talks of 'undue partisanship' by public servants straining the principles of Westminster. The pictures they paint are apocalyptic. The old principles have been rejected, and the new precepts, according to academic critics, lack accountability and principle.

We do not share this doomsday vision. Rather, we see traditions under challenge that reshape reforms as reforms reshape them. Indeed, what some academics see as revolutionary and discomforting, the practitioners see as evolutionary and normal adaptation. The latter are reflecting on what specific legacies are important to them and the parts of the managerial public sector systems they will run with. Patently, the new public management tradition is not a total replacement for traditional Westminster ideas. It is grafted on to the previous set of beliefs. So, the generalist public service tradition had to be – and was – rescued by reinvention. And in the process of reinvention, practitioners are being candid and making myths at the same time. For their voice to carry conviction it must appeal to shared beliefs and practices. For their message to resonate, it must inspire, so the appeal is to the glories of the past and the public service as the heir to the generalist tradition.

The rise of the new public management in its various guises in the 1980s led to recurring challenges to administrative traditions for the next two decades. In early stages of these reforms, senior public servants would not have referred to their traditions and such nineteenth-century notions as permanence and impartiality. These ideas would have sounded anachronistic, self-serving, and reactionary. The mood of the day stressed the need for the 'can-do manager', motivated by results-based achievement, managerial competence, and performance-driven commitment. New public management arrived, and was eagerly embraced by a professional public service and talk of Westminster was largely suspended by the architects of reform.

Today, the pendulum has swung too far for many (see Podger 2007) and these same civil servants are prepared to discuss whether – or how far – we have moved from Westminster, and from the Northcote–Trevelyan ideals. Current and former heads of the civil service have each mused about which aspects of their respective traditions still survive, how the traditions shape today's practices, and how Westminster traditions provide both a defence from powerful critics and coping mechanisms for future changes. So in the 2000s, historical legacies are increasingly seen as important. Thus, Shergold (2004*a*, 8) was anxious to stress today's continuity with the previous norms of the public service but in different contexts:

> The Westminster tradition today, just as fifty years ago, refers to a complex set of balanced relationships, marked by subtleties and nuances. For that reason the sign of a good Secretary is not marked alone by the independence of his mind or the robustness of her advice. Rather it is indicated by the extent to which they fully appreciate the respective roles of elected government and appointed public servant. Nowhere is the necessary balance of Secretarial responsibility better articulated than in the key public service value set out in the bipartisan *Public Service Act 1999*, namely that: 'The APS [Australian Public Service] is responsible to the Government in providing frank, honest, comprehensive, accurate and timely advice and in implementing the Government's policies and programmes'.

In addition, the set of ideas and myths surrounding, say, Northcote–Trevelyan are called upon as a means of legitimizing change and defending practices. It is resistance, albeit by gentlemen and writ small. Turnbull, Shergold, and Himelfarb each defended the confluence of political and nonpartisan advice to ministers. There was benefit in having separate 'political' advice at the centre while preserving the expertise of bureaucratic advisers. Himelfarb stated that 'good policy' emerged from the combination of political advice from the Prime Minister's Office (PMO) and a non-partisan source of advice from the Privy Council. He argued that the PMO has

> a Policy Research Unit where they assess a range of issues that come to their attention from departments or from the outside in terms of their constituency with the government's overall agenda, and they provide advice independently of the Public Service to the Prime Minister on a range of policy issues that they themselves have researched and assessed, generally in close communication with departments and the PCO [Privy Council Office].... PCO provides non-partisan advice.... PMO provides a political lens on policy advice. It is not duplicative. It often converges as good policy, is often good politics. But the Prime Minister has access to both a political lens, in particular, a partisan political lens, and a non-partisan source of advice often on the same issues. (Cited in Gomery 2004*a*, 1833)

Equally, Turnbull (2005, 3) welcomed 'the fact that we are much more open to ideas from think-tanks, consultancies, governments abroad, special advisers, and front-line practitioners'. He ventured: 'in developing policy we not only consult more widely than we used to but involve outsiders to a far greater degree in the policy making process'. He then quoted Shergold approvingly:

> Let me make it clear that I extol the fact that the public service policy advice is increasingly contested. I welcome it intellectually: our perspectives and strategies benefit from challenge. I also welcome it professionally, as a public servant. In my view, more Ministerial advisers does not represent the 'politicisation of the APS' (Australian Public Service), still less the demise of an independent public service or undermining of the Westminster tradition. (Turnbull 2005, 3)

For civil servants the challenge now is to know whom the minister has consulted, and from what direction they approach the problem. Civil servants now have to justify their involvement and contribution, argue for their expertise, and prove their worth to their political bosses. They are not accepted as merely part of the infrastructure. Indeed, one Canadian political chief of staff challenged the right of bureaucrats to be there at all. He argued they 'should get back to their real job – to implement decisions and see to it that government operations run smoothly and leave policy to us' (cited in Savoie 2003, 124). Alternatively, as one Australian secretary noted, the growth in the number of ministerial advisers

> fundamentally transformed the role of a secretary. I constantly have to compete for the policy attention of the minister with those in the minister's office. No two ways about it; I have to fight for my position at the table. (Cited in Weller 2001, 103)

We are not charting a convergence of traditions in Westminster-derived jurisdictions as they wrestle with new challenges to their understanding of the changing state and their role in it. Rather, we can see empirically that the heads of the civil services have found 'space' or 'voice' to articulate innovative ways of combining past traditions with new organizing principles of governance. In each case, Australia, Canada, and the UK, it is not a question of 'in with the new, out with the old', but of 'in with the new alongside key components of the old'.

The speeches serve a complex of motives. They serve bureaucratic self-interest by defending the standing of the public service. They reassure the troops by identifying continuities. They spot snags. They resist too much change, implemented too soon and too rapidly. They inspire through myth making. They forestall further change by identifying the world that could be lost. They fudge core elements in the Westminster tradition, emphasizing what they want to hold on to. Sometimes, they cling to the myths of Westminster. At other times, they are simply not specific about which aspects they continue to consider legitimate. Sometimes they disagree – while Himelfarb is anxious to hold on to anonymity at all costs, Shergold views the new requirements holding public servants personally to account as a positive attribute to open scrutiny consistent with the Westminster tradition. Turnbull was critical of much of the old trappings of what he saw as the Northcote–Trevelyan legacy, but does not want to discard many of the most important attributes. He cherishes the impartiality of the civil service; the greater degree of permanency than Australia; the close accountability between ministers, officials, and parliament; the promotion of staff by merit; and the advantages of departments as non-statutory organizations of state. Innovation is central to preserving traditions. To paraphrase Shergold, if Westminster was never 'Camelot', this does not mean that some of the myths that sustain the Camelot legend do not remain germane to the modern public service.

Notes

1. Central government ministerial codes and guidelines exist in Australia (Department of Prime Minister and Cabinet 1998); Canada (Treasury Board of Canada Secretariat 2008); and the United Kingdom (Cabinet Office 2007*a*, 2007*b*).
2. For the collective portrait of these senior officials (such as Oscar Skelton, Clifford Clark, Norman Robertson, Graham Towers, Lester Pearson, Louis Rasminsky, Mitchell Sharp, and Robert Bryce), see Granatstein (1982) and Savoie (2003, 62–9). Interestingly, many of these senior administrators made the transition into elected office, becoming ministers and, in Pearson's case, prime minister.
3. See, for example, Weller (2001, 37–52 and 183–88; and 2007, 100 and 113). There is no collective study of the 'Seven Dwarfs' (Henry Bland, Alan Brown, H. C. Coombs, John Crawford, Richard Randall, Frederick Shedden, and Roland Wilson), but some individual studies include Coombs (1981), Cornish (2002), Horner (2000), and Rowse (2002).
4. For a more detailed account of the origins of Britain's 'constitutional bureaucracy', see Chapman and Greenaway (1980), Chester (1981), MacDonagh (1977), Parris (1969), and Rhodes (1994).
5. We are indebted to Rodney Lowe (2005) for his seminar at the Australian National University on 'Western Public Administration and the Myth of Northcote Trevelyan', 12 October. The ideas in this paragraph were developed as a result of his seminar.
6. Turnbull said about Gordon Brown's style of leadership: 'There has been the absolute ruthlessness with which Gordon Brown has played the denial of information as an instrument of power. He has maintained an iron grip on spending and on the distribution to departments. ... Do those ends justify the means? It has enhanced Treasury control, but at the expense of any government cohesion and any assessment of strategy. You can choose whether you are impressed or depressed by that, but you cannot help admire the sheer Stalinist ruthlessness of it all' (Timmins 2007).
7. For a more detailed account of the origins of Australia's 'constitutional bureaucracy' and administrative professionalism, see Caiden (1967, 1990), and Finn (1987).
8. Three significant scandals raising issues of propriety and professionalism by both ministers and officials impacted on Australian politics between 2001 and 2006. These were the 'children overboard' affair, where convenient untruths were told and left uncorrected (Weller 2002; Marr and Wilkinson 2003); the scandals over wrongful detention by the Immigration department (Palmer 2005); and the Australian Wheat Board Ltd scandal in which (known) kickbacks were paid to the Iraqi regime under Saddam Hussein and covered up (Botterill 2007).

9. For a more detailed account of the origins of Canada's 'constitutional bureaucracy', see Sossin (2006), but also note Aucoin's depiction (1995, 30) of the Canadian bureaucracy as the 'administrative state' that was supposed to remain 'constitutionally subordinate to its political masters', but was often perceived to have 'become an independent power in its own right'.
10. The 'sponsorship scandal' refers to the Canadian federal government's 'sponsorship program' in the province of Quebec, established originally as an effort to raise awareness of the Government of Canada's contributions to Quebec industries and other activities and counter the efforts of Quebec's Parti Québécois government to promote Quebec separatism. For more information see: http://www.cbc.ca/news/background/groupaction/gomeryreport_phaseone.html (last accessed 30 July 2009).

Chapter 9

Bringing People Back In

Introduction

This chapter explores how customers, employees, and managers of the English state understand the managerial rationalities of the past two decades. We tell three stories based on factions, elite interviews, and fieldwork. The first story takes the form of three factions based on the files of a local authority in Northern England and written by the social workers involved. After discussing the drafts with the social workers, we edited them. They then agreed the version produced below. All names have been changed to protect the anonymity of customers,[1] the social workers, and the local authority. The second story takes the form of extracts from interviews with the Chair of a Primary Care Trust (PCT) in the English National Health Service. To resort to shorthand, he represents the 'new public management' in the UK public sector. We discuss how he understands the managerial rationalities of New Labour. The published text was the product of negotiations with the manager. The reader hears his 'voice' filtered through our selection of extracts and the subsequent negotiations. The extract is an agreed construction of how he saw his world. The final story is based on fieldwork in a government office. We observed how the Private Offices of Ministers and Permanent Secretaries coped with the management tasks they confronted. Here, we tell a confessional, impressionistic tale as in Chapter 6. In all three stories, our aim is to show that there are significant differences in the way the rationality of managerialism is experienced and understood. These different narratives are stories of resistance in that they show either the several understandings of central intentions or the unintended consequences arising from the local reasoning of many individuals. Such stories are central to understanding what elites term the 'implementation gap' in the reform of public services.

Customers

Case 1: Mr. and Mrs. R – familiar faces

Mr. and Mrs. R live in a two-bedroom house in the suburbs of a town with a population of some 200,000. Mr. R is 83 years old, and wheelchair bound following a stroke six months ago. Mrs. R is 79 years old, still active mentally and physically but not strong enough to help with her husband's personal care without help from one other person.

For the past six months, they have had a care assistant from a private agency to help Mr. R with getting up, toileting, washing and dressing every morning. A local authority Home Help calls at lunch to help with toileting, and personal care tasks if necessary. The Home Help also calls twice weekly to do shopping, as Mrs. R can't leave Mr. R, because he gets distressed when left on his own. Mr. R has a catheter that is managed by his wife and checked by a Community Nurse twice weekly. Three nights a week (Friday, Saturday, and Sunday) a private agency care assistant calls to help Mr. R to go to bed. The local authority's Home Help service assists on the four remaining evenings a week. The evening call can take place any time from 7.00 pm to 9.00 pm depending on daily demand on staff. The local authority care manager arranged and purchased the private agency.

Mr. and Mrs. R moved their double bed into the lounge because the bathroom is downstairs at the back of the kitchen and Mr. R cannot get upstairs. They live and entertain in their small kitchen. Mr. R cannot get out without being lifted because there are three steep steps at the front and at the back of the house that make it difficult to install a ramp.

To make themselves more comfortable their care manager suggested moving to a new comfortable sheltered housing complex in the centre of town. They have an offer of a one-bedroom flat with a kitchen and living room on the first floor. There are lifts. There is a communal room with regular activities.

Mr. R would be able to move freely around the flat and use the kitchen, as the units are wheelchair height. He would be able to use the lift and attend the activities at the communal room. He would need assistance at home for personal care. Mrs. R would be able to get out to do some shopping while her husband is joining in the communal activities. She would not be so isolated, as she would be able to join in the communal activities with her husband.

Mr. R will not consider looking at the flat until he knows he can have the same carer from a private agency who calls every morning. This will not be possible because his care arrangements will be provided by different locally based staff. His wife needs help to explain this. The Home Care Manager responsible for the new area visits the couple to reassure Mr. R that he and his wife will get all the help that they need. The couple visit the new flat and accept the offer.

Case 2: Mrs. T – whose choices?

Mrs. T is 80 years old, and arthritic. Her local GP has referred her case, asking for Home Help. She lives on her own in a bungalow. She uses a walking frame to help with walking. She can no longer manage pans and cooking for herself. She was coping well until she fell five days previously, fracturing her wrist. She visited the hospital casualty department for treatment on the wrist and was discharged home. A friend has been helping but she is elderly and finding the constant help that Mrs. T needs too much of a struggle for her.

The Home Care Manager visits and assesses Mrs. T. She is slow and finds holding the frame difficult because of the arthritis in her hands and fractured wrist. She has difficulty with washing, dressing, toileting, bathing, preparing food, cooking, and shopping.

The friend who calls in has been cooking and shopping and helping with personal care. She would still like to visit her friend twice a week and will do small amounts of shopping and get Mrs. T's pension when she gets her own. Mrs. T's three children all live away from their hometown, have their own families and work. The eldest expects to retire in the next year. The family arranged to take turns to visit on Sundays, keep the house and garden tidy and in good repair.

The Home Care Manager asks for an urgent visit from the Occupational Therapy Services to assess Mrs. T for equipment for daily living. While waiting for this assessment a Home Help will call at mealtimes and help with dressing in the morning. The friend will call about 7.00 pm to help with undressing.

Two days later an Occupational Therapy Assistant (OTA) calls to assess for equipment to help with daily living. Mrs. T can eat with special cutlery and a plate guard. She can manage a cup of tea with a kettle tipper if it is laid out for her. Mrs. T can manage toast or cereal for breakfast if put out beforehand. Tea is manageable with bread, butter, cheese, or cold meats. Mrs. T can manage her gas cooker with the help of replacement dials. The kitchen is well organized. With a perching stool she can sit at the work surface next to the cooker to eat her meals. She can wash and dress herself with equipment but needs help with doing up buttons, laces, and zips and putting on stockings. With carefully selected clothing from the wardrobe, Mrs. T will need minimum help to dress and undress. She needs a raised toilet seat and frame in the bathroom and a bath board on the bath with a grab rail on the wall. The equipment, except the grab rail, is provided later that day. An emergency warden call system will be installed by the end of the week by the local authority's housing services. The Gas Board will call within 48 hours to replace the dials on the cooker.

The Home Care Manager rearranges the Home Help. She provides a morning call from her own services Monday to Friday, and arranges a private agency on Saturdays. The Home Help will help with buttons and to collect shopping and pension or to do some basic cleaning. They will do the laundry and ironing. One hour a day is allowed. The home carer helps Mrs. T to use her bath board to have a bath one morning a week. Breakfast and tea are laid out and the kettle is filled for the day. A twilight service will call any time between 7.00 and 9.00 p.m. Monday to Saturday to help with undressing; fifteen minutes are allowed. These services are arranged and purchased by the Home Care Manager.

The Women's Royal Voluntary Service (WRVS) delivers Meals-on-Wheels Mondays and Fridays. Frozen meals are cooked at a local primary school and delivered by the Home Help. On Saturdays Mrs. T will treat herself to a meal cooked and delivered by a local hotel.

Mrs. T does not get out at all and with increasing disability does not feel that she can consider going out. She is isolated. Various local centres have activities for the elderly run either by the local authority or by voluntary agencies such as Age Concern, which runs a post-hospital discharge support service. Used to her own company, Mrs. T is nervous about mixing with others. She is so grateful for all the help she gets she does not want to be a nuisance and does not like to ask for information and more help. She also has no savings, getting only her pension. The Home Care Manager is busy and now all the arrangements are in place will make a quick visit to check every six months.

The social worker concerned wondered if Mrs. T's quality of life would be improved if a social worker assessed her. Is the quality of Mrs. T's life improved by the range of services provided by the Home Care Manager and OTA? Social workers may have other resources at their fingertips. Could someone take her to a local lunch club or a day centre? She may like playing bingo or whist. What about a stay in a residential home or a holiday with her friend perhaps? Is Mrs. T entitled to more money? What about Income Support, Attendance Allowance, and Council Tax Benefit? Would Mrs T have more choice about the services she would like if she had more income? Would she have to pay more for some of the services?

Case 3: Mrs. K – 'seems like a railway station'

Mrs. K was admitted to the local psychiatric hospital having become aggressive towards her daughter. Mrs. K was 78 years old, and had been suffering from dementia for two years. She lived alone in a large detached Victorian house in a village some 10 miles from the local town.

Before admission, Mrs. K's family, particularly her daughter and two children, visited daily and Mrs. K had been coping well. The GP and Consultant Psycho-Geriatrician kept in regular contact with the family and a community psychiatric nurse visited once a week. Mrs. K attended the specialist day hospital one day a week and the local elderly persons' day care centre one day a week. The social services Home Help service called in the morning (Monday–Friday) to see that Mrs. K was dressed, breakfasted, and ready for any transport that would be calling. On the days Mrs. K was at home, the Home Help called at lunchtime to make sure that she had eaten the hot meal delivered by WRVS or the Home Help (prepared at the local elderly persons home). The family called in at teatime and again later in the evening to check Mrs. K was all right. Mrs. K tended not to sleep at night and would telephone neighbours in the middle of the night for help. She had been known to wander out in the middle of the night disturbing the neighbours.

To give the family a break, Mrs. K was admitted to the local elderly persons' home for a two-week short stay. After two days, Mrs. K became confused and disorientated, demanding to go home. The home manager became concerned when Mrs. K began to wander outdoors, something she had not done while attending day care. Mrs. K hit a member of staff who had tried to escort her indoors. A decision was made to allow Mrs. K to go to the day hospital as usual and arrangements were made for her to return home.

On returning home Mrs. K became even more disorientated, wanting to return to her home to be with 'mummy and daddy'. She hit her daughter when her daughter tried to take her around the house to convince her that she was at home. The daughter broke down saying that the family could no longer cope and that she could not allow her children to visit if Mrs. K was going to be violent.

The Consultant visited and decided that Mrs. K needed reassessment and a review of her medication. She was admitted to the psychiatric hospital. The assessment showed that Mrs. K's condition had deteriorated rapidly into a delusional and challenging phase. No long-term beds were available from the health trust but, with the correct medication, Mrs. K's condition and behaviour could be reasonably well controlled. Mrs. K was referred for permanent care to the social services care manager attached to the hospital.

The care manager decided that Mrs. K needed 24-hour supervision and assistance with all aspects of daily living and personal care. The care manager discussed this with the family who were clearly distressed at the idea of nursing home care for Mrs. K. With the new medication, Mrs. K was less aggressive and they believed that they could manage with a full package of care for Mrs. K. They insisted that Mrs. K returned home.

The Care Plan was complicated and expensive. Cover for each hour of 24 hours was worked out for two-week blocks. The Care Plan involved the health trust's psychiatric day services, private nursing home day care, private agency home care, voluntary home care sitting services, social services home care, and several transport services supporting the daughter to provide 24-hour care at home. The social services felt that it would be more cost-effective for Mrs. K to go into a nursing home. Following recent case law, the local authority was within its rights to offer nursing home care to meet the need. They could have asked the family to supplement the cost of the care.

Because there were continuing health care issues, the care manager was able to secure funding from the joint-finance continuing care fund for the first four weeks. The care manager was unhappy about the arrangements because it is widely known, and particularly in the case of Mrs. K, that constant changes in carers and location add to disorientation and confusion for people with dementia.

The daughter was concerned that she would have to give up work and asked if a private agency could be bought in for the equivalent amount of money. This would not help. There would continue to be many carers visiting. The house would seem like 'a railway station' with so many people calling.

The arrangements were set up on discharge but quickly become difficult to manage as Mrs. K would not attend day care some days and more care had to be bought in from the private home care agency. There were frequent problems with maintaining regular home care support with home carers being ill, late, or not turning up and replacements being difficult to find in a rural area. Mrs. K's son and daughter-in-law did what they could to help but they did not live locally and were not as committed as their sister.

After one month, the care manager decided to approach Community Service Volunteers (CSV), a national volunteer agency that provides young volunteers as full-time live-in carers. Four weeks later, two young volunteers began providing 24-hour care and supervision for Mrs. K. The care plan covered a three-week block with supplementary help for the CSVs. The cost of the care was similar. Two months later the young volunteers were feeling the stresses and strains of caring full time for an elderly person with dementia. They were fighting among themselves and one young person began taking the medication prescribed for Mrs. K and drinking alcohol. She was asked to leave.

One week later Mrs. K died.

Managers: 'we are in the shit if we don't'

This story is from an interview with the Chair of a Primary Care Trust (PCT). He has been in post for less than a year. He is soberly dressed and the interview is businesslike. It takes place in his study in his modern house in an exclusive housing development aimed at the executive and professional classes. We sit at opposite sides of the table. His job is to provide strategic leadership for the primary care sector of the National Health Service (NHS). Primary care comprises the services provided in a specific geographic area by family or general practitioners and the community health services, such as midwifery, which look after people in their own homes. The account is in the manager's own words. We have edited it into a continuous text. At a few points we have left our questions or prompts in the text (marked **Q**). The backcloth against which the manager speaks is New Labour's public sector reforms. We described in Chapter 5, the shift from first-wave to second-wave governance. New Labour accepted the first-wave account that managerialism and marketization had the unintended consequence of fragmenting the systems for delivering public services. Its response was to bring the state back in by promoting networks, partnerships, and joined-up government (Bevir 2005, chapter 2). The manager had to find ways of putting this general initiative by the central state into local practice.

> *Our major partner is the local authority as a whole, not just social services. One of the first people I met was the chief executive of a local authority. I rang him up and said I'd like to see him and he and the leader of the local authority came round to see me. The chief executive talks about the town and, I mean, he is strongly committed to the notion of the local authority as community leader but is very, very keen to have as many meetings as possible outside the local authority offices. One of the first things I talked to them about was developing a common planning capacity to support the community plan. We are a small organization and I'm keen for us to play a part right across the community because the potential impact of what they do on us is great and vice versa. Within a few weeks they asked me if I would be the vice-chair of the community safety partnership and that, it turned out, was really to chair it because the person who chairs it, who is the former leader of the local authority, was never there. Whenever I've been there, which is three times now, I've chaired it. So, yeah, they were very keen to get us into things like that. I knew the former director of social services very well. He moved on to a job in the Department of Health at Christmas. Yeah, I've known him for years and years, and I guess he knows a lot about what I've done in the past and I'm sure he's passed that on to people in the local authority.*

I certainly see the director of the community services, who is the chief officer responsible for community safety, regularly. I see the guy who – he has chief officer status – is responsible for the local strategic partnership in the community plan. There's a lot of issues about mental health and crime and only this week I discovered a whole set of issues around prison health. We primarily meet in a partnership group. It is one of five task groups. It reports to the overall local strategic partnership. The local strategic partnership is the overarching liaison, strategic, planning mechanism that brings together all the elements of the community plan, but if we need to have a one-to-one, yes. For example, I wanted to see the local commander and again he came around to the office for about an hour just to chat.

Apart from the local authority and the community plan, the other key actors are the provider trusts and in our case there is an acute trust, a mental health and learning disabilities trust. Then, in addition, there's the whole primary care sector. Obviously in some respects they are major providers but in the main they are still independent contractors and they are not on a contract with us, but they are our partners, they are part of the trust.

There are separate meetings of all the chief executives, and there are separate meetings of all the chairs, though as a result of a proposal I made at the last chairs' meeting, we're going to have some joint meetings. But most of the business is done through bilaterals. There are some exceptions that sort of prove the rule, like there was a review of acute services. There is the financial agreement each year, what's called the Service and Financial Framework (SAFF), which is certainly the centre of the financial frameworks. Essentially that's where each purchaser agrees with the local providers what the envelope cash is in the coming year, and what targets they will meet in terms of delivering their services, and that is a politicized process with a small 'p', which has been brokered by the health authority. This year because there are lots of deals that have to be done around the two big acute trusts – which have implications for the rest of the services, as they tend to swallow up a lot of the growth – those deals have to be brokered on an area-wide basis.

The health authority is also a major actor. We have to sign an annual accountability agreement with it. The essential element of it is that we will meet the targets laid down in the national NHS plan. We meet them on a quarterly basis. There's the regional office of the NHS executive, to which we are accountable via the health authority. Our provider trusts are directly accountable to the regional office. The regional office has to broker the SAFFs if the health authority can't do it, and the regional offices in our region put a lot of pressure on the health authorities to get everything signed up by the end of March. The regional office monitors us through the quarterly returns that we make to the health authority and then the regional office monitors the health authority.

I mentioned the meetings of the chairs of the trust and the health authority. The first meeting I went to, it was absolutely clear that we've got a major problem with the East acute trust, which has been built up to provide regional specialties. It was saying that it couldn't meet its cost reduction targets and if it can't do that, then there is no growth money available to use to develop some other areas of service in which I'm strongly interested. So I've used a combination of informal lobbying of some of the other chairs, plus the meetings to say, 'actually, I don't think we can let this happen'. We can't have the chair of another trust coming along and saying I'm sorry but we're not going to meet these targets. What I've done so far is I have been careful to build up a relationship with the acute provider on the West bank who provides most of our acute services and who also suffers if East gets all this cash; and with the community mental health trust who will lose a lot. You know we've got poor mental health services which I'd like to see improved and there's no way they'll get improved if we can't get this money out of the trust. It hasn't been necessary to take it outside the area so far. It may be, it may be.

Within the town, all the major players work in offices within 10 minutes walk of one another. Domestically and socially, everybody knows where you live and where you went. At the senior level, a number of people meet for lunch and have drinks during the day and things like that. I've met the director of social services to have a pub meal. There is, undoubtedly, a local network which is beginning to self-consciously think about organizing itself, rationalizing a lot of the activities. I think it was Wednesday I was chairing the community safety thing, and we talked about rationalizing the way that youth offending, drugs, and community safety are handled, so now its all going to be within a single framework.

The voluntary or the private sectors are not immensely significant for decision making in the arenas that I operate in. It is not as significant in this area as in some places because of the long tradition of municipal Labourism. If not alive and well, it's still there [laughs]. The voluntary sector is, however, a major player in service delivery although it is not a major player in terms of strategic development.

We have a responsibility to consult with and involve the public in setting priorities and getting feedback about health services and we've got what we call the communications forum, which meets about every two months. We can get as many as 60 people into a meeting. We've invested a lot of time in developing good relationships with a wide range of community groups.

***Q.** There really is a local area network that has to be worked, managed, and learnt?*

***A.** Absolutely. Yes. Every week I will be involved in a meeting with some part of it, which will be a decision-making meeting in the main.*

We haven't talked also about the interrelationship between my other roles because I'm part of national and regional networks by virtue of my job, which plays directly into my PCT role as well.

Q. *You are actually plugging the local network into a bigger network?*

A. *Oh yeah. A very large part of my role is networking, ambassadorial. I was reflecting on this over the last couple of weeks, perhaps partly because we were gonna talk and you know partly because I was reflecting on the job because I've been doing it for a while. It's almost entirely self-managed. There's no requirement on me to make a lot of all my links.*

Q. *What are the benefits and costs of this kind of management?*

A. *The time issue. We have a central government that is behaving proactively in relation to a whole range of issues. So people on the ground are suffering from initiative-itis. The benefits are (long pause). The way I conceive of health, and the role of health organizations, means that it's impossible to achieve any goals without working with and through other organizations and other key actors regionally, and especially locally, and to some extent nationally. It would not be possible to do the work that I do, it wouldn't fulfil the goals I have, unless I was approaching it in that way. I guess I am trying to turn this into more of a managed network. I'm hoping to talk to the chief executive of the local authority in the next week or so about how we can rationalize some of our activities and how we can get this common planning support capacity.*

The cost of it? You know it obviously is time-consuming. I guess if you didn't naturally enjoy this kind of work then it could be difficult – if you were a sort of shrinking violet as it were, did not have the personal qualities that go with this [long pause]. I guess there have to be costs in terms of juggling so many things at the same time. It would be easy to burn out yourself as well as the organization. There's no question about that. So you have to keep it within limits. I can't... I mean... I suppose, to be honest, the honest answer is that it is so new and I'm enjoying it so much that it doesn't have any obvious costs at the moment but over time they may become much more evident.

Q. *Networks presuppose some agreement on values and that agreement on values is very elusive?*

A. *That's absolutely right. There is an agreement on some basic values on the part of most of the people I meet and the major one goes back to the old thing about city pride. You know it's the really old thing; we are working on behalf of the people of the area. There's a public service ethos, there's no doubt about that. Unless we work together, then we can't actually manage ourselves out of some of the difficulties we've got because if you want to do what you want to do, you have to work with them. There's a strong recognition that we are in the shit if we don't.*

The office: 'It's pretty impossible'[2]

This section reports on everyday life in the office. It is a subset of the data on the day in the life of a Minister and we follow the same reporting conventions. The existing literature always talks of the Private Office and focuses on the Minister, the PPS, and his immediate Private Office. Some departments talk of the 'central secretariat', which covers all the Private Offices and the supporting units. We would argue it is more accurate to talk of the department's core executive or 'departmental court' (Rhodes 2009*a*; see also Blunkett 2009). This phrase draws attention to the beliefs and practices of the court, to the court politics surrounding Ministers and senior civil servants, to the competition between Ministers, to the tensions within the court, to conflicts between the sections of the department, and to the relationship between civil servants and SpAds. The term shifts the focus from positions and offices to relationships both inside and outside the department.

One immediate consequence of this shift is that it highlights the size of the court. As well as the Private Office of the Minister, it also comprises ministerial or special advisers (SpAds) who have their own Private Secretary; the Private Offices of Ministers of State; the Permanent Secretary's Private Office, and some permutation of Parliamentary, Correspondence, and Business Support units. So, one department had eight Ministers and about eighty people supporting them. In other words, the PPS not only looks after the Minister but also has the major task of managing the court. It is that task we focus on.

Expectations change. Once upon a yesterday, the budding civil servant learnt on the job. The traditional pattern of training was a series of postings to challenging jobs. In each posting, the high-flyer had a mentor, usually informal, commonly a Principal (now Grade 6 or 7 Deputy Director or Team Leader). Nowadays there is more formal training. One PPS was keenly aware of the challenges of blending old and new.

> *They sent me off to do an MBA at Imperial College, which was a very good experience for me, followed by a short stint working on HR [human resources] strategy and then I got promoted to the Senior Civil Service when I led one of the reviews of the Department and then for 18 months after that I project managed the implementation programme.* [PPS 14/4/04]

He felt the culture in which he had been socialized was

> *much more a new public management [NPM] one. Most of my more senior colleagues have been schooled through the 80s and those people have traditionally always been through policy jobs and have ended up being the mandarins we all recognise, but I'm not a classic old-fashioned mandarin.* [PPS 14/4/04]

He resisted any simple NPM versus mandarin dichotomy, admitting he had some of the features of a mandarin: 'and as I get older I seem to have more'. Nonetheless, he insisted:

> *There is already an understanding that to be an effective civil servant, he's not in it just to be clever, you also have to manage the processes around the delivery of policy.* [PPS 14/4/04]

When we summarized his account as 'twin track' training, combining manager, and mandarin, he commented 'I think it's very fair' [PPS 14/4/04].

So, both the PSS and the PSs have to cope with new ideas about managing the department and its service delivery. Yet managing is not their primary task, which remains looking after the Minister or the Permanent Secretary. One PS found the demands of being a manager frustrating and vented at some length.

> *I find [management] the most challenging bit. That's the bit that I worry about. Managing [the Office] out there is hugely difficult, given the volume of work. The core tasks of the job have to sit alongside your management responsibility. I know exactly what I ought to be doing to be the perfect manager. And short of sacrificing my future health, I physically can't do that; for example, finding time to sit down and have formal 'round the table' meetings. Or knowing there is a particular document on the [internal reform], which everybody has received a copy of, which I ought to be sitting down and talking to them about. Because of time pressures it's impossible to do that. I have to make sure that I have some kind of substitute for it, which is making sure that wherever I can, I give them feedback on how they are doing. I make sure we observe the formal processes, although to be honest, even now it is a struggle. None of them have got completed [performance appraisals] although they all have objectives.... That side is really hard to do justice to. And it's a particular struggle in this [Private Office] compared to other Private Offices in that I am the sole manager of the unit, and I am also the Private Secretary. In other Offices, the Private Secretary will manage two more junior people [APSs] who then manage the most junior people. And the burden of trying to make sure that [the recruits] develop as they should when they are both very new to the job and need simple things explaining to them and need to know how [the Department] operates, why they're here, what the bigger picture is. I mean it just sends me spare sometimes*

> *because I spend the core day helping [the Permanent Secretary] or answering the phone or shuffling papers. If I am spending time with them, then when do I do the notes of meetings, when do I do the stuff that [the Permanent Secretary] wants me to do? It's quite difficult. And the [internal reforms]! What difference does the [internal reform] make to you in your job? Trying to bring that alive to people. It's pretty impossible, to be honest.* [PS 14/11/02]

This commentary sees the Permanent Secretary's Private Office as a separate part of the court. Some PPSs had a different view.

> *We should be looking at ourselves as a team and as a management outfit and talking about how we get together. You see it is important to the way I run it, I think that the whole Private Office thing comes together in this office, and in many ways comes together in my seat. I think it's a bit like jazz.* [PPS 14/4/04]

His metaphor of the Private Office as a jazz band that must allow, even encourage, solos while remaining a coherent ensemble is an illuminating one.

> *There's an old-fashioned way of running a Private Office and I've seen it, and I've worked with Principal Private Secretaries who've done this – you control everything. You can do that. You can do it but I think it's a suboptimal way to do it. In a modern world where you've got all these different bits of information lying around, especially when you've got a switched on Minister like this one, it is desperately suboptimal. Instead what I want to say to colleagues is 'I understand it's a bit frightening, it's a bit brinky, but there are a lot of things going on that I can't see. I'm going to sit here and I'm going to say to you "Let's all play this game together and let's jam together and what we get at the end will sound good". You've got to trust me to be the one in the middle. If people don't trust me then it will break down. And that goes back to what I said about my skill with relationships.* [PPS 14/4/04]

However, this PPS was the only one who so described the Private Office and his tasks. Others had a more circumscribed view, focusing mainly on the needs of the Minister or the Permanent Secretary, not internal management. Individual Private Offices could become isolated: '*I move from my desk to the loo, to the kitchen, to my desk*' [PS 14/11/02]. The PS '*sticks her head down and ignores you*'. The PPS worries that 'people need to realise we are all part of the same team' (Departmental induction video).

As in any Office there are tensions, mainly around the role of the PS, and the culture of long hours.

The turnover of Private Secretaries

Most PPSs agreed there was a problem with the rapid turnover of PSs:

> *We're trying to make it longer now. There's been a policy until relatively recently of getting young, whizzy 'fast streamers' in, who have been placed here rather than through the Department's internal advertising scheme. I have moved away from that and said that we will recruit through the advertising scheme, which apart from anything else means you can fish in a wider pool and you give opportunity to other people who might not normally think about coming into Private Office. I've also stipulated that I want people staying here longer, so 18 months or 2 years.* [PPS 10/8/03]

One PS suggested she was the equivalent of a supply teacher, who irritated the long-stay members of the Private Office with her views about how the Office really ought to work.

> *They always have the knowledge that you are going to go and there is going to be another one coming through. So you know you are just passing through the [Private Office] and they are permanent and you are not. Which I don't think is very healthy and is a big barrier.* [PS 10/4/03]

Others are less temperate:

> ***Q***. *How irritating is it to have all these young men flying through every 18 months to two years? You've had 17; it must have got irritating on occasion?*
> ***A***. *The eager, maniacal, arrogant, little horrors.* [DS 25/4/02]

It is not confined to the PS:

> *There is a tension between the Private Secretary, Diary Secretary half, and the clerical correspondence half (of the departmental court).* [PPS 14/4/04]

The PS side of the court refers to the 'corres girls' and they are not being nice. The correct title should be 'Correspondence Managers' (CM). When we ask about allocating mail, we are told the 'corres girls' have a list of the subjects covered by each PS but '*they ask all the bloody time*'. The 'corres girls' reply '*That's not the way it's done*' [PS 10/4/03].

There are targets for handling mail and they too are a source of stress. The system automatically flags any late responses. There are also cross-departmental targets for dealing with correspondence and they are taken seriously because the Cabinet Office publishes a 'league table' of departmental performance; for example, an MP must have a reply within ten working days. When the Minister was told the Department would not meet its targets, letters were sent to those Ministers who were slow to reply, telling them, 'Come on, up your game'. Even the Prime Minister gets involved:

> *The Prime Minister makes a big thing of correspondence. I go over to No. 10 on a regular basis, every three–six months. They have a seminar over there for all the Correspondence Managers around Whitehall and he always makes a point of coming to speak to us, which he doesn't have to do.* [CM 10/4/03]

The ten-day target proved impossible to meet because of the volume of letters, so the target was changed to fifteen days, which brought the department into line with other large Whitehall departments. The combination of targets, league tables, and prime ministerial interest was a source of pressure and failing to meet the target was a source of stress.

Such tensions are all too common in any Office – a case of 'so it goes'. However, the problems around the PS are more intractable. It is not simply that that they come and go but some, during their short stay, never fit in. We saw one PS struggle. The scene is a mistake that will seem minor to an outsider but mistakes undermine the rationale of the Office. Papers had gone to the Permanent Secretary for the meeting but not to the rest of the Department's Management Board. The PS was upset: 'whenever things go wrong I feel terrible not just because I like to do things right' but because 'I am thinking all the time about not letting him down'. We asked if she received any mentoring – no. There was no regular monitoring or appraisal while learning the job. The PS was learning the preferences of the Permanent Secretary and trying to win his confidence. It seemed obvious to us that the PS was not succeeding.

The PS commented that 'there are people who have been very close to [the Permanent Secretary]', who are 'finding it hard to let go of that personal relationship', so 'they service the [Permanent Secretary] directly'. In other words, the Diary Secretary (DS) went direct to the Permanent Secretary and ignored the PS. On a couple of occasions, the DS simply refused to do what the PS asked. The PS was 'only just beginning to relax' and to act on the problem; 'I have set up some team building events'. The PS's confidence was shaken: 'I do have access to him, and I can put something in the diary *if she (the DS) will let me*' (emphasis added). When we asked about her successes in the job, she um-ed and ah-ed before saying, 'I guess I have established myself as Private Secretary' [PS 21/5/02].

By this time we knew everyone in the Office well. We nattered about this and that, including 'teamwork'; the preferred, understated euphemism for the Office's little local difficulties. No one was prepared to criticize the PS. And no one helped. The PS was flailing and failing, so everyone else backed off. The body language was stiff. Much was said with glances between desks. The language was determinedly polite. The Private Office coped by keeping its distance. When the PS asked if everyone had had a lunch break, they all said 'yes', but none had and she must have known that. At one point, we asked her why her desk faced the wall instead of the Office. The next day she had turned the desk to face the Office, and there was a deal of muttering. Distance had been breached. Now the glances between desks had to be rationed. When we returned to this Private Office on a repeat visit, the PS was gone. Why? She had done the usual stint in the Private Office and returned to the Department. It was a short stint and rapid return.

Such problems can prompt drastic action. Another Private Office member commented, 'We have had two horrors', referring to Private Secretaries. So,

> *We call 'total honesty sessions'. You basically shut the door and it's 'no holds barred', no recrimination, no repercussion and everybody gets it off their chest. They say 'I can't stand what you do and the way you do it'. And the times we've had to do it with some of the Private Secretaries, it actually worked, and some of the people that we've done it with I am still friends with.* [DS 25/4/03]

Long hours' culture

As one Minister of State observed:

> My girls in the office are working all hours and it is not fair to them. It's all right for me. I asked for it but they didn't. (Currie 1989, 19)

There is an entrenched culture of long hours that has repercussions for recruitment, training, and morale.[3]

> *It's the culture of the [Private Office]. You can't, you couldn't, it's so busy, the volume of business within the [Private Office], you couldn't work on a 9–5 basis. You just couldn't.* [DS 20/5/02]

Long hours and the related stress are harder to manage at the lower end of the departmental hierarchy:

> *when I was up here before it was stressful and I remember when, just before Christmas, I went home and I was very upset because I just found it so stressful and people had been ringing me up and had been talking in this rapid way to me about things I didn't understand – it was always stressful. I was always aware that if I got something wrong it would be damaging, it would be embarrassing, people would shout. So when I came back I was ready for all that again. I find it a breeze actually.* [PPS 14/4/04]

He offered a couple of reasons for this change. First, *'It's probably also something to do with me being a bit older and a bit more confident'*. Second, he has *'more clout. I mean nobody messes with me now'*. As a result, *'If you ask my wife how do I seem, she would say that I seem completely relaxed. I sleep well and everything is fine'* [PPS 14/4/04].

Others are not so calm.

> *I find I will have physiological reactions to the stress sometimes. I will have weeks where I will have awful skin and my heart rate doesn't want to go down. Yesterday it was [the Minister] being in a bad mood. And that's stressful just because the service element of the job comes in. None of us knew how to make him feel better about his day.* [PS 10/4/03]

One DS works *'say 9 am to 7 pm. I enjoy the job. I enjoy the work. I have no kids. I have a flexible husband'*. There are rewards. She enjoys working with the Minister; *'I've had the good fortune of working with five Secretaries of State who I have got on with and seem to be able to bear me'* [DS 9/3/03].

But the novelty wears off:

> *I have done a year-and-a-half, and you get 'burn out' in the job. Meeting [the Minister] or the Chancellor or the Prime Minister has worn off so then the hard work kicks in and sometimes you feel like 'I don't want to be in work at 8:00 am because I will have to sit and listen to [work colleague]. You know it's a very negative attitude but the novelty has worn off.* [PS 10/4/03]

When we asked about their social life, the responses were almost identical.

> *Social life? I have not lost friends, but I have friends who are exhausted with saying, 'Let's go out Wednesday', and me saying, 'Yes', and ringing them up 20 minutes before we are to go out saying, 'It's absolutely no way I can make it to the cinema. Absolutely no way.'* [PS 10/4/03]
>
> *I mean that's the worst side of it, I mean you 'pack in' a social life.* [PS 26/4/02]
>
> *There is none.* [PPS 21/5/02]

For members of the Private Office, it is hard to strike a decent work–life balance. They leave:

> *My partner is pregnant. We are expecting our first baby in a month and I knew that I wouldn't physically be able to do these hours and have a family.*[4] [APS 21/5/02]

The clerical staff works fewer hours; *'I don't class it as a long hours culture'* [Clerk]. Core hours are normally 10–12 and 2–4. They can make up the rest on flexitime. Some have part-time jobs – bingo caller three nights a week. One is a martial arts expert who has appeared in cage fighting on TV. His prowess is the cause of much Private Office hilarity; they get a kick out of his Warholian fifteen minutes of fame. But the culture of long hours affects this group as well. An Assistant PS left home at 6.30 am and did not get back until 9 pm. He lived some way out because *'it's just too damned expensive'* to live in London [APS 21/5/02]. One DS explained she had one early evening a week, leaving at 5 pm but commented *'you just can't plan anything'*. Most get the weekends free, but many, including the DS, take work home [DS 20/5/02].

So, the top of the department court may be an exciting place to work but it is also exacting for those who fail and for those with families. One Permanent Secretary told his Private Office, 'Go home some of you, I don't want a long hours culture in the book'. The remark simply confirmed its existence. And no one left.

Conclusions

Our stories are simple tales. Consumers experience the state and its managerial rationalities in different ways. For Mr. and Mrs. R, they want the same familiar face to look after them. They have little interest in forms of institutional care. Mrs. T has choices about the care she receives. The case ought to exemplify the government's 'choice and voice' agenda. But who makes the choice? Who has the information for choosing? Whatever the answers to these questions, one point is clear – it is not Mrs. T. They are dependent on the Home Care manager for information and advice, and like many customers they also see the services as 'given' in the sense of gifts, and they are grateful. Gratitude sustains dependence, thereby sustaining the immutable quality of the state. Mrs. K's daughter sees her mother's house as a railway station because of its endless stream of visitors. The state is a complex, confusing structure that seems as if it is fixed and immutable, while the care manager rails against constraints she seeks to change.

British government recognizes this complexity as a problem for citizens (Cm 4310 1999). The call for joined-up government and partnerships is their response. Thus, the Chair of the PCT sees himself as constructing – that is, designing, building, and managing – a network not just for his organization but also for the local area. Indeed, during our conversations, the Chair worked out he was constructing an *area* network. It was not an explicit part of his strategy at the start of our conversation. He recognized that he is not required to build the linkages but believes he will be 'in the shit' if he doesn't. He exemplifies the first wave of governance in his understanding of the state and its role and he seeks to adapt it to local, area conditions.

We found evidence of the new culture of targets in the handling of letters and in managing the PCT. Not one Permanent Secretary or PPS mentioned that they had personal targets. Of course, there were departmental targets for PSAs and delivery but the responsibility for them fell mainly on the DGs. This finding should not be a surprise. Such managerial tools are used by senior management to control others. They apply to 'everybody but us'. That said, one PS said the absence of targets was a result of a heavy workload. She simply did not have time to conduct the performance appraisals because the work of the Minister and the Permanent Secretary always came first.

The new managerial rationalities changed not only some office practices but also the work of senior managers. Their workload was greater because they were now explicitly office managers. One PPS, for example, had direct line responsibility for sixteen people and signed off on another sixty. Anyone who has taken the performance appraisal of staff seriously, rather than 'ticked and flicked', will recognize the demands of such numbers. Just as the PPS now had twin-track training that combined manager and mandarin, he also had a dual responsibility to political management for the Minister and to the canons of the new managerialism. The unintended consequences of this combination were a culture of long hours, high staff turnover, and stress. Managerial rationalities were experienced as control not, as is sometimes claimed, the freedom to manage.

The word 'resistance', or the capacity to oppose or withstand, comes in many forms, little and big, passive and active. As we noted in Chapter 4, power can refer to the restrictive consequences of the actions of others in defining what we can and cannot do. Unintended consequences are evidence of the actions of others in resisting, for example, the stated intentions of state actors. Here, we provide examples of power and resistance: Mr. and Mrs. R refuse to move unless they keep their favourite carer; the care manager struggles to provide a care package; the manager strives to build a local network within a regional policy; the office workers vote with their feet and leave; and the PPS combines old and new expectations into his jazz band view of management. No one of these examples is major, and that is part of our point. Implementation deficits arising from unanticipated actions by actors in long chains of decision making are a long-standing feature of top-down views of policy implementation (see Pressman and Wildavsky 1973). In Chapter 8, we describe how the Heads of the Civil Service defend it from the incessant clamour for reform. Elsewhere, we have provided examples of the important consequences for the policies of the central state of police officers and doctors actively resisting reforms (Bevir and Rhodes 2006, chapters 8 and 9). But the cumulative effect of continuous, minor adjustments by actors with lowly positions in the hierarchy can be just as great. Indeed, it is precisely these endless minor adaptations that characterize living traditions and their impact on state policies and managerial rationalities through the everyday actions of customers, employees, and managers.

Our overall conclusion for these short stories is a simple one. The term 'state' has different meanings for each respondent, and the study of managerial rationalities must capture these different meanings, not read them off from the beliefs and practices we assume adhere to a specific position. There is no essentialist account of managerial rationalities that can be used either to produce law-like generalizations or to legitimate advice to policy makers. Rather, to understand managerial rationalities and their effects, we need decentred accounts that give due recognition to the creative individual. Individual actors construct managerial rationalities even as governments seek to create them, and researchers seek to impose their definition of the situation on both. Nearly twenty years ago, Fenno (1990, 128) commented, 'not enough political scientists are presently engaged in observation'. He was correct then. He is correct now. Our account of rule, rationalities, and resistance make the case for decentred theory and observational methods. In the final chapter, we essay an overall assessment of our theory and methods.

Notes

1. The local authority care workers were told to refer to the users of their services as 'customers'. We follow local practice.
2. All the material from the fieldwork notebooks is taken from FWNBs Nos. 1–5, dated 25–26 April, 20 May, 16–18 September, 19–20 September, and 13–14 November 2002.

3. On the long hours' culture, see also Blunkett (2006, 673 and 729), Bruce-Gardyne (1986, 34), Henderson (2001, 182), and Lawson (1992, 385).
4. Some of today's senior civil servants had to make similar decisions earlier in their careers. Gus O'Donnell, Head of the Home Civil Service at the time of writing, turned down the opportunity to become Nigel Lawson's PPS at the Treasury for the same reason (Lawson 1992, 385).

Chapter 10

Conclusions

Introduction

In this chapter, we provide a summary of the state as cultural practice; 'the stateless state'. We then reflect on the several issues posed by this analysis. Obviously, we claim it is novel. So, we highlight our key findings to justify that claim. Our observational methods are also novel in political science, if not in other social sciences. They have their limits and weaknesses as with all social science research methods. We discuss the several pitfalls, making the pragmatic judgement that our methods are among the best available for studying cultural practices. Finally, we reflect on the normative implications of our analysis for the tradition of representative democracy.

The stateless state

We began with an interpretive approach to political science. Political life consists of meaningful activity. The flow of politics is speech and other actions infused with the intentionality of the actors. To discuss and explain meaningful activity is to ascribe desires and beliefs to the relevant actors. Actions can be understood only by referring to the conscious, unconscious, and subconscious reasoning of the actors.

Our interpretive approach to political science involves a historicist emphasis on situated agency. People act against the backcloth of inherited traditions that influence them. But people can vary these traditions for reasons of their own in response to circumstances, so these traditions do not determine what they come to believe and do. Also, actors have beliefs about governing and the ways other actors are likely to respond to what they do. These beliefs influence their reasoning and actions. But these beliefs are not necessarily correct, so social norms and social contexts do not have any direct impact on people's actions. Political scientists should not mistake traditions, beliefs, and practices for structures or discourses that allegedly define or fix behaviour. To the contrary, meaningful activity is inherently historically contingent as well as historically situated.

This interpretive and historicist approach to political science leads to a theory of the state as cultural practice. The state, like all political life, consists of meaning in action. The state is a practice because it is just contingent activity. The state is a cultural practice because this activity is meaningful. Indeed, we should say the state is a *set* of cultural practices. The state is not monolithic. It consists of all kinds of practices from everyday polite exchanges over cups of tea, through symbolic displays of authority and status, to decisions about policy and its implementation. Yet each of these practices too is anything but monolithic. Polite exchanges over tea do not have a fixed form. Their nature is not determined by some abstract norm. Rather, the exchanges again consist of the speech and other actions of the participants, who are acting on contingent beliefs and desires, including those about what is appropriate and what one another will do. Everyday rituals, like all activity, are contingent and undetermined. As practices are not monolithic, they do not have natural boundaries. Political scientists decide what to and what not to include in a practice depending on what actions interest them, and the way they want to explain those actions. The state is meaningful activity. Political scientists pick out patterns in that activity to identify contingent and contested cultural practices.

Our theory of the state as cultural practice stands in sharp contrast to the theories that dominate the literature. Compared with these theories, we depict a stateless state. The dominant theories of the state are reifications. They abstract the state from meaningful activity, presenting it as an almost monolithic entity able to act by making policy or undertaking metagovernance. They postulate the state as an institution or structure that determines practices and explains outcomes. Our emphasis on situated agency precludes such reification. The state is merely an aggregate descriptive term for a vast array of meaningful actions that coalesce into contingent, shifting, and contested practices. The state is stateless, therefore, in that it has no essence, no structural quality, and no power to determine the actions of which it consists. These actions are explained instead by the beliefs actors inherit from traditions and then change for reasons of their own.

So, the stateless state consists solely of contingent practices. These practices are meaningful in that they embody the intentionality – the beliefs – of the actors. Political scientists explain these actions and beliefs by locating them against the background of traditions that are modified in response to dilemmas. Part II of this book explores some of the cultural practices that make up the stateless state, from the mundane and the ordinary to the grand public performance. We suggested that much of the mundane everyday activity embodied traditions of politeness that are widespread in other practices at least in Britain. We also suggested that three more obviously political traditions informed much of this activity: a lingering monarchical or court tradition; the Westminster tradition with its implicit debt to Whig historiography; and a newer managerial tradition. These traditions conflict with one another. Actors struggle to manage the dilemmas that arise form the conflict. The result is a complex pattern of ruling, rationalities, and resistance. Ministers and senior civil servants are still trying to rule in terms defined by the Westminster tradition and its monarchical roots. But they also seek the alleged efficiencies of managerial rationalities. All kinds of civil servants struggle to combine these competing demands, often moderating and resisting the imperatives of managerialism. Street-level bureaucrats try to apply the resulting policies and languages to their own work, again often transforming them and resisting at least some of the aims of policy makers.

Political life is an endless stream of activity infused with beliefs. No method can guarantee that political scientists rightly identify the actions that most interest them or explain the consequences that most interest them. And no method can guarantee that political scientists attribute the correct beliefs to actors to explain a practice. Nonetheless, the contingency of meaning in action should make political scientists wary of all attempts to reduce beliefs, actions, and practices to monolithic norms or discourses. Instead, we believe political scientists would be well advised to privilege textual analysis and ethnographic observations as ways of identifying beliefs, actions, and practices. Texts often provide sophisticated statements of possible beliefs. Observation provides a way of checking such statements against people's actions and, at least as importantly, of identifying beliefs, actions, and practices of which there is little or no written record. So, in Part II we used observation, interviews, and textual analysis to explore some of the diverse beliefs, actions, and practices that make up the stateless state in Britain.

Key findings

How novel is our analysis of the stateless state in its British guise? We have been asked, 'what do we know from our observational fieldwork, from being there and focusing on everyday practices that we do not know from existing research or our experiences of working in any organization?'

The 'so what' question reflects the bias of mainstream political science to 'hard' evidence. We find it odd that we are expected to answer the question because the answer is obvious. Such methods are common in anthropology, organization theory, and sociology. It would seem that only political science has a problem. 'Thick descriptions' in particular and case studies in general are well-established tools in the social sciences, valuable both in their own right and as a corrective to approaches that read off beliefs from social structure. It is as foolish to dismiss thick descriptions as survey methods. As Agar (1996, 27) comments, 'no understanding of a world is valid without representation of those members' voices'. Similarly, knowledge of one's own organization is not the same as evidence about the beliefs and practices of another organization. No one would dream of mistaking one's own organization for the universe of organizations. We study organizations to identify both the common and the unique. So, we seek to show that the ethnographic tool kit has manifold uses for research in political science and to counter the mainstream bias to ostensibly 'hard' evidence.

Second, our research strategy, when allied to an interpretive approach, resolves the theoretical difficulties that beset more positivist versions of government. An interpretive approach uses texts, interviews, and observation to decentre institutions. It avoids the unacceptable suggestion that institutions fix the behaviour of individuals rather than being products of that behaviour. Our observations of how ministers and civil servants play their parts in the daily dramas of departmental life show that even when their overall roles are spelt out for them by the shared understandings of the Westminster tradition, it is individuals' understandings of their roles, shaped by their beliefs and personalities, which breathe life into the institution. Their beliefs determine the nature and quality of the collaboration between politicians and bureaucrats. The observational study of public elites leads one to unpack catch-all phrases such as 'path-dependency' and 'context' to provide accounts of stability and change rooted in the beliefs and practices of individual actors as they struggle to renegotiate policies and practices in the face of changing circumstances. And yet, as we show in Chapter 8 and our analysis of how top civil servants reinterpret their traditions, our theory and methods allow us to offer aggregate studies by using such concepts as tradition to explain how they come to hold those beliefs and perform those practices.

Third, observation has two long-established principal features as a source of data. It gets below and behind the surface of official accounts by providing texture, depth, and nuance, so our stories have richness as well as context. Also, it lets interviewees explain the meaning of their actions, providing an authenticity that can only come from the main characters involved in the story. As the interview with the PCT manager shows, face-to-face interviews can be revealing for both interviewer *and* interviewee alike. It was an example of 'how do I know what I think until I hear what I say'. In explaining to us that he was building an area network, he explained it to himself. With observation, such interviews are central to producing thick descriptions.

Fourth, 'being there' admits of surprises, of moments of epiphany, which can open new research agendas. It accepts serendipity and happenstance. It is fruitful, progressive, and open. We were staggered when the PPS talked about language in use and language games while musing on whether he was embedded in a web of words or a web of relationships. Although we focus on elites, ethnography opens a wide range of new areas and styles of research about the beliefs, preferences, and practices of diverse political actors – from Prime Minister to individual citizens – as they preserve and modify traditions and practices.

Fifth, our methods help us to identify and analyse the symbolic dimensions of political action. Most political behaviour has a strong symbolic dimension. Indeed, symbols are the bedrock of everyday political life with even our most basic political concepts such as the 'state', 'nation', 'government', and 'the people' often appearing in symbols. Symbols do not simply 'represent' or reflect political 'reality', they actively constitute that reality. By drawing out the negotiated, symbolic, and ritual elements of political life, ethnographic analysis draws attention to principles of organization that are not visible to empiricist or positivist approaches. For the Minister the activity of ruling is mainly about 'the appearance of rule'. Of course, Ministers can and do make policy. But as our account of their daily life shows, it is not their main activity. They are mainly the public face of government. They represent its authority. They must appear as men and women of stature and standing. The Minister is the Queen's minister and accorded due homage. His office has a long history of grandeur. The Minister is called Minister or Secretary of State and rarely addressed by his first name by officials. Outsiders display equivalent verbal and physical deference. He is the centre of attention, a celebrity, and this simple fact is displayed in language, beliefs, and practices. As a celebrity, he is escorted everywhere in a chauffeur-driven car, greeted at doorways on red carpets by respectful hosts.

Finally, interviews and observation confront researchers with the challenges of their research roles and the limitations of their data. The usual methodological qualifications and cautions found in standard modernist-empiricist accounts can seem insignificant. The frailty of elite research cannot be hidden when researchers are forced to negotiate, and often repeatedly renegotiate, access to the corridors of power. Cleaning a data set is nothing compared to elites shutting doors as they decide to draw a veil over what they will allow the observer to see. Or there is that sinking feeling after you submit a draft of your findings and the Minister turns on you, disparaging your work. They are embarrassed by how close you have come to capturing on paper what they do and why they do it, including the mundane nature and hypocrisy of life at the top (see the discussion on speaking truth to power later).

So far, so general. What do we know about elites and their beliefs and practices that we did not know before? Two seemingly contradictory findings stand out; the ordinariness of it all, and public servants and ministers as performers. The contradiction is more apparent than real.

Everyday practices are ordinary. The lifestyle is prosaic. It is so familiar we can overlook it. It is made up of meetings, paper pushing, and staring at desktop screens. Chapters 6 and 9 comment on the culture of long hours, the office routines, and the ever-present, time-consuming committee meetings, where the clear and present danger is boredom. Gossip, humour, and politeness sustain these routines.

In the political science literature, everyday practices are often described as routines, which are well known and unremarkable features of bureaucracies. Bureaucracies are governed by rules (or red tape) that underpin standardized service delivery. But that is not the function of the routines we highlight. Routines are, in our view, a way of making a complex and often anarchic world seem manageable.

Ministers living in the goldfish bowl created by the mass media are cocooned by their rule-driven departments. Civil servants are socialized into the kinds of gossip, humour, and politeness that sustain this everyday world. It is not taught in business schools to MBAs, yet the British government unthinkingly recruit outsiders. Ministers strive to reduce risk and uncertainty while calling for less risk-averse behaviour by civil servants. Do they mean that civil servants should increase the uncertainties in the minister's life, because it is him they seek to protect? They know not what they ask, preferring the allure of 'modernization' and 'results-driven government' to the certainties and safety offered to their otherwise chaotic and dangerous existence by the routines of the 'bureaucracy' they are expected to criticize in public.

This world of routines is also a closed world. Decisions are made by small groups of elite actors. Everyday life may be ordinary but in elite groups with embedded routines sustained by long-standing socialization practices, such domesticity can have significant consequences. Groupthink means that ministers do not have to instruct their civil servants because they know what is expected before it is spoken. They get 'anticipatory compliance' ('t Hart, Stern, and Sundelius 1997), as the closed world imposes severe punishments on insiders, such as Clive Ponting and David Kelly, who go public.

Politicians and bureaucrats perform on both public and private stages. The minister is a combination of royalty and celebrity. He is an actor on several public stages with the ability to wear the various masks his role demands. Even the more invisible top officials who operate in mundane, routinized administrative worlds still 'perform'. For example, a Private Secretary commented:

> *There were moments that are unbeatable, you know, when something goes right. I can remember the last rows with the Treasury. I love the [Chancellor] and [the Minister] on the phone to one another. You get to listen in and you hear [the Minister] really 'kick-ass' with him. And [the Minister] comes out and goes, 'Right get those words over to him. You send them over.' And the great thing is the Private Secretaries go into theatrical mode. So [the PS] over at the Treasury, he is then the Chancellor, and I am then [the Minister]. You have these phone conversations and you are horrible to each other in this diplomatic way. It hones your skills. You know you have to do the diplomatic thing and there is a real thrill to it. There is a real absolute thrill.* [PS 10/4/03]

Performing is not only about public, visible, and even exciting performances, but it is also about the ordinary, everyday performances of not-so-public figures.

Pitfalls in the field

We are keenly aware of the limits and weaknesses of observational methods, although they are no more severe than with most other research methods in the social sciences. We believe it is imperative to have a reflexive critical stance to our methods. Therefore, we discuss the several issues we faced in our fieldwork using the headings: speaking truth to power; secrecy and spies; we are not journalists; maintaining standards; don't talk, listen; working together; what do we know; and I want to tell you a story.

Speaking truth to power

Aaron Wildavsky's epigrammatic story (1979, 402) about speaking truth to power summarizes our point:

> The King said: 'Venerable Nagasena, will you converse with me?'
> Nagasena: 'If your Majesty will speak with me as wise men converse I will; but if your Majesty speaks with me as kings converse, I will not.'
> 'How then converse the wise, venerable Nagasena?'
> 'The wise do not get angry when they are driven into a corner, kings do.'

The metaphor of 'village' may describe Whitehall but the cosy metaphor should not mislead. We are studying elites and the village inhabitants are powerful men and women. Ministers and permanent secretaries can refuse interviews, deny access to the organization, declare documents secret, and insist on anonymity for both themselves and their organization. All the interviews and periods of observation took place with informed consent but as the work unfolded we had to negotiate constantly to keep that cooperation. Consider the following letter.

> I am afraid I was completely dismayed to read your draft. You assured me – and my permanent secretary – that this was a serious piece of research and that the participants would not be identified or identifiable. In fact, both I and the Department are clearly recognisable and as a result, I believe that many of your quotations and observations will inevitably be used in a way that neither of us intended, or believed you intended, when we agreed to participate. The result, I am afraid, is extremely unfair to our departmental colleagues. I am therefore not prepared to give my permission either for my name to be used or for the quotes to be attributed.

This quote tells us something about the cast of mind elites adopt when reading accounts of their beliefs and practices by outsiders.

A degree of self-serving, self-important defensiveness creeps in. Politicians know they are public figures, comparable to celebrities. They act to defend that public image irrespective of whether the comments are accurate. To be fair, the Private Office staff can be even worse, defending their boss come hell or high water. This pitfall is not specific to studying government elites; for example, 'horror stories' from the field abound in sociology (see Bell and Newby 1977; Burns 1977; and Punch 1986).

Speaking truth to power is never easy. An ethnographic study of elites holds up an acute mirror to them. It shows them not just their on-stage but also their 'off-stage' or 'backstage' behaviour. It echoes their ways of 'making sense'. It would be naive to think that they are invariably delighted to look into such a mirror. And they have the power to complicate the research effort. The important point is that such trepidation and tensions are there to be managed, not avoided.

Secrecy and spies

Whether spy-like behaviour to get to the bottom of things is defensible admits of no easy answer. On the one hand, we deal with the powerful, not the dependent. We confront a stacked deck. In the era of spin, 'truth' is negotiable and negotiated. Covert behaviour is one way of redressing the imbalance of power. On the other hand, if we are deemed to have 'cheated', then we could make life more difficult for future researchers.

It is commonly argued that ethnographic research on the powerful encounters the endemic secrecy of government. It permeates everything; for example, permanent secretaries in Britain are not supposed to talk publicly about their membership of the honours committees in case they get lobbied. To breach the veil, covert behaviour may be the only means 'open' to us.

The problem should not be overstated. Almost everyone was willing to speak on tape. At the end of most long interviews, the elite were relaxed, willing to chat about anything, historical or present-day. Many have a need to talk. As Rawnsley (2001, xi) observes, 'they have to tell an outsider because they are so worried about whether it makes sense or, indeed, whether they make sense'. The interviewer is cast in the role of providing reassurance, if not a form of therapy, for the stressed-out, the frustrated, and the humiliated.

In studying the powerful, therefore, we are spies to the extent they are secretive. For much research, most of the time, there is no issue. When problems arise, they win. Getting information by covert means is our equivalent of guerrilla warfare (and on social scientists, subversion, and the powerful, see Punch 1986 and Hammersley 2000). It signals the end of trust and consensual access and heralds the arrival of exit strategies and the stance and tactics of investigative journalism.

We are not journalists – building and keeping trust

A leading UK journalist in his book on Tony Blair's first government 'chose to conduct all interviews on a background basis' because on-the-record interviews would suffer from a lack of candour (Rawnsley 2001, xvii–xviii). He quotes a senior UK Minister, Robin Cook, on the art of the interview: 'to talk for an hour without saying anything too interesting'. Jeremy Paxman (2002, 207) is a prominent UK television journalist and interviewer. He met a similar lack of candour when seeking to shadow Alan Milburn when he was the Secretary of State for Health. Despite many letters and phone calls, Paxman not only failed to get a day on which he could shadow the minister, he could not even get a decision. After six months, he was granted a day, six weeks after the deadline for his book. That is not our experience. Paxman and Rawnsley are reporting the lot of the journalist, not the academic. There are significant differences between us. As remarked above, ethnographic researchers are to some degree 'spying' on elites, but our aims are different from those of investigative journalists. Our starting point was cooperation, not spying. We presumed good intentions, not secrecy. We presumed good faith, not deception and duplicity. So, we allowed respondents to comment on our work. Interviewees had transcripts of their interviews to check any quotes. Interviewees read a draft of the manuscript, commented on our interpretation and approved all attributed quotes. We publish long after the events described, striving for accuracy and not the banner headline. We focus on 'everyday life' and the commonplace, not the feeding frenzy of a crisis beloved of journalists. Everyday detail adds flesh to their story. For us the detail is the story. These differences mean we can be trusted; but trust is not a constant, it has to be constantly renegotiated.

Maintaining standards – reliability and validity

We seek to show our approach is both thorough and systematic by reporting such details as the number and length of interviews and the total hours of observation. We checked the veracity and reliability of our data in three ways. First, we interviewed many officials and politicians, allowing us to cross-check their varying accounts. Second, we had access to the written records of both individuals and organizations. Third, we observed elites at work, and observation is an essential complement to interviews. Interviews recorded at a different time from observation are a way of corroborating the claims of a speaker. Finally, we sought to 'reconfirm' our account by encounters with practitioners who commented on the fieldwork-based chapters. We spared them encounters with anti-foundationalism! In short, objectivity lies in the intersubjective agreement built from comparing the different narratives. This process of reflexive, iterative reconfirmation lends credence to our stories (see Rhodes 1997*a*, chapter 10; Bevir 1999).

Don't talk, listen

Interviews are said to be an unreliable source of data because interviewees 'unselfconsciously project an official self-image' (Lee 1995, 149–50) and politicians are seen as self-serving to the point of misleading:

> The author frequently had reason to wonder whether some former ministers had served in the same administration so at variance were their accounts of the way coordination took place at the heart of Whitehall. (Seldon 1995, 126)

We have to decode the official self-image and politicians' management of their public image. We do so in three ways. First, we locate the official ethos and language in its historical context by comparing texts, whether official publications, files, or interview transcripts. Second, we compare the statements made in interviews with observed behaviour. Finally, all of us during our everyday lives develop skills in interpreting what others mean when they speak to us. Thus, we judge whether someone is lying by many verbal and body cues. We do not leave such skills at the door of the interview room. Every interview involves such judgements.

Working together

It is all too easy to affect the relationship between yourself and the observed, causing them to behave differently. The aim of the so-called non-participant observer is to remain the outsider. However, for lengthy on-site visits and extensive repeat interviews, you have to have a conversation and engage with the people around you. You have to establish rapport. You are sucked into events, even if it is only casual badinage to ease tension. For example, a Permanent Secretary gave us a copy of his diaries. The analysis of his engagements and committee work showed he was spending about one-third of his time on corporate civil service business outside the department. He was surprised. He had no clear picture of the distribution of his workload. Immediately, he began to reduce his corporate commitments. It is a tricky balancing act to remain both distant and to keep their confidence; to keep critical detachment, and empathize and not go native. That said, the ersatz native eventually withdraws from the field and a reflexive stance to one's work should enable the researcher to become once again the professional stranger.

What do we know – generalization

It is claimed that ethnography's idiographic thick descriptions preclude generalizations. Thus, in mainstream political science, case studies were often criticized as of little or no scientific value because one cannot use them either to test hypotheses or to generalize. Over thirty years ago, Eckstein (1975, 116) demonstrated that case studies can be used to test theories, and he was working with the natural science model of the social sciences. The common error is to equate generalization with the formal generalization associated with a natural science model of research. Yin (2003) contrasted such 'empirical generalization' requiring some form of statistical sampling with 'theoretical generalization', where selecting a case study and interpreting its findings are guided by our prior theories (see also George and Bennett 2005). Geertz (1973; 1983) describes ethnography as a soft science that guesses at meanings, assesses the guesses, and draws explanatory conclusions from the better guesses. And it is thus possible to make general statements. Theory provides a vocabulary with which to express what symbolic action has to say about itself. Political scientists can offer accounts that explain practices and actions by pointing to the conditional connections between, beliefs, practices, interactions, traditions, and dilemmas.

I want to tell you a story

Writing is not the end of research but the start of a new phase that is just as challenging. In effect, we seek detachment and distance by trying to make the familiar strange and the strange familiar. We turn a critical eye not only on our material but also on ourselves as we write our part in the story. We have to beware of 'secondary ethnocentrism', that is, we cannot accept that our informants give us a higher order of truth or accuracy. Rather, we must think about why people say and do the things they do. We have to twist and turn the data as we interrogate our fieldwork. Everyone has to interrogate their fieldwork. Everyone has to decide the extent to which they should be present in their story. It is hard to strike the balance in deciding how much personal reflection to include, if any. We tread warily between the 'diary disease' (Geertz 1988, 90) and 'the doctrine of immaculate perception' (Van Maanen 1988, 74). Too little reflection and there is no point. Too much reflection and there is the danger of provoking the response, 'I don't care'.

Every method has limits and weaknesses. Observation is no exception. All any researcher can do is come clean and face up to those limits and weaknesses. So, we incline to Fox's practical and pragmatic assessment (2004, 4):

> While participant observation has its limitations, this rather uneasy combination of involvement and detachment is still the best method we have for exploring the complexities of human cultures, so it will have to do.

In short, what works is best. We have shown that it does work in analysing the state as cultural practice.

Democratic governance

Decentring governance has led us to give an account of the state as cultural practice – a stateless state in contrast to a sovereign state. Sovereignty is not, and cannot be, monolithic. The concept of the sovereign state has become increasingly inaccurate because of, for example, the growth of national and transnational, network governance, and changes in managing and delivering public services.

A fragmented view of sovereignty poses challenges for our historical ideas of representative and parliamentary democracy. Even if legislatures are the dominant law-making body in formal constitutions, the processes that result in policies commonly take place in policy networks connected to departments and the core executive. Parliaments may pass legislation, but they do not dominate the processes that decide what goes into legislation. In the UK, parliamentary sovereignty is a legal norm barely seen in everyday political processes. The doctrine of parliamentary sovereignty reflects a dated faith in the formal laws and institutions of Westminster parliamentary governments. Everyday political processes are better understood using the behavioural ideas flagged by Wallas (1948 [1908]), developed throughout the last century, and now embedded in the network governance narrative (Bevir and Rhodes 2003). But we do not intend to draw a sharp dichotomy. If some proponents of a governance narrative present it in sharp contrast to the Westminster narrative, we have suggested the Westminster narrative still matters because so many political actors believe in it and act on it. While some political scientists still tackle behavioural topics such as interest groups, policy networks, and bureaucratic behaviour using formal techniques and explanations, we have argued for an interpretive approach that explores these topics by focusing on the beliefs and practices of actors.

To what extent should we accept that the stateless state undermines the legal norms associated with the Westminster story? To what extent does the stateless state pose dilemmas for historical concepts of representative democracy? We worry that representative democracy is often a thin veneer covering rule through networks of unelected officials and experts. To conclude, therefore, we argue for supplementing representative institutions with participatory democracy, collaborative forms of governance, and dialogic policy making.

Participatory democracy

Participatory democracy is a form of government in which the citizens themselves have the opportunity to decide public policy. Participatory democrats try to promote a form of self-rule in which individuals decide how they are to be governed. Citizens play a powerful role in making particular decisions through, for example, public discussion, negotiation, and voting. When participatory democrats assign a role to the state, they often want it to educate citizens and provide spaces for communication. Most participatory democrats have been inspired at least in part by dissatisfaction with the limited opportunities for participation provided in modern representative democracies (Pateman 1970; Barber 1984). In representative democracies, citizens delegate the tasks of decision making and policy implementation to elected politicians and appointed bureaucrats. Their participation is largely restricted to electing politicians who then 'represent' the interests of their constituents in decision making and holding the bureaucracy to account.

Although participatory democracy can be seen as an alternative to liberal democracy, it is perhaps more helpful to think of participation as a continuum, and participatory democrats as demanding an increase in current levels of participation. Common forms of participation include electoral participation, group participation, citizen–government participation, and direct participation. The electoral process allows citizens to select their representatives. Group participation allows citizens to combine in associations within civil society to form groups that have a voice in policy making: common groups include churches, businesses, and trade unions. Citizen–government interaction refers to a diverse set of mechanisms by which citizens may convey their opinions and preferences to politicians; for example, public meetings, congressional hearings, and citizen surveys. Although participatory democrats value all of these forms of participation, they often place a particular emphasis on more direct forms of participation; for example, the initiative, the referendum, and citizen juries.

Discussions about network governance and metagovernance raise several questions about participation and democracy. One obvious question is whether or not either form increases participation. Some commentators suggest the spread of markets increases choice and so the opportunities for citizens to participate in public decision making. Neo-liberals might argue, for example, that whenever citizens choose to use one public hospital or one school rather than another, they participate in determining a public outcome. In sharp contrast, we think market activity rarely has democratic value. It is more plausible to argue that the spread of networks increases opportunities for participation. Citizens and social movements can involve themselves in all kinds of networks (Braithwaite 1997). However, critics rightly suggest that the spread of networks may undermine the democratic effectiveness of participation. By multiplying networks, decision making is shifted to actors who lack proper legitimacy and who are barely accountable to citizens. The challenge is, therefore, to create opportunities for participation in networks that preserve legitimacy and accountability (Considine 2002; Minow 2003). We need new forms of collaborative governance.

Collaborative governance

Collaborative governance refers to attempts to create policies and conduct policy making by involving non-governmental and non-traditional political actors (Ansell and Gash 2007). At times, it refers to attempts to bring all the relevant stakeholders together for face-to-face discussions during which policies are developed. The actors from civil society who are interested in a policy play an active role in the policy process from initial discussions over the agenda to completion. Examples of relevant non-governmental organizations include not only businesses and unions but also citizen groups such as local residents and activist groups. Collaborative governance is an interactive process in which myriad actors with various interests, perspectives, and knowledge are brought together. The hope is that the resulting policies will be better designed, more suitable to the local context, more workable, and more legitimate than would policies formed through more closed policy-making processes.

Collaborative governance parallels a broader trend away from top-down hierarchical approaches to public policy – a trend that also includes marketization and joined-up government. Yet collaborative governance differs from other moves away from hierarchy in its emphases on discussion and cooperation among stakeholders. Unlike marketization, collaborative governance relies on negotiation, not competition, to define acceptable outcomes. Unlike joined-up governance, collaborative governance focuses on involving citizens' groups in the policy process, not the bringing together of the diverse government agencies involved in a given policy area.

Supporters of collaborative governance argue it has several advantages (Healey 1997; Meadowcroft 1999; Wondolleck and Yaffe 2000). First, it accelerates the policy-making process because more actors are involved in the earlier stages, creating more support for the policy when it is enacted and implemented. Second, involving diverse actors leads to a more thorough exploration of any proposed policy. There is less chance that an aspect or consequence of a policy will be overlooked or ignored. Third, collaborative governance brings new skills, expertise, and perspectives into the policy-making process. It increases the number of people involved, and it might lead to more innovative policies. Fourth, collaborative governance can increase the legitimacy of public policies. It opens up the policy-making process, increasing transparency, accountability, and trust. Finally, collaborative governance can widen participation in the policy-making process.

Critics of collaborative governance rightly suggest that it may represent only the interests of the few selected groups that participated in the policy process. Some interests are too diffuse to be readily organized and voiced. Collaborative processes may favour groups with better finances and more knowledge. The challenge is, therefore, to change the culture and practices of policy networks. Public officials need to rethink their role as one that facilitates dialogue rather than advising politicians, managing departments, and implementing decisions (see, e.g. Wamsley *et al.* 1990).

Dialogic policy making

Dialogic policy making is a process in which citizens actively participate in creating public policies (Fischer and Forester 1993; Forester 1999; Hajer and Wagenaar 2003). To be more specific, dialogic and deliberative approaches to policy give citizens an opportunity to exchange relevant viewpoints and arguments before adopting a policy. The dialogic process might be overseen or facilitated by public officials. Alternatively, public officials might provide one voice among the many in the dialogue. The dialogic process might be a way of deciding, or an exercise in consultation. Typically, dialogic policy making is an iterative process. The repeated negotiation of conflicting beliefs discourages participants from remaining stubbornly uncompromising. Dialogue may move participants towards substantial compromises and agreements (Roberts 2002). These compromises and agreements may increase satisfaction with policy outcomes.

Many commentators highlight several preconditions for the success of dialogic policy making. First, public officials should set the stage for a dialogue; in particular, they should make sure the participants all have clear roles. Second, the participants should enter the dialogue with openness; they should not hold hidden agendas since these undermine the trust that is crucial for meaningful deliberation and negotiation. Third, public officials should express their sincerity and confidence in the process, because it encourages citizens to treat their own participation as relevant and important. Finally, the dialogue should concentrate on concrete policies of direct concern to the participants.

When dialogic ideals first arose among political scientists, they appeared far removed from democratic practice. More recently, however, the gap between ideals and practices has shrunk. On one hand, some political scientists have begun to run deliberative (and less frequently dialogic) experiments, at times with the support and funding of social movements or television channels.[1] On the other hand, a few states have begun to toy with small-scale uses of deliberative (and again less frequently dialogic) measures. The last two decades have seen considerable falls in the electoral turnout in many states. The decline in the percentage of eligible voters who vote is often perceived as a threat to states' legitimacy. Policy actors are increasingly concerned that the falling rates of voter participation reflect a growing discontent with government and even a growing distrust of politicians. Some believe dialogic policy making may provide a means of renewing civic life and enhancing political legitimacy.

Over the years we have coined several phrases to encapsulate our arguments, including 'from government to governance' and 'the differentiated polity'. It is a way of stating arguments baldly, before adding the necessary qualifications. We have added 'the stateless state' to this arsenal, but our aims remain constant. In every case, after Rorty (1980, 360), we sought 'new, better, more interesting, more fruitful ways of speaking about' British government; after Van Maanen (1988, 35), we sought 'more, not fewer, ways to tell of culture'; and after Geertz (1973, chapter 1), we sought for a refinement of debate so 'what gets better is the precision with which we vex each other'. Each is a part of our ambition in decentring the state.

Note

1. For examples, see the Centre for Deliberative Democracy at: http://deliberativedemocracy.anu.edu.au/papers.php (last accessed 30 July 2009).

References

Abel, T. 1948. 'The operation called *verstehen*', *American Journal of Sociology* 54 (3): 211–18.

—— 1974. 'A reply to Professor Wax'. In M. Truzzi, Ed. *Verstehen: Subjective understanding in the social sciences*. Reading, MA: Addison-Wesley, pp. 83–6.

Abrams, P. 1988. 'Notes of the difficulty of studying the state', *Journal of Historical Sociology* 1 (1): 58–89.

Adcock, R., M. Bevir, and S. Stimson 2007. 'Historizing the new institutionalism(s)'. In R. Adcock, M. Bevir, and S. Stimson, Eds. *Modern political science: Anglo-American approaches to a historical political science since 1880*. Princeton, NJ: Princeton University Press, pp. 259–89.

Agar, M. 1996. *The professional stranger*, 2nd edition. San Diego, CA: Academic Press.

Agranoff, R. 2007. *Managing within networks: adding value to public organizations*. Washington, DC: Georgetown University Press.

—— and M. McGuire 2004. *Collaborative public management: new strategies for local governments*. Washington, DC: Georgetown University Press.

Almond, G. 1960. 'A functional approach to comparative politics'. In G. Almond and J. Coleman, Eds. *The politics of the developing areas*. Princeton, NJ: Princeton University Press, pp. 3–64.

—— 1965. 'A developmental approach to political systems', *World Politics* 17 (2): 183–214.

—— 1988. 'The return to the state', *American Political Science Review* 82 (3): 853–74.

Ansell, C. and A. Gash 2007. 'Collaborative governance in theory and practice', *Journal of Public Administration Theory and Practice* 18 (4): 543–71.

Aristotle. 1946. *The Politics*, trans. E. Barker. Oxford: Clarendon Press.

Aucoin, P. 1995. *The new public management: Canada in comparative perspective*. Quebec, Canada: Institute for Research on Public Policy.

Bagehot, W. 1963 [1867]. *The English constitution*. With an introduction by R. H. S. Crossman. London: Fontana.

Ballard, J. G. 2006. *Kingdom come*. London: Fourth Estate.

Barber, B. 1984. *Strong democracy: participatory politics for a new age*. Berkeley, CA: University of California Press.

Barber, M. 2007*a*. *Instruction to deliver. Tony Blair, public services and the challenge of targets*. London: Politico's Publishing.

Barber, M. 2007*b*. 'Education Reform Lessons from England'. An interview with Sir Michael Barber at: http://www.educationsector.org/analysis/analysis_show.htm?doc_id = 344385 (last accessed 30 June 2009).

—— 2007*c*. 'Why giving the prime minister more power, not less, must be new leader's first step', *The Times*, 14 May at: http://www.timesonline.co.uk/tol/news/politics/article1784690.ece?print = yes

Barker, E. 1915. *Political thought in England from Herbert Spencer to present day*. New York: Holt.

—— 1944. *The development of public services in Europe, 1660–1930*. New York: Oxford University Press.

—— 1956. *From Alexander to Constantine: passages and documents illustrating the history of social and political ideas 336 BC–AD 337*. Translated with introductions, notes, and essays by Ernest Barker. Oxford: Oxford University Press.

Barry, A., T. Osborne, and N. Rose, Eds. 1996*a*. *Foucault and political reason*. London: UCL Press.

—— 1996*b*. 'Introduction'. In A. Barry, T. Osborne, and N. Rose, Eds. *Foucault and political reason*. London: UCL Press, pp. 1–18.

Barthes, R. 1977. 'Death of the Author'. In *Image, music, text*, trans. S. Heath. London: Fontana.

Bates, D. 1996. 'Rediscovering Collingwood's spiritual history (in and out of context)', *History and Theory* 35 (1): 29–55.

Bates, R. H. 1981. *Markets and states in tropical Africa: the political basis of agricultural policies*. Berkeley, CA: University of California Press.

—— 1983. *Essays on the political economy of rural Africa*. Cambridge: Cambridge University Press.

Beckett, F. and D. Hencke 2004. *The Blairs and their court*. London: Aurum Press.

Beer, S. 1956. 'Pressure groups and parties in Britain', *American Political Science Review* 50 (1): 1–23.

—— 1963. *Modern British politics: a study of parties and pressure groups*. London: Faber.

Bell, C. and H. Newby, Eds. 1977. *Doing sociological research*. London: Allen & Unwin.

Bevir, M. 1999. *The logic of the history of ideas*. Cambridge: Cambridge University Press.

—— 2001. 'Prisoners of professionalism: on the construction and responsibility of political studies', *Public Administration* 79 (2): 469–89.

—— 2005. *New Labour: a critique*. London: Routledge.

—— and R. A. W. Rhodes 2003. *Interpreting British governance*. London: Routledge.

—— —— 2006. *Governance stories*. London: Routledge.

—— and F. Trentmann 2002*a*. 'Critique within capitalism: historiographical problems, theoretical perspectives'. In M. Bevir and F. Trentmann, Eds. *Critiques of capital in modern Britain and America: transatlantic exchanges 1800 to the present day*. Basingstoke, UK: Palgrave Macmillan, pp. 1–25.

—— —— Eds. 2002*b*. *Critiques of capital in modern Britain and America: transatlantic exchanges 1800 to the present day*. Basingstoke: Palgrave Macmillan.

—— —— Eds. 2004. *Markets in historical contexts: ideas and politics in the modern world.* Cambridge: Cambridge University Press.

—— —— Eds. 2007. *Governance, consumers, and citizens: agency and resistance in contemporary politics.* Basingstoke: Palgrave Macmillan.

Blair, T. 2004. 'Civil service delivery and values event', speech, ExCeL Centre, London, 24 February, at: www.civilservice.gov.uk/archive/delivery_and_reform/publications/rtf/PM_speech.rtf

Blunkett, D. 2006. *The Blunket tapes: my life in the bear pit.* London: Bloomsbury.

—— 2009. 'The ambiguity of civil service loyalty' in 'Editorial and Debates', *Public Money and Management* 29 (4): 203–8.

Bluntschli, J. 1885. *The theory of the state.* Oxford: Clarendon Press.

Blyth, M. 2002*a*. *The great transformations.* Cambridge: Cambridge University Press.

—— 2002*b*. 'Institutions and ideas'. In D. Marsh and G. Stoker, Eds. *Theory and methods in political science.* Basingstoke, UK: Palgrave, pp. 292–310.

Bogdanor, V. 1999. 'Comparative politics'. In J. Hayward, B. Barry, and A. Brown, Eds. *The British study of politics in the twentieth century.* Oxford: Oxford University Press for the British Academy, pp. 147–79.

—— Ed. 2005. *Joined-Up Government.* Oxford: Oxford University Press, 2005.

Bosanquet, B. 1965. *The philosophical theory of the state.* London: Macmillan.

Botterill, L. C. 2007. 'Doing it for the growers in Iraq? The AWB oil-for-food and the Cole Inquiry', *Australian Journal of Public Administration* 66 (1): 4–12.

Bovaird, T. and K. Russell 2007. 'Civil service reform in the UK, 1999–2005: revolutionary failure of evolutionary success?' *Public Administration* 85 (2): 301–28.

Bower, T. 2007. *Gordon Brown: prime minister.* London: Harper Perennial. Revised and expanded edition.

Braithwaite, J. 1997. 'On speaking softly and carrying big sticks: neglected dimensions of a Republican separation of powers', *University of Toronto Law Journal* 47 (3): 305–61.

Bridges, E. 1950. *Portrait of a profession.* Cambridge: Cambridge University Press.

—— 1956. Administration: what is it and how can it be learnt? In A. Dunsire, Ed. *The making of an administrator.* Manchester, UK: Manchester University Press, pp. 1–24.

Brown, G. 1999. 'Modernising the British economy: the new mission for the Treasury', speech, Institute of Fiscal Studies, London, 27 May, at: http://www.hm-treasury.gov.uk/newsroom_and_speeches/speeches/chancellorexchequer/speech_chex_270599.cfm (last accessed 30 July 2009).

Brown, P. and S. C. Levinson 2000. *Politeness: some universals in language use.* Cambridge: Cambridge University Press.

Bruce-Gardyne, J. 1986. *Ministers and mandarins: inside the Whitehall village.* London: Sidgwick & Jackson.

Bryce, J. (1st Viscount Bryce). 1888. *The American commonwealth*, 3 volumes. London: Macmillan.

Burchell, G., C. Gordon, and P. Miller, Eds. 1991. *The Foucault effect: studies in governmentality.* London: Harvester Wheatsheaf.

Burns, T. 1977. *The BBC: public institution and private world*. London: Macmillan.

Butler, J., E. Laclau, and S. Zizek 2000. *Contingency, hegemony, and universality*. London: Verso.

Butler, Sir Robin (Lord Butler of Brockwell). 1992. 'Managing the new public services: towards a new framework?' *Public Policy and Administration* 7 (3): 1–14.

—— 1993. 'The evolution of the civil service', *Public Administration* 71 (3): 395–406.

Cabinet Office. 2001. *Better policy making*. London: Cabinet Office.

—— 2006*a*. *Capability review of the Cabinet Office*. London: Cabinet Office.

—— 2006*b*. *Capability reviews tranche 2: common themes and summaries*. London: Cabinet Office.

—— 2007*a*. *Code of Conduct for Special Advisers*. http://webarchive.nationalarchives.gov.uk/ + http://www.cabinetoffice.gov.uk/propriety_and_ethics/special_advisers/code/index.asp (last accessed 30 July 2009).

—— 2007*b*. *Ministerial Code*. http://webarchive.nationalarchives.gov.uk/ + http://www.cabinetoffice.gov.uk/propriety_and_ethics/publications/pdf/ministerial_code_current.pdf (last accessed 30 July 2009).

—— and Performance and Innovation Unit. 2000. *Wiring it up*. London: Cabinet Office.

Caiden, G. E. 1967. *The Commonwealth bureaucracy*. Melbourne: Melbourne University Press.

—— 1990. Australia's changing administrative ethos: an exploration. In A. Kouzmin and N. Scott, Eds. *Dynamics in Australian public management*. Melbourne: Macmillan, pp. 29–49.

Campbell, A. 2007. *The Blair years: extracts from the Alastair Campbell diaries*. London: Hutchinson.

Campbell, C. and G. Wilson 1995. *The end of Whitehall: death of a paradigm?* Oxford: Blackwell.

Campbell, J. and O. K. Pederson, Eds. 2001. *The second movement in institutional analysis*. Princeton, NJ: Princeton University Press.

Centre for Contemporary Cultural Studies. 1982. *The empire strikes back: race and racism in 70s Britain*. London: Hutchinson.

Chapman, R. A. 1988. *Ethics in the British civil service*. London: Routledge.

—— and J. R. Greenaway. 1980. *The dynamics of administrative reform*. London: Croom Helm.

Chester, N. 1981. *The English administrative system 1780–1870*. Oxford: Clarendon Press.

Chevallier, J. 1996. 'Public administration in statist France', *Public Administration Review*, 56 (1): 67–74.

—— 2002. *Science Administrative*, 3rd edition. Paris: PUF, Coll. Thémis.

Clarke, J. 2007. 'It's not like shopping': citizens, consumers and the reform of public services. In M. Bevir and F. Trentmann, Eds. *Governance, consumers, and citizens: agency and resistance in contemporary politics*. Basingstoke, UK: Palgrave Macmillan, pp. 97–118.

Clifford, J. 1983. 'On ethnographic authority', *Representations*, Number 2, Spring: 118–46.

—— and G. E. Marcus, Eds. 1984. *Writing culture: the poetics and politics of ethnography.* Berkeley, CA: University of California Press.

Cm 2627. 1994. *The civil service: continuity and change.* Cabinet Office: Office of Public Service and Science. London: HMSO.

Cm 4310. 1999. *Modernising government.* London: Stationery Office.

Cmnd 3638. 1968 [1854]. *Report on the organisation of the permanent civil service.* (S. H. Northcote and C. E. Trevelyan). Reprinted in: Committee on the Civil Service (Fulton), *Report.* London: HMSO, Appendix 3.

Collingwood, R. 1946. *The idea of history.* Oxford: Clarendon Press.

—— 1978 [1939]. *An autobiography.* Oxford: Oxford University Press.

Committee on Political Behavior. 1950. 'Committee briefs: political behavior', *Social Science Research Council Items* 4.

Conservative Party Democracy Task Force. 2007. *An end to sofa government.* London: Conservative Party.

Considine, M. 2002. 'The end of the line? Accountable governance in the age of networks, partnerships, and joined-up services', *Governance* 15 (1): 21–40.

Coombs, H. C. 1981. *Trial balance.* Melbourne: Macmillan.

Cornish, S. 2002. *Sir Roland Wilson: a biographical essay.* Canberra: ANU.

Crossman, R. H. S. 1975. *The diaries of a cabinet minister, Volume 1: Minister of Housing 1964–66.* London: Hamish Hamilton and Jonathan Cape.

Currie, E. 1989. *Life lines.* London: Sidgwick & Jackson.

Dahl, R. 1956. *A preface to democratic theory.* New Haven, CT: Yale University Press.

Davidson, D. 1980. 'Actions, reasons, and causes'. In *Actions on essays and events.* Oxford: Clarendon Press, pp. 3–20.

Dean, M. 1998. *Governmentality: power and rule in modern society.* London: Sage.

—— 2007. *Governing societies.* Maidenhead, UK: Open University Press.

—— and B. Hindess, Eds. 1998. *Governing Australia: studies in contemporary rationalities of government.* Cambridge and Melbourne: Cambridge University Press.

Department of the Prime Minister and Cabinet. December 1998. *A guide on key elements of ministerial responsibility.* http://www.pmc.gov.au/guidelines/docs /ministerial_responsibility.pdf (last accessed 30 July 2009).

Derrida, J. 1976. *Of grammatology,* trans. G. Spivak. Baltimore, MD: Johns Hopkins University Press.

Dicey, A. V. 1914. *Lectures on the relations between law and public opinion during the nineteenth century,* 2nd edition. London: Macmillan.

Dilthey, W. 1996. 'On understanding and hermeneutics: student lecture notes (1867–68)'. In R. Makkreel and F. Rodi, Eds. *Selected works, Volume 4: hermeneutics and the study of history.* Princeton, NJ: Princeton University Press, pp. 229–34.

—— 2002*a*. 'Plan for the continuation of the formation of the historical world in the social sciences'. In R. Makkreel and F. Rodi, Eds. *Selected works, Volume 3: the* *formation of the historical world in the human sciences*. Princeton, NJ: Princeton University Press, pp. 211–311.

—— 2002*b*. 'The rise of hermeneutics'. In R. Makkreel and F. Rodi, Eds. *Selected works, Volume 4: hermeneutics and the study of history*. Princeton, NJ: Princeton University Press, pp. 235–60.

DiMaggio, P. J. and W. W. Powell 1991. 'Introduction'. In W. W. Powell and P. J. DiMaggio, Eds. *The new institutionalism in organizational analysis*. Chicago, IL: University of Chicago Press, pp. 1–38.

Dray, W. 1957. *Laws and explanation in history*. Oxford: Oxford University Press.

—— 1995. *History as re-enactment: R. G. Collingwood's idea of history*. Oxford: Clarendon Press.

Duhamel, O. and J. L. Parodi, Eds. 1985. *La constitution de la Cinquième République*. Paris: Presses de la FNSP.

Dunleavy, P. and B. O'Leary, Eds. 1987. *Theories of the state*. Houndmills, Basingstoke, UK: Macmillan.

Duverger, M. 1959 [1954]. *Political Parties*, 2nd revised edition. London: Methuen.

—— 1980. 'A new political system model: semi-presidential government', *European Journal of Political Research* 8 (2): 165–87.

Dworkin, D. 1997. *Cultural Marxism in post-war Britain: history, the New Left, and the origins of cultural studies*. Durham, NC: Duke University Press.

Easton, D. 1953. *The political system: an inquiry into the state of political science*. New York: Knopf.

Eckstein, H. 1960. *Pressure group politics*. Palo Alto, CA: Stanford University Press.

—— 1963. 'A perspective on comparative politics, past and present'. In H. Eckstein and D. E. Apter, Eds. *Comparative politics: a reader*. London: The Free Press of Glencoe, pp. 3–32.

—— 1975. 'Case study and theory in political science'. In F. I. Greenstein and N. Polsby, Eds. *Handbook of political science, Volume 7: strategies of inquiry*. Reading, MA: Addison-Wesley, pp. 79–137.

—— 1979. 'On the "science" of the state', *Daedalus* 108 (4): 1–20.

Eldersveld, S., A. Heard, S. Huntington, M. Janowitz, A. Leiserson, D. McKean, and D. Truman, 1952. 'Research in political behavior', *American Political Science Review* 46 (4): 1003–45.

Elgie, R. 1996. 'The French presidency: conceptualizing presidential power in the Fifth Republic', *Public Administration*, 74 (2): 275–91.

Evans, P. 1979. *Dependent development: the alliance of multinational, state, and local capital in Brazil*. Princeton, NJ: Princeton University Press.

—— D. Rueschemeyer, and T. Skocpol, Eds. 1985. *Bringing the state back in*. New York: Cambridge University Press.

Fawcett, P. 2009. 'Government, governance and metagovernance in the British core executive'. PhD thesis. University of Birmingham (UK).

Fenno, R. F. 1990. *Watching politicians: essays on participant observation*. Berkeley, CA: Institute of Governmental Studies, University of California.

Ferlie, E., L. E. Lynn, and C. Pollitt, Eds. 2005. *The Oxford handbook of public management*. Oxford: Oxford University Press.

Finer, H. 1932. *Theory and practice of modern government*, 2 volumes. London: Methuen.

Finer, S. E. 1958. *Anonymous empire: a study of the lobby in Great Britain*. London: Pall Mall Press.

—— 1997. *The history of government from the earliest times*, 3 volumes. Oxford: Oxford University Press.

Finlayson, A. 2003. *Making sense of New Labour*. London: Lawrence & Wishart.

—— and J. Martin 2006. 'Post-structuralism'. In C. Hay, M. Lister, and D. Marsh, Eds. *The state: theory and issues*. Houndmills, Basingstoke, UK: Palgrave Macmillan, pp. 155–71.

—— —— 2008. '"It ain't what you say ...": British political studies and the analysis of speech and rhetoric', *British Politics* 3 (4): 445–64.

Finn, P. D. 1987. *Law and government in colonial Australia*. Melbourne: Oxford University Press.

Finnemore, M. 1996. 'Norms, culture, and world politics: insights from sociology's institutionalism', *International Organization* 50 (2): 325–47.

Fischer, F. and J. Forester, Eds. 1993. *The argumentative turn in policy analysis and planning*. Durham, NC: Duke University Press.

Fleming, J. and J. Wood, Eds. 2006. *Fighting crime together: the challenges of policing and security networks*. Sydney: UNSW Press.

Fodor, J. and E. LePore 1992. *Holism: a shopper's guide*. Oxford: Blackwell.

Forester, J. 1999. *The deliberative practitioner: encouraging participatory planning processes*. Cambridge, MA: MIT Press.

Foucault, M. 1973. *Birth of the clinic: archaeology of medical perception*. London: Tavistock.

Foucault, M. 1977. *Discipline and punish: the birth of the prison*. Harmondsworth, UK: Penguin.

—— 1978–85. *The history of sexuality, Volume 1: an introduction, Volume 2: the use of pleasure, Volume 3: the care of the self*, trans. R. Hurley. New York: Pantheon Books.

—— 1989. *Madness and civilization: a history of insanity in the age of reason*. London: Routledge.

—— 1991. 'Governmentality'. In G. Burchell, C. Gordon, and P. Miller, Eds. *The Foucault effect: studies in governmentality*. London: Harvester Wheatsheaf, pp. 87–104.

—— 2004. *Naissance de la biopolitique: cours au Collège de France (1978–1979)*. Paris: Gallimard.

Fox, K. 2004. *Watching the English: the hidden rules of English behaviour*. London: Hodder & Stoughton.

Frances, J., R. Levacic, J. Mitchell, and G. J. Thompson 1991. 'Introduction'. In G. Thompson, J. Frances, R. Levacic, and J. Mitchell, Eds. *Markets hierarchies and networks: the co-ordination of social life*. London: Sage, pp. 1–19.

Frank, A. G. 1967. *Capitalism and underdevelopment in Latin America: historical studies of Chile and Brazil*. New York: Monthly Review Press.

Friedrich, C. 1937. *Constitutional government and politics*. New York: Harper.

—— 1941. *Constitutional government and democracy*. Boston, MA: Little, Brown.

—— 1952. *The age of the Baroque, 1610–1660*. New York: Harper.

Gadamer, H.-G. 2002. *Truth and method*, trans. J. Weinsheimer and D. Marshall. New York: Continuum.

Garceau, O. 1951. 'Research in the political process', *American Political Science Review* 45 (1): 69–85.

Geertz, C. 1973. *The interpretation of culture*. New York: Basic Books.

—— 1983. *Local knowledge*. New York: Basic Books.

—— 1988. *Works and lives: the anthropologist as author*. Palo Alto, CA: Stanford University Press.

George, A. L. and A. Bennett 2005. *Case studies and theory development*. Cambridge, MA: MIT Press.

Gershon, P. 2004. *Releasing resources for the front-line: independent review of public sector efficiency*. London: Stationery Office.

Gilroy, P. 1987. *There ain't no black in the Union Jack: the cultural politics of race and nation*. London: Hutchinson.

—— 1993. *The black Atlantic: modernity and double consciousness*. Cambridge, MA: Harvard University Press.

Gomery, J. H. 2004*a*. Public hearing before the *commission of inquiry into the sponsorship program and advertising activities* (Gomery Commission), Volume 12, 27 September. Ottawa, Canada: Canadian Government Publishing.

—— 2004*b*. Public hearing before the *commission of inquiry into the sponsorship program and advertising activities* (Gomery Commission), Volumes 47 and 48, 8 and 9 December. Ottawa, Canada: Canadian Government Publishing.

—— 2005. *Who is responsible? Fact-finding report: phase 1 of the report of the commission of inquiry into the sponsorship program and advertising activities* (Gomery Commission). Ottawa: Canadian Government Publishing.

—— 2006. *Restoring accountability: phase 2 of the report of the commission of inquiry into the sponsorship program and advertising activities* (Gomery Commission). Ottawa, Canada: Canadian Government Publishing.

Goss, S. 2001. *Making local governance work*. Houndmills, Basingstoke, UK: Palgrave Macmillan.

Government Communications Review Group. 2003. *Interim Report* at: http://archive.cabinetoffice.gov.uk/gcreview/News/interimreport.pdf

Granatstein, J. L. 1982. The *Ottawa men: the civil service mandarins 1935–1957*. Toronto: Oxford University Press.

Griffith, E., Ed. 1948. *Research in political* science. Chapel Hill, NC: University of North Carolina Press.

Griggs, S. and D. Howarth 2000. 'New environmental movements and direct action protests: the campaign against Manchester Airport's second runway'. In

D. Howarth, A. Norval, and Y. Stavrakakis, Eds. *Discourse theory and political analysis: identities, hegemonies and social change*. Manchester, UK: Manchester University Press, pp. 52–69.

Gunnell, J. 2007. 'Making democracy safe for the world: political science between the wars'. In R. Adcock, M. Bevir, and S. Stimson, Eds. *Modern political science: Anglo-American exchanges since 1880*. Princeton, NJ: Princeton University Press, pp. 137–57.

Habermas, J. 1988. *On the logic of the social sciences*, trans. S. Nicholsen and J. Stark. Cambridge, MA: MIT Press.

Hajer, M. A. and H. Wagenaar, Eds. 2003. *Deliberative policy analysis: understanding governance in a networked society*. Cambridge: Cambridge University Press.

Hall, J. A. and G. J. Ikenberry, 1989. *The state*. Milton Keynes, UK: Open University Press.

Hall, P. A. 1986. *Governing the economy: the politics of state intervention in Britain and France*. New York: Oxford University Press.

—— 1989. 'Conclusion: the politics of Keynesian ideas'. In P. A. Hall, Ed. *The political power of economic ideas*. Princeton, NJ: Princeton University Press, pp. 351–91.

—— and R. Taylor 1996. 'Political science and the three institutionalisms', *Political Studies* 44 (5): 936–57.

Hall, S. 1983. 'The great moving right show'. In S. Hall and M. Jacques, Eds. *The politics of Thatcherism*. London: Lawrence & Wishart, pp. 19–39.

—— 1986. 'Cultural studies: two paradigms'. In R. Collins, Ed. *Media, culture and society*. London: Sage, pp. 33–48.

Hall, S. 1988. *The hard road to renewal: Thatcherism and the crisis of the Left*. London: Verso.

—— 2003. 'New Labour's double shuffle', *Soundings* 24 (Summer): 10–24.

—— and T. Jefferson Eds. 1993. *Resistance through rituals: youth subcultures in post-war Britain*. London: Routledge.

—— B. Lumley and B. McLennan 1978. 'Politics and ideology: Gramsci'. In *On ideology*. University of Birmingham Centre for Contemporary Cultural Studies Working Papers in Cultural Studies, No. 10, London: Hutchinson, pp. 45–76.

Hammersley, M. 2000. *Taking sides in social science research: essays on partisanship and bias*. London: Routledge.

—— and P. Atkinson 1995. *Ethnography: principles in practice*, 2nd edition. London: Routledge.

Harris, J. 1990. 'Society and state in twentieth century Britain'. In F. M. L. Thompson, Ed. *The Cambridge social history of Britain 1750–1950, Volume 3: social agencies and institutions*. Cambridge: Cambridge University Press, pp. 63–117.

Hartz, L. 1955. *The Liberal tradition in America: an interpretation of American political thought since the revolution*. New York: Harcourt Brace & World/Palgrave Macmillan.

Hay, C. 1996. *Re-Stating social and political change*. Buckingham, UK: Open University Press.

Hay, C. 2002. *Political analysis: a critical introduction*. Houndmills, Basingstoke, UK: Palgrave Macmillan.

—— 2006. 'Constructivist institutionalism'. In R. A. W. Rhodes, S. Binder, and B. Rockman, Eds. *The Oxford handbook of political institutions*. Oxford: Oxford University Press, pp. 56–74.

—— and M. Lister 2006. 'Introduction: theories of the state'. In C. Hay, M. Lister, and D. Marsh, Eds. 2006. *The state: theory and issues*. Houndmills, Basingstoke, UK: Palgrave Macmillan, pp. 1–20.

—— M. Lister and D. Marsh, Eds. 2006. *The state: theory and issues*. Houndmills, Basingstoke, UK: Palgrave Macmillan.

Heady, B. 1974. *British cabinet ministers*. London: Allen & Unwin.

Healey, P. 1997. *Collaborative planning: shaping places in fragmented societies*. London: Macmillan.

Hempel, C. 1965. *Aspects of scientific explanation, and other essays in the philosophy of science*. New York: Free Press.

—— 1966. 'Explanation in science and in history'. In W. Dray, Ed. *Philosophical analysis and history*. New York: Harper & Row, pp. 95–126.

Henderson, S. N. 2001 [1984]. *The private office*. London: Profile Books.

Hennessy, P. 1998. 'The Blair style of government', *Government and Opposition* 33 (1): 3–20.

—— 2000. *The Blair revolution in government*. Leeds, UK: University of Leeds, Institute for Politics and International Studies.

—— 2001 [1989]. *Whitehall*, revised edition. London: Secker & Warburg.

—— 2005. 'Rulers and servants of the state: the Blair style of government 1997–2004', *Parliamentary Affairs* 58 (1): 6–16.

Herring, P. 1929. *Group representation before Congress*. Baltimore, MD: Johns Hopkins University Press.

Heseltine, M. 2000. *Life in the jungle: my autobiography*. London: Hodder & Stoughton.

Hill, C. 1965. *Intellectual origins of the English Revolution*. Oxford: Clarendon Press.

HM Treasury. 2002. *Securing our future health: taking a long-term view* (Wanless Review). London: HM Treasury.

—— 2007. *Transforming government procurement*. London: Stationery Office.

—— and Cabinet Office. 2004. *Devolving decision making: delivering better public services: refining targets and performance management*. London: Stationery Office.

—— and Department for Communities and Local Government. 2006. *Barker review of land use planning*. London: Stationery Office.

—— and Department for Education and Skills. 2006. *Prosperity for all in the global economy – world class skills*. London: Stationery Office.

Hodgson, L. C., M. Farrell, and M. Connolly 2007. 'Improving UK public services: a review of the evidence', *Public Administration* 85 (2): 355–82.

Hoggart, R. 1957. *The uses of literacy: aspects of working class life*. London: Chatto & Windus.

Horner, D. 2000. *Defence supremo: Sir Frederick Shedden and the making of Australian defence policy*. Sydney: Allen & Unwin.

House of Commons 2004. *Report of the inquiry into the circumstances surrounding the death of Dr David Kelly C.M.G. by Lord Hutton*. HC 247. London: The Stationery Office, 28 January. See also http://www.the-hutton-inquiry.org.uk (last accessed 30 July 2009) and http://en.wikipedia.org/wiki/David_Kelly_(weapons_expert) (last accessed 30 July 2009).

Howarth, D. 2000. *Discourse*. Buckingham, UK: Open University Press.

—— and J. Torfing, Eds. 2005. *Discourse theory in European politics: identity, policy and government*. Basingstoke, UK: Palgrave.

—— A. Norval, and Y. Stavrakakis, Eds. 2000. *Discourse theory and political analysis: identities, hegemonies, and social change*. Manchester, UK: Manchester University Press.

Howe, G. 1994. *Conflict of loyalty*. London: Macmillan.

Huntington, S. P. 1981. *American politics: the promise of disharmony*. Cambridge, MA: Harvard University Press.

Inglis, F. 2000. *Clifford Geertz: culture, custom and ethics*. Oxford: Blackwell.

Jackson, R. J. and D. Jackson 2006. *Politics in Canada: culture, institutions, behaviour and public policy*, 6th edition. New York: Pearson Prentice Hall.

Jacobs, K. and T. Manzi 2000. 'Performance indicators and social constructivism: conflict and control in housing management', *Critical Social Policy* 20 (1): 85–103.

James, O. 2004. 'The UK core executive's use of public service agreements as a tool of governance', *Public Administration*, 82 (2): 397–419.

James, S. 1999. *British cabinet government*, 2nd edition. London: Routledge.

Jary, C. 2004. *Working with ministers*. London: Cabinet Office/CMPS.

Jessop, B. 1990. *State theory: putting capitalist states in their place*. Cambridge: Polity.

—— 2000. 'Governance failure'. In G. Stoker, Ed. *The new politics of British local governance*. Houndmills, Basingstoke, UK: Macmillan, pp. 11–32.

—— 2005. 'Critical realism and the strategic-relational approach', *New Formations* 56 (1): 40–53.

—— 2007*a*. *State power*. Cambridge: Polity.

—— 2007*b*. 'Governance and metagovernance: on reflexivity, requisite variety, and requisite irony'. In M. Bevir, Ed. *Public governance, Volume 1: theories of governance*. London: Sage, pp. 230–45.

Kant, I. 1949. *The philosophy of Kant*, trans. C. Friedrich. New York: Modern Library.

Katzenstein, P. J. 1976. 'International relations and domestic structures: foreign economic policies of advanced industrial states', *International Organization* 30 (1): 1–45.

—— Ed. 1978. *Between power and plenty: foreign economic policies of advanced industrial states*. Madison, WI: University of Wisconsin Press.

—— Ed. 1996. *The culture of national security: norms and identity in world politics*. New York: Columbia University Press.

Katznelson, I. 1994. 'The state to the rescue? Political science and history reconnect', *Social Research* 59 (4): 719–37.

Kaufman, G. 1980. *How to be a minister.* London: Sidgwick & Jackson.

Kavanagh, D. and A. Seldon 2000. *The powers behind the prime minister: the hidden influence of Number Ten.* London: HarperCollins.

Kelly, J. 2006. 'Central regulation of English local authorities: an example of meta-governance?' *Public Administration*, 84 (3): 603–21.

Kenny, M. 1995. *The first New Left.* London: Lawrence & Wishart.

Keohane, R. O. 1988. 'International institutions: two approaches', *International Studies Quarterly* 32 (4): 379–96.

Kerr, P. and S. Kettell 2006. 'In defence of British politics: the past, present and future of the discipline', *Journal of British Politics*, 1 (1): 3–25.

Koppernjan, J. F. M. and E. H. Klein 2004. *Managing uncertainties in networks: a network approach to problem solving and decision making.* London: Routledge.

Kramer, R. M. and T. Tyler, Eds. 1996. *Trust in organizations: frontiers of theory and research.* London: Sage.

Krasner, S. D. 1976. 'State power and the structure of international trade', *World Politics* 28 (3): 317–47.

—— 1978. *Defending the national interest: raw materials investments and U.S. foreign policy.* Princeton, NJ: Princeton University Press.

—— 1984. 'Approaches to the state: alternative conceptions and historical dynamics', *Comparative Politics* 16 (2): 223–46.

Kratochwil, F. and J. G. Ruggie 1986. 'International organizations: a state of the art on an art of the state', *International Organization* 40 (4): 753–75.

Laclau, E. 1990. *New reflections on the revolution of our time.* London: Verso.

—— and C. Mouffe 1985. *Hegemony and socialist strategy: towards a radical democratic politics.* New York: Verso.

Landau, M. 1979 [1972]. *Political theory and political science: studies in the methodology of political inquiry.* Brighton, UK: Harvester Press.

Lange, D. 1992. *Broadsides.* Wellington, NZ: Jonathan Hudson.

Lasswell, H. and A. Kaplan 1950. *Power and society: a framework for political inquiry.* New Haven, CT: Yale University Press.

Lawson, N. 1992. *The view from No. 11.* London: Bantam Press.

Lee, M. 1995. 'The ethos of the Cabinet Office: a comment on the testimony of officials'. In R. A. W. Rhodes and P. Dunleavy, Eds. *Prime minister, cabinet and core executive.* London: Macmillan, pp. 149–57.

Leiserson, A. 1951. 'Systematic research in political behavior', *Social Science Research Items* 5: 29–32.

Lemke, T. 2001. 'The birth of bio-politics: Michel Foucault's lecture at the Collège de France on neo-liberal governmentality', *Economy and Society* 30 (2): 190–207.

Levi, M. 1987. 'Theories of historical and institutional change,' *PS* 20 (3): 684–8.

—— 1988. *Of rule and revenue.* Berkeley, CA: University of California Press.

Lipsky, M. 1979. *Street level bureaucracy.* New York: Russell Sage Foundation.

Lowe, R. 2005. 'Western public administration and the myth of Northcote Trevelyan'. Seminar presented to the Political Science Program, Research School of Social Sciences, Australian National University, 12 October.

Lowell, A. 1908. *The government of England*, 2 volumes. New York: Macmillan.

Lowndes, V. 1996. 'Varieties of the new institutionalism: a critical appraisal', *Public Administration*, 74 (2): 181–97.

MacDonagh, O. 1977. *Early Victorian government*. London: Weidenfeld & Nicolson.

Mackenzie, W. J. M. 1955. 'Pressure groups in British government', *British Journal of Sociology* 6 (2): 133–48.

Management Advisory Committee (MAC). 2004. *Connecting government: whole of government response to Australia's priority challenges*. Canberra: Australian Public Service Commission.

Mandelson, P. and R. Liddle, 1996. *The Blair revolution: can New Labour deliver?* London: Faber & Faber.

March, J. G. and J. P. Olsen 1984. 'The new institutionalism: organizational factors in political life', *American Political Science Review* 78 (3): 734–49.

—— —— 1989. *Rediscovering institutions*. New York: Free Press.

Marinetto, M. 2003. 'Governing beyond the centre: a critique of the Anglo-Governance School', *Political Studies*, 51 (3): 592–608.

Marr, D. and M. Wilkinson 2003. *Dark victory*. Crows Nest, New South Wales, Australia: Allen & Unwin.

Marsh, D. 1999. 'Resurrecting Marxism'. In A. Gamble, D. Marsh, and T. Tant, Eds. *Marxism and social science*. London: Macmillan, pp. 320–40.

Marsh, D. 2008*a*. 'Understanding British government: analysing competing models', *British Journal of Politics and International Relations*, 10 (2): 251–68.

—— 2008*b*. 'What is at stake? A response to Bevir and Rhodes', *British Journal of Politics and International Relations* 10 (4): 735–39.

—— and M. Smith, 2000. 'Understanding policy networks: towards a dialectical approach', *Political Studies* 48 (1): 4–21.

—— D. Richards, and M. J. Smith 2001. *Changing patterns of governance in the United Kingdom*. Houndmills, Basingstoke, UK: Palgrave.

Marshall, G. 1986. *Constitutional conventions: the rules and forms of political accountability*. Oxford: Clarendon Press.

Massey, A. and R. Pyper 2005. *Public management and modernisation in Britain*. Houndmills, Basingstoke, UK: Palgrave Macmillan.

McAnulla, S. 2006. 'Challenging the new interpretivist approach: towards a critical realist alternative', *British Politics*, 1 (1): 113–38.

McKinlay, A. and K. P. Starkey, Eds. 1998. *Foucault, management and organization theory: from panopticon to technologies of self*. London: Sage.

Meadowcroft, J. 1999. 'Cooperative management regimes: collaborative problem solving to implement sustainable development', *International Negotiation* 4 (2): 225–54.

Meyer, J. W. and B. Rowen 1977. 'Institutionalized organizations: formal structure as myth and ceremony', *American Journal of Sociology* 83 (2): 340–63.

Milgrom, P. R., D. C. North and B. R. Weingast 1990. 'The role of institutions in the revival of trade: the law merchant, private judges, and the champagne fairs', *Economics and Politics* 2 (1): 1–23.

Miliband, R. 1969. *The state in capitalist society*. London: Weidenfeld & Nicolson.

—— R. 1970. 'The capitalist state: reply to Nicos Poulantzas', *New Left Review* 59 (1): 53–60.

Miller, P. and N. Rose 2008. *Governing the present: administering economic, social and personal life*. Cambridge: Polity.

Minow, M. 2003. 'Public and private partnerships: accounting for the new religion', *Harvard Law Review* 116 (1): 1229–70.

Moe, T. M. 1984. 'The new economics of organization', *American Journal of Political Science* 28 (4): 739–77.

Moss, G. and O'Loughlin, B. 2005. 'New Labour's Information Age policy programme: an ideology analysis', *Journal of Political Ideologies* 10 (2): 165–83.

Mouffe, C. 1993. *The return of the political*. London: Verso.

—— 2000. *The democratic paradox*. London: Verso.

Mulgan, G. 2005. Interview on 'Looking back at power', BBC Radio 4, 5 September at: http://www.bbc.co.uk/radio4/news/look_back_at_power.shtml (last accessed 30 July 2009).

—— 2006. *Truth in government and the politicisation of public service advice*, Policy and Governance Discussion Papers 06–02. Canberra: ANU.

Naughtie, J. 2002. *The rivals. The intimate story of a political marriage*, revised edition. London: Fourth Estate.

Noon, M. and R. Delbridge. 1993. 'News from behind my hand: gossip in organizations', *Organization Studies* 14 (1): 23–36.

O'Donnell, G[uillermo]. 1978. 'Reflections on patterns of change in the bureaucratic authoritarian state', *Latin American Research Review* 13 (1): 3–38.

O'Donnell, Sir Gus 2006*a*. 'Gus Vision; the 4Ps' at: http://www.civilservice.gov.uk/about/work/vision.aspx (last accessed on 30 July 2009).

—— 2006*b*. 'Our 21st century civil service – creating a culture of excellence', Public Service Reform Conference, QE II Conference Centre, London, 6 June, at: http://www.civilservice.gov.uk/publications/doc/psr_speech060606.doc

O'Halpin, E. 1989. *Head of the civil service: a study of Sir Warren Fisher*. London: Routledge.

Oakeshott, M. 1996. *The politics of faith and the politics of scepticism*, ed. T. Fuller. New Haven, CT: Yale University Press.

Odegard, P. 1928. *Pressure politics: the story of the anti-saloon league*. New York: Columbia University Press.

Office of Public Services Reform (OPSR). 2002. *Reforming our public services – principles into practice*. London: Cabinet Office.

—— 2005. *Putting people at the heart of public services*. London: Cabinet Office.

Palmer, M. J. 2005. *Inquiry into the circumstances of the immigration detention of Cornelia Rau report*. Canberra: Commonwealth of Australia.

Parris, H. 1969. *Constitutional bureaucracy: the development of British central administration since the eighteenth century*. London: Allen & Unwin.

Part, A. 1990. *The making of a mandarin*. London: Deutsch.

Pateman, C. 1970. *Participation and democratic theory*. Cambridge: Cambridge University Press.

Paxman, J. 2002. *The political animal*. London: Michael Joseph.

Perri 6, D. Leat, K. Seltzer, and Stoker, G. 2002. *Towards holistic governance: the new reform agenda*. Houndmills, Basingstoke, UK: Palgrave.

Peston, R. 2005. *Brown's Britain*. London: Short Books.

Peters, B. G. 1996. *The future of governing: four emerging models*. Lawrence, KS: University Press of Kansas.

—— 1999. *Institutional theory in political science: the 'new institutionalism'*. London: Pinter.

—— R. A. W. Rhodes, and V. Wright, Eds. 2000. *Administering the summit: administration of the core executive in developed countries*. Houndmills, Basingstoke, UK: Macmillan.

Pierre, J. and B. G. Peters, 2000. *Governance, politics and the state*. Houndmills, Basingstoke, UK: Macmillan.

Pierson, P. 2000. 'Increasing returns, path dependence, and the study of politics', *American Political Science Review* 94 (2): 251–67.

Pierson, P. 2004. *Politics in time: history, institutions, and social analysis*. Princeton, NJ: Princeton University Press.

Podger, A. 2007. 'What really happens: departmental secretary appointments, contracts and performance pay in the Australian public service?' *Australian Journal of Public Administration* 66 (1): 131–47.

Poguntke, T. and P. Webb 2005. 'The presidentialization of politics in democratic societies: a framework for analysis'. In T. Poguntke and P. Webb, Eds. *The presidentialization of politics: a comparative study of modern democracies*. Oxford: Oxford University Press, pp. 1–25.

Pollard, S. 2005. *David Blunkett*. London: Hodder & Stoughton.

Pollitt, C. 2003. 'Joined-up government: a survey', *Political Studies Review* 1 (1): 34–49.

Popkin, S. L. 1979. *The rational peasant: the political economy of rural society in Vietnam*. Berkeley, CA: University of California Press.

Popper, K. 1959. *The logic of scientific discovery*. New York: Basic Books.

—— 1972. *Conjectures and refutations: the growth of scientific knowledge*. London: Routledge.

Poster, M. 2007. 'Manifesto for a history of the media'. In S. Morgan, K. Jenkins, and A. Munslow, Eds. *Manifestos for history*. London: Routledge, pp. 39–49.

Poulantzas, N. 1969. 'The problem of the capitalist state', *New Left Review*, 1/58: 67–78.

Poulantzas, N. 1973. *Political power and social classes*, trans. T. O'Hagan. London: New Left Books.

Powell, W. 1991. 'Neither market nor hierarchy: network forms of organization'. In G. Thompson, J. Frances, R. Levacic, and J. Mitchell, Eds. *Markets, hierarchies and networks: the coordination of social life*. London: Sage, pp. 265–76.

Power, M. 1994. *The audit explosion*. London: Demos.

Prescott, J. 2008. *Prezza. My story: pulling no punches*. London: Headline Review.

Pressman, J. and A. Wildavsky 1973. *Implementation*. Berkeley, CA: University of California Press.

Prime Minister's Strategy Unit (PMSU). 2002. *The energy review*. London: Cabinet Office.

—— 2006. *The UK government's approach to public service reform – a discussion paper*. London: Cabinet Office.

—— 2007. *Building on progress: public services*. London: Cabinet Office.

Privy Council Office (PCO). 1993. *Responsibility in the constitution*. Submission to the Royal Commission on Financial Management and Accountability. Ottawa Ministry of Supply and Services Canada. Available at: http://www.pco-bcp.gc.ca/ (last accessed 30 July 2009).

Proctor, J. 2004. *Stuart Hall*. London: Routledge.

Public Administration Select Committee (PASC). 2001. *Making Government work: the emerging issues*, Session 2000–01 HC 94 London: Stationery Office.

—— 2002. *'These unfortunate events': lessons of recent events at the former DTLR. Eighth Report. Minutes of evidence*. Thursday, 7 March, HC 303 Session 2001–02. London: Stationery Office.

—— 2005. *Choice, voice and public services*, 2004–05 HC 49-I. London: Stationery Office.

—— 2007. *Governing the future*, 2006–07 HC 123-I. London: Stationery Office.

Punch, M. 1986. *The politics and ethics of fieldwork*. Newbury Park, CA: Sage.

Quine, W. 1961. 'Two dogmas of empiricism'. In *From a logical point of view*. Cambridge, MA: MIT Press, pp. 20–46.

—— and J. Ullian 1970. *The web of belief*. New York: Random House.

Rawnsley, A. 2001. *Servants of the people: the inside story of New Labour*, revised edition. London: Penguin Books.

Rentoul, J. 2001. *Tony Blair: prime minister*. London: Little, Brown.

Resch, R. 1992. *Althusser and the renewal of Marxist social theory*. Berkeley, CA: University of California Press.

Rhodes, R. A. W. 1988. *Beyond Westminster and Whitehall*. London: Unwin Hyman.

—— 1994. 'State-building without bureaucracy'. In I. Budge and D. McKay, Eds. *Developing democracy: research in honour of Jean Blondel*. London: Sage, pp. 165–78.

—— 1995. 'From prime ministerial power to core executive'. In R. A. W. Rhodes and P. Dunleavy, Eds. *Prime minister, cabinet and core executive*. London: Macmillan, pp. 11–37.

—— 1997*a*. *Understanding governance: policy networks, governance, reflexivity and accountability*. Buckingham, UK: Open University Press.
—— 1997*b*. 'It's the mix that matters: from marketisation to diplomacy', *Australian Journal of Public Administration*, 56 (2): 40–53.
—— Ed. 2000. *Transforming British governance*, 2 volumes. London: Macmillan.
—— 2001. 'The civil service'. In A. Seldon, Ed. *The Blair effect*. London: Little, Brown, pp. 97–116.
—— 2009*a*. 'From private office to departmental court', *Public Money and Management* 29 (3): 191–4.
—— 2009*b*. 'Scenes from the departmental court', *Public Policy and Administration* 24 (4): 437–56.
—— 2011. *Everyday Life in British Government*, Oxford: Oxford University Press.
—— and P. Dunleavy, Eds. 1995. *Prime minister, cabinet and core executive*. London: Macmillan.
—— and P. Weller, Eds. 2001. *The changing world of top officials: mandarins or valets?* Buckingham: Open University Press.
—— S. Binder, and B. Rockman, Eds. 2006. *The Oxford handbook of political institutions*. Oxford: Oxford University Press.
—— P. 't Hart and M. Noordegraaf, Eds. 2007. *Observing government elites: up close and personal*. Houndmills, Basingstoke: Palgrave Macmillan.
Rhodes, R. A. W., J. Wanna, and P. Weller 2009. *Comparing Westminster*. Oxford: Oxford University Press.
Richards, D. 2007. *New Labour and the civil service: reconstituting the Westminster model*. Houndmills, Basingstoke, UK: Palgrave Macmillan.
—— and M. J. Smith 2002. *Governance and Public Policy in the UK*. Oxford: Oxford University Press.
—— —— 2003. 'The 'hybrid state': New Labour's response to the challenge of governance'. In S. Ludlam and M. J. Smith, Eds. *Governing as New Labour*. London: Palgrave, pp. 106–25.
Riddell, P. 2001. 'Blair as prime minister'. In A. Seldon, Ed. *The Blair effect*. London: Little, Brown, pp. 21–40.
—— 2005. *The unfulfilled prime minister: Tony Blair and the end of optimism*. London: Politico's.
Riker, W. H. 1980. 'Implications from the disequilibrium of majority rule for the study of institutions', *American Political Science Review* 74 (2): 432–46.
Roberts, N., Ed. 2002. *The transformative power of dialogue*. Oxford: Elsevier.
Rorty, R. 1980. *Philosophy and the mirror of nature*. Oxford: Blackwell.
Rose, N. 1989. *Governing the soul: the shaping of the private self*. London: Routledge.
—— 1998. *Inventing ourselves: psychology, power, and personhood*. Cambridge: Cambridge University Press.
—— 1999. *Powers of freedom: reframing political thought*. Cambridge: Cambridge University Press.

Rowse, T. 2002. *Nugget Coombs: a reforming life*. Melbourne: Cambridge University Press.

Royal Commission on Australian Government Administration (RCAGA). 1976. *Report*. Canberra: Government Printer.

Royal Institute of Public Administration (RIPA). 1987. *Top jobs in Whitehall: appointments and promotions in the senior civil service*. London: RIPA.

Ruggie, J. G. 1975. 'International responses to technology: concepts and trends', *International Organization* 29 (3): 557–83.

—— 1998. *Constructing the world polity: essays on international institutionalization*. London: Routledge.

Sait, E. M. 1938. *Political institutions: a preface*. New York: Appleton-Century.

Salamon, L. M., Ed. 2002. *The tools of government: a guide to the new governance*. Oxford: Oxford University Press.

Sanjek, R. 2000. 'Keeping ethnography alive in an urbanizing world', *Human Organization* 593: 280–8.

Saussure, F. de 1966. *Course in general linguistics*, ed. C. Bally and A. Sechehaye, trans. W. Baskin. New York: McGraw-Hill.

Savoie, D. J. 2003. *Breaking the bargain: public servants, ministers and parliament*. Toronto: University of Toronto Press.

Scharpf, F. W. 1997. *Games real actors play: actor-centred institutionalism in policy research*. Boulder, CO: Westview Press.

Schattschneider, E. 1935. *Politics, pressures, and the tariff*. New York: Prentice-Hall.

Seidman, H. 1975. *Politics, position and power*, 2nd edition. Oxford: Oxford University Press.

Seldon, A. 1995. 'The Cabinet Office and coordination, 1979–87'. In R. A. W. Rhodes and P. Dunleavy, Eds. *Prime minister, cabinet and core executive*. London: Macmillan, pp. 125–48.

—— 2004. *Blair*. London: Free Press.

—— with P. Snowden and D. Collings 2007. *Blair unbound*. London: Simon & Schuster.

Shepsle, K. A. 1979. 'Institutional arrangements and equilibrium in multidimensional voting models', *American Journal of Political Science* 23 (1): 27–60.

—— 1995. 'Studying institutions: some lessons from the rational choice approach'. In J. Farr, J. S. Dryzek, and S. T. Leonard, Eds. *Political science in history: research programs and political traditions*. New York: Cambridge University Press, pp. 276–96.

—— 2006. 'Rational choice institutionalism'. In R. A. W. Rhodes, S. Binder, and B. Rockman, Eds. *The Oxford handbook of political institutions*. Oxford: Oxford University Press, pp. 23–38.

Shergold, P. 2004*a*. 'Once was Camelot in Canberra? Reflections on public service leadership'. *Sir Roland Wilson Lecture*, 23 June, Canberra. Available at: http://dspace.anu.edu.au/bitstream/1885/44503/2/Newshergold.pdf (last accessed 30 March 2009).

—— 2004*b*. 'Can governments be strategic? The role of the public service'. Address to the ANZSOG Public Policy Program, 30 July, Canberra.
—— 2005. 'Goodbye to all that power?' *The Canberra Times*, 5 April.
Skinner, Q. 1978. *The foundations of modern political thought*, 2 volumes. Cambridge: Cambridge University Press.
Skocpol, T. 1978. *States and social revolutions: a comparative analysis of France, Russia, and China*. Cambridge: Cambridge University Press.
—— 1985. 'Bringing the state back in: strategies of analysis in current research.' In P. B. Evans, D. Rueschemeyer, and T. Skocpol, Eds., *Bringing the state back in*. New York: Cambridge University Press, pp. 3–43.
Skowronek, S. 1982. *Building a new American State: the expansion of national administrative capacities, 1877–1920*. Cambridge: Cambridge University Press.
Smith, A.-M. 1994. *New Right discourse on race and sexuality: Britain, 1968–1990*. Cambridge: Cambridge University Press.
—— 1998. *Laclau and Mouffe: the radical democratic imaginary*. London: Routledge.
Smith, M. J. 1999. *The core executive in Britain*. London: Macmillan.
Sorsensen, E. and J. Torfing, 2007. 'Theoretical approaches to metagovernance'. In E. Sorsensen and J. Torfing, Eds. *Theories of democratic network governance*. Houndmills, Basingstoke, UK: Palgrave Macmillan, pp. 169–82.
Sossin, L. 2006. 'Defining boundaries: the constitutional argument for bureaucratic independence and its implication for the accountability of the public service'. In *commission of inquiry into sponsorship program and advertising activities (Gomery), Phase II, restoring accountability. Research studies, Volume 2: the public service and transparency*. Ottawa, Canada: Canadian Government Publishing.
Stanley, M. 2008*a*. 'How to be a civil servant' at: http://www.civilservant.org.uk/
—— 2008*b*. 'Mandarin English Part 1' at: http://www.civilservant.org.uk/jargon.pdf
Stedman Jones, G. 1983. 'Rethinking Chartism'. In *Languages of class*. Cambridge: Cambridge University Press, pp. 90–178.
—— 1996. 'The determinist fix: some obstacles to the further development of the linguistic approach to history in the 1990s', *History Workshop*, 42 (Spring): 19–35.
Stepan, A. 1978. *The state and society: Peru in comparative perspective*. Princeton, NJ: Princeton University Press.
Stewart, J. 2004. *The decline of the tea lady*. Kent Town, SA: Wakefield Press.
Stivers, C. 2008. 'Governance's new spectacles', *Public Administration Review* 68 (5): 941–43.
Stoker, G., Ed. 1999. *The new management of British local governance*. London: Macmillan.
—— Ed. 2000. *The new politics of British local governance*. London: Macmillan.
—— 2004. *Transforming local governance*. Houndmills, Basingstoke, UK: Palgrave Macmillan.
Stothard, P. 2003. *30 days: a month at the heart of the Blair war*. London: HarperCollins.

Sundquist, J. L. 1983. *Dynamics of the party system: alignment and realignment of political parties in the United States*. Washington, DC: Brookings Institute.

Taylor, C. 1961. 'Explanation by purpose and modern psychological theory', DPhil thesis, University of Oxford.

—— 1964. *The explanation of behaviour*. London: Routledge & Kegan Paul.

—— 1967. 'Neutrality in political science'. In P. Laslett and W. Runciman, Eds. *Philosophy, Politics, Society*, 3rd series. Oxford: Blackwell, pp. 25–57.

—— 1971. 'Interpretation and the sciences of man', *Review of Metaphysics* 25(1): 3–51.

Taylor, M. 1989. 'Structure, culture and action in the explanation of social change', *Politics and Society* 17 (2): 115–62.

't Hart, P., E. K. Stern, and B. Sundelius, Eds. 1997. *Beyond groupthink: political group dynamics and foreign policy making*. Ann Arbor, MI: University of Michigan Press.

Thelen, K. 1999. 'Historical institutionalism in comparative politics', *Annual Review of Political Science* 2: 369–404.

Thelen, K. and S. Steinmo 1992. 'Historical institutionalism in comparative politics', In S. Steinmo, K. Thelen, and F. Longstreth, Eds. *Structuring politics: historical institutionalism in comparative analysis*. New York: Cambridge University Press, pp. 1–32.

Thompson, E. P. 1978. 'The poverty of theory: or an orrery of errors'. In *The poverty of theory and other essays*. London: Merlin, chapter 1.

Thompson, E. P. 1981. *The making of the English working class*. London: Harmondsworth.

Tilly, C. Ed. 1975. *The formation of national states in Western Europe*. Princeton, NJ: Princeton University Press.

Timmins, N. 2007. 'Stalinist Brown', *Financial Times*, 20 March. Also at http://www.ft.com (last accessed 30 July 2009).

Torfing, J. 1999. *New theories of discourse: Laclau, Mouffe, and Zizek*. Oxford: Blackwell.

Treasury Board of Canada Secretariat. 2008. Policies and guidelines for ministers' offices, at: http://www.tbs-sct.gc.ca/pubs_pol/hrpubs/mg-ldm/gfmo-eng.asp (last accessed 30 July 2009).

Treasury Select Committee. 2000. 'Minutes of evidence, annex 1, Treasury aims and objectives', Session 2000–2001, 11 May 2000. http://www.publications.parliament.uk/pa/cm199900/cmselect/cmtreasy/492/0051103.htm (last accessed 30 July 2009).

—— 2001. *HM Treasury*, Session 2000–01 HC 73-II. London: Stationery Office.

—— 2005. *Performance targets and monitoring*, Session 2004–05 HC 331-i. London: Stationery Office.

Truzzi, M., Ed. 1974. *Verstehen: subjective understanding in the social sciences*. Reading, MA: Addison-Wesley.

Trimberger, E. K. 1978. *Revolution from above: military bureaucrats and development in Japan, Turkey, Egypt and Peru*. New Brunswick, NJ: Transaction Books.

Truman, D. B. 1951. 'The implications of political behaviour research', *Social Science Research Council Items* 5: 37–9.

Turnbull, A. 2005. Valedictory lecture, 27 July 2005. *Guardian Unlimited*. Available at: http://www.guardian.co.uk/politics/2005/jul/27/Whitehall.uk (last accessed on 30 July 2009).

Uebel, T. 1996. 'Anti-Foundationalism and the Vienna circle's revolution in philosophy'. *British Journal of the Philosophy of Science* 47 (3): 415–40.

Van der Dussen, J. 1995. 'The philosophical context of Collingwood's re-enactment theory', *International Studies in Philosophy* 27 (2), 81–99.

Van Maanen, J. 1988. *Tales of the field: on writing ethnography*. Chicago, IL: University of Chicago Press.

Vinzant, J. C. and L. Crothers, 1998. *Street level leadership: discretion and legitimacy in front line public service*. Washington, DC: Georgetown University Press.

Walker, P. G. 1970. *The cabinet*. London: Jonathan Cape.

Wallas, G. 1948 [1908]. *Human nature in politics*. London: Constable.

Wallerstein, I. M. 1874. *The modern world system: capitalist agriculture and the origins of the European world-economy in the sixteenth century*. New York: Academic Press.

Wamsley, G. L., C. T. Goodsell, J. A. Rohr, C. A. Stivers, O. F. White, and J. F. Wolf 1990. 'Public administration and the governance process: shifting the political dialogue'. In G. L. Wamsley and J. F. Wolf, Eds. *Refounding democratic public administration: modern paradoxes, postmodern challenges*. London: Sage, pp. 31–51.

Weller, P. 2001. *Australia's mandarins: the frank and the fearless?* Crow's Nest, NSW, Australia: Allen & Unwin.

—— 2002. *Don't tell the prime minister*. Carlton North, Vic.: Scribe Publications.

—— 2003. 'Cabinet Government: an elusive ideal?' *Public Administration*, 81 (4): 701–22.

—— and M. Grattan 1981. *Can ministers cope? Australian federal ministers at work*. Melbourne: Hutchinson.

Wendt, A. 1992. 'Anarchy is what states make of it: the social construction of power politics', *International Organization* 46 (2): 393–94.

—— 1999. *Social theory of international politics*. Cambridge: Cambridge University Press.

White, H. 2007. 'Afterword; manifesto time'. In S. Morgan, K. Jenkins, and A. Munslow, Eds. *Manifestos for history*. London: Routledge, pp. 220–31.

Wildavsky, A. 1979. *The art and craft of policy analysis*. London: Macmillan.

Williams, R. 1958. *Culture and society*. London: Chatto & Windus.

—— 1961. *The long revolution*. London: Chatto & Windus.

Wilson, R. 1999. 'The civil service in the new millennium'. Speech delivered at City University, London, 5 May.

—— 2003. 'Portrait of a profession revisited', *Public Administration* 81 (2): 365–78. Published version of a speech delivered on 26 March 2002 at Admiralty Arch, London.

Winch, P. 1958. *The idea of a social science and its relation to philosophy*. London: Routledge & Kegan Paul.

Wittgenstein, L. 1972*a*. *The blue and brown books*. Oxford: Blackwell.
—— 1972*b*. *Philosophical investigations*, trans. by G. Anscombe. Oxford: Basil Blackwell.
—— 2008. *Wittgenstein in Cambridge: letters and documents 1911–1951*, ed. B. McGuinness, 4th edition. Oxford: Wiley–Blackwell.
Wondolleck, J. and S. Yaffee 2000. *Making collaboration work: lessons from innovation in natural resource management*. Washington, DC: Island Press.
Wright, V. and J. Hayward 2000. 'Governing from the centre: policy co-ordination in six European core executives'. In R. A. W. Rhodes, Ed. *Transforming British government, Volume 2: changing roles and relationships*. London: Macmillan, pp. 27–46.
Wulff, H. 2002. 'Yo-yo fieldwork: mobility and time in multi-local study of dance in Ireland', *Anthropological Journal of European Cultures* 11: 117–36.
Yanow, D. 2006. 'Dear reviewer, dear author: looking for reflexivity and other hallmarks of interpretive research'. Paper to the Annual Meeting of the American Political Science Association, 30 August–3 September 2006, Philadelphia.
Yin, R. K. 2003. *Case study research: design and methods*, 3rd edition. London: Sage.

Name Index

Subject Index